新东方 NEW ORIENTAL

MW01677136

新东方雅思(IELTS)考试指定辅导教材·基础培训

IELTS Reading

雅思阅读胜经

新东方教育科技集团
雅思研发团队 编著

群言出版社

图书在版编目(CIP)数据

雅思阅读胜经 / 新东方教育科技集团雅思研发团队编著. —北京：群言出版社，2006

ISBN 7-80080-581-6

Ⅰ. 雅...　Ⅱ. 新...　Ⅲ. 英语—阅读教学—高等学校—入学考试，国外—自学参考资料　Ⅳ. H319.4

中国版本图书馆 CIP 数据核字(2006)第 052977 号

责任编辑　于　薇
封面设计　王　琳
出版发行　群言出版社
地　　址　北京东城区东厂胡同北巷 1 号
邮政编码　100006
联系电话　65263345　65265404
电子信箱　qunyancbs@dem-league.org.cn
印　　刷　北京画中画印刷有限公司
经　　销　全国新华书店
版　　次　2006 年 6 月第 1 版　2006 年 6 月第 1 次印刷
开　　本　787×1092　1/16
印　　张　14
字　　数　300 千字
书　　号　ISBN 7-80080-581-6
定　　价　30.00 元

[版权所有　翻印必究]

如有缺页、倒页、脱页等印装质量问题，请拨打服务热线：010－62605166。

新东方 NEW ORIENTAL

图书策划委员会

主任 俞敏洪

委员 （按姓氏笔划为序）

王　强　王文山　包凡一　仲晓红　汪海涛

周成刚　徐小平　钱永强　铁　岭　窦中川

新东方 NEW ORIENTAL

雅思考试基础培训教材编委会

（按姓氏笔划为序）

王　毓　冯　鹤　任　林　孙　涛

何　钢　金培娜　郝　斌　戚霄睿

Mark Allen

心中的罗马(代序)

在人生发展的道路上，人们总希望有更多的选择，有更多的改变命运的机会，从而使自己的生活变得更加丰富多彩。

上世纪80年代的中国学生还没有太多的选择，他们毕业后通常都是由国家分配工作。大多数学生都是“本分”孩子，高高兴兴地走上了他们被分配的工作岗位，继而在祖国最需要的地方认认真真干一辈子。

90年代的学生开始有了选择。随着中国的改革开放，国家鼓励出国留学，学生们开始把眼光投向了国外。或为了知识或为了生活，留学成了中国学生的重要追求之一。90年代的留学，大家的眼光多关注于美国，因为只有美国能够给中国学生奖学金，使一些贫困的中国学生在不需要自己花费的情况下就能够得到很好的教育。为了能够争取到美国读书，中国学生使尽浑身解数，把两门到美国去的必经考试TOEFL、GRE考到了奇迹般的水平，出现了很多的满分，中国学生的互相竞争到了白热化的程度。

2000年以后，中国学生有了更多的选择。随着中国的发展，有一些家庭变得富有起来，已经能够自费出国留学。在美国固执地认为中国人太穷付不起学费时，他的兄弟国家如英国、澳大利亚等却像猎狗一样，敏锐地嗅到了中国学生出国留学的热情和其中的商机，开始大量地录取中国学生到他们的国家去读书。中国学生面对突然出现的众多选择，一时眼花缭乱，蜂拥而出。和TOEFL相对应的英联邦国家的语言水平考试IELTS便成了中国学生选择的另一门重要的留学必经考试。

当美国人满足于他们自己的既定标准，并且坚持认为TOEFL是全世界最好的语言测试系统时，IELTS却向更实用的方向发展，强调学生的听、说、读、写四大能力在语言测试中的重要性。这一方向赢得了英联邦国家大学的认可，甚至越来越多的美国大学也开始认可雅思考试。于是，在短短的几年内，雅思考试成为中国学生出国的首选考试，考试人数在一段时间内超过了TOEFL考试人数。

当美国人意识到自己所犯的错误，开始对TOEFL考试进行改革时，已经有成千上万的中国学生到英联邦国家去读书了。由于相对宽松的录取政策，还有更多的学生正在准备到这些国家去读书，很多学生甚至到了牛津、剑桥这样的名牌大学。到英联邦国家去留学这一选择，已经成为越来越多的中国学生的日常思维。美国大学不再是中国学生的惟一选择。这一情况的出现，给中国学生至少带来了两大好处：一是IELTS和TOEFL这两门考试的不断改革，使其更加切合实际，中国学生通过对于这两门考试的准备，能够真正提高英语水平，不再存在高分低能的现象；二是美国的骄傲心态开始改变，开始愿意给中国学生更宽松的政策和更多的学习机会。

这无疑是一件好事，中国学生有了更多的选择，也许会出现更多的惊喜，生命也许会更加灿烂。而IELTS和TOEFL这两门考试的竞争将会给中国学生带来更多的方便，比如考试形式更加灵活、服务更加周到等。总之，选择带来希望，竞争造就优质。也许，中国学生的未来还有更多的选择，现在很多学生已经开始到法国、德国和其他非英语国家去留学。从大趋向上来说，无论是对于个人还是对于国家，这肯定是一件好事。

只是希望中国学生不要在选择中迷失了自己，不要为了选择而选择。生命的道路有很多，最好一开始就选对道路，否则回头重走会倍加艰难。也许你会问：选择哪一条道路好呢？条条大路通罗马，关键是你要知道罗马在什么地方。罗马，就是你心中最割舍不下的理想。

新东方也在为心中割舍不下的理想而努力，那就是在中国学生前进的道路上出一把力，成为中国学生越过人生障碍的垫脚石或者加速前进的助推器。这套雅思书籍的出版，就是我们所做努力的一点小小的证明。也许这不一定是最好的雅思书，但是它们倾注了新东方雅思老师的全部心血，融入了老师们近十年的教学经验。这些心血和经验，在全书的字里行间都能够读出来。

生命的梦想需要很多努力才能实现，雅思考试本身尽管无聊，但背后包含的意义是丰富的，它是你为自己的梦想努力过的证明。也许因为这一努力，你的生命将会从此与众不同。

目 录

雅思考试总论

1. 什么是雅思(IELTS)考试

雅思(IELTS: International English Language Testing System)是专门为准备进入以英文教学的学院或大学深造的学生而设的英文水平测试。雅思注重学生在专业范畴内需具备的英语能力，所以许多英语国家的学校都鼓励学生参加雅思测试。雅思测试由澳洲大学联盟（IDP Education Australia)、英国文化协会(British Council)以及剑桥大学测试中心(UCLES)共同举办，由剑桥大学测试中心统筹管理。

2. 雅思的测试对象

凡计划前往英语国家就读本科、研究生、专科技术学院或预科等课程的考生，以及想要申请赴澳洲、新西兰、加拿大等地移民的移民者都可参加雅思考试。目前，全世界共有40多个国家或地区认可雅思成绩，主要包括英、美、加、澳、新西兰、爱尔兰和南非等英语国家，此外还有很多欧洲及亚洲国家，如瑞士、挪威和新加坡等都认可雅思；而且，它是赴澳大利亚、荷兰留学受认可的惟一的语言测试；所有的加拿大教育机构都认可雅思成绩；根据雅思考试官方网站透露，在美国，现在已经有380余所大学和研究生院正式认可雅思成绩。目前，全球120个国家的400多个测试中心定期举办雅思考试。

3. 雅思的计分方式及考题类别

(1) **计分方式**：雅思分Listening、Reading、Writing、Speaking四大项目，各项目独立计分，最后所得成绩取四项成绩的平均值。IELTS满分为9分，成绩能达至9分者，代表其英语能力与母语为英语的人能力相当，反之，若只得1分则表明其不具有英语能力。

(2) **考试组别分类**：Reading与Writing部分采取分组方式，共分为Academic和General Training两组；Listening和Speaking两项则不分组。

(A) **Academic**：适用于申请正式课程者，例如研究所、大学、专科学校或要求此组别者。

(B) **General Training**：适用于申请移民者及欲申请学校要求此组别者。

4. 雅思的测试方式及时间

测试时间：约2小时45分

测试顺序如下：

笔记区

雅思测试顺序	
(1)Listening 听力	测试时间：约30分钟，另有10分钟誊写答案 测试方式：分4段进行，每大题前会有30秒时间阅读题目及答案选项，每段测试之后，还会有30秒时间检查答案。 测试题数：4道大题，共40个问题
(2)Reading 阅读	测试时间：60分钟 测试方式：填空/选择/问答/匹配
(3)Writing 写作	测试时间：60分钟 测试方式：第一篇作文至少需写150字，主要是对所提供的数据、图表加以描述；第二篇作文至少需写250字，主要是就某个主题发表自己的想法及意见。 测试题数：2篇
(4)Speaking 口试	测试时间：10~15分钟 测试方式：口试官和考生进行一对一的口试。

5. 考试流程

考生(candidate)在考试当天必须携带身份证原件和准考证，在8:30之前到考场门外等候，然后逐个验证入场。入场后考生可依次找到自己的座位。考场大多是语言实验室，使用耳机。桌上有一张印有考生姓名(拼音)、考号、生日和类别(Academic类还是General Training类)的纸条、一支HB铅笔和一块橡皮。待全体考生就座，主考官介绍考试规则后分发答题卡和听力考试的试题本(booklet for the listening test)。

在答题卡的正面答听力题，背面答阅读题。考生应在答题卡的正面填写自己的姓名(拼音)和考号(candidate number)，并用铅笔将相应的长方形小框涂黑。之后，听力考试开始。

听力考试结束后由监考人员收走听力试题本，然后分发阅读试题本。考生应在答题卡背面标明考试类别（Academic类还是 General Training类），然后开始阅读考题。

需特别指出的是，听力磁带约为30分钟，考生答题时，需先将答案写在试题本上，待磁带上的试题内容放完后，有10分钟的时间将答案誊写到答题卡上。

阅读考试的答题则应直接写在答题卡上。阅读考试的时间为60分钟，考生不再有额外的时间誊写答案。在做阅读题时，可以用笔在试题本上划线或做标记。考官会在阅读考试进行到30分钟和55分钟时提醒考生考试时间。阅读考试结束后监考人员将试题和答题卡收走。考生要注意的是，从2003年9月开始，阅读与写作之间没有休息时间，考生不得以任何理由离开考场。监考人员会分发作文题和作文纸。同样，考生需填写candidate name，candidate number，date，centre name，module。作文考试的时间也是60分钟，考官会在考试进行到20分钟、55分钟时提醒考生时间。作文考试结束后，笔试部分全部结束。

考生考完笔试后，监考人员会提醒考生有关口试的注意事项。口试的时间

笔记区

写在考生桌子上的一张小纸条上。考生应记住自己口试的日期（是当天或是第二天）、时间(几点几分)和地点(口试考场房间号)。口试顺序的安排一般是先外地考生,再本地考生。但这只是一般原则,具体安排会因两部分考生的比例不同而有所不同。一般而言,考生尽量不要在笔试的第二天(一般是星期日)安排其他活动,以免与口试发生冲突。

口试时应提前一个半小时左右到达考场附近,因为前面的考生可能会迟到,或者因笔试考得不理想而放弃口试。出现这种情况时,后面的考生应能够及时补上,以避免考场出现空档。

6. 考试成绩

考试结束的第十个工作日之后考生可以登录http://ielts.etest.edu.cn查询成绩。雅思考试成绩有效期为两年。

（1）每名考生只有一份考试成绩单原件,需妥善保存。成绩单的真实性可以通过网络进行核查。详情请登录www.ielts.org查阅。

（2）考试结束两周后,英国使馆文化教育处考试部会将考生的成绩单寄往考生报名时提交的邮寄地址。

（3）考生如需额外成绩单,需向英国使馆文化教育考试部提交申请。

7. 2006年雅思考试新变化

2006年,雅思考试在考务方面进行了一系列的改进,包括通过电子邮件寄送成绩单、成绩复议费下调和取消90天内不得重考的规定。

从2006年4月1日起,雅思成绩单的寄送效率有了显著提高,不仅寄送时间大为缩短,而且考生还可以向英国文化协会中国办公室考试部提交寄送考试成绩单申请。考生提交的寄送成绩单申请经受理后,成绩单就可以立刻以Email的形式送至考生指定的成绩单接收机构。这种快速操作过程给考生和接收机构都带来了便利。考生除在考后提出申请外,还可以选择在报名考试时填写指定成绩接收人地址。此外,考生也无须再承担寄发成绩单的邮资。如果需要以国际航空平信形式寄送,相应邮资也无须考生承担。雅思的免费“额外成绩单”代寄最多可达5份。

另外,雅思成绩复议价格也有所降低。根据雅思考试规则,对分数有疑义的考生可以在成绩公布28天内提出复议,从4月1日起,复议的费用由过去的950元降为860元。复议后如成绩确实存在误差,该费用将退还给考生。

雅思考试还取消了考生在考试90天以后才能够重新报考的限制。考生可以根据自己的情况随时报名重考。据悉,目前世界各地有大量机构采用雅思成绩、他们不仅对考生的总分有要求,对单项成绩也有要求,考生有可能总分达到了要求,但是单项成绩不合格,而“90天不得重考”这个规定的取消,无疑给考生带来了方便。

笔记区

8. 雅思考试评分标准细则

成绩评分标准

BAND9 Expert User：能自如地运用英语，表达恰当、准确、流畅并且理解透彻。

BAND8 Very Good User：能自如地运用英语，只是偶尔会有语言不够连贯、不够准确的问题。偶尔会无法理解不够熟悉的情景。能较好地掌握复杂的说理论辩。

BAND7 Good User：在某些情景中偶尔会有语言不准确、不恰当以及不理解的情况，但具备语言实际运用能力。基本上可以较好地理解较复杂的英语和详细的论证，尤其在熟悉的场景中。

BAND6 Competent User：大体上能比较有效地运用英语。虽然有时出现表达不准确、不恰当和不理解的情况，但能够理解和运用较复杂的英语，尤其是在熟悉的场景中。

BAND5 Modest User：具有部分运用英语的能力，在大多数情况下可大致了解大意。虽然出现不少错误，但是基本可以在自己所熟悉的领域内沟通。

BAND4 Limited User：只限于在熟悉的情景中具有基本交际能力，理解和表达方面经常会出现错误，无法使用复杂的英语。

BAND3 Extremely Limited User：只能在简单的情况下表达和理解大概含义。频繁出现交流障碍。

BAND2 Intermittent User：无法进行真正的交流。只能在极熟悉的场景中用只字片语来满足紧急需求。理解书面语和口语方面有重大障碍。

BAND1 Non User：仅能说几个不关联的单词，根本无法沟通。

成绩评分标准细则

按照《IELTS评分标准、分数报告和解释》，考生成绩从1~9共分为九个等级。成绩报告单上有听、说、读、写四个单项的得分和总分（四个部分所得分数的平均分四舍五入之后就是考生的总分）。

总分、听力以及阅读部分的分数是整级或半级。例如，如果四项平均分等于或大于6.25分，则取6.5分；如果平均分等于或大于6.75分，则取7分。写作和口语部分的分数只按整级计算。

听力和阅读部分各包含40道题，每答对一道得一分。考生这两部分满分的原始分均为40分，考生依据其原始分获取1~9的等级分。

等级分/原始分如何换算

部分等级分及原始分换算表（听力/阅读）

听力		学术类阅读		普通培训类阅读	
等级分	原始分	等级分	原始分	等级分	原始分
5	16	5	15	4	15
6	23	6	23	5	23
7	30	7	30	6	30
8	35	8	35	7	34

笔 记 区

写作评分细则示例

雅思写作通常有Task1和Task2两个部分，考官给以下四项分别评等级分：任务完成(Task 1)/任务反应(Task 2)、连贯与衔接、词汇以及句式多样性和语法准确性。

以Task1为例，一名在雅思学术类考试中写作部分获得6分的考生，其这一分数所对应的写作水准应是：

(A) 任务完成方面：达到写作任务各项要求、能确切选择有用信息进行全面评述、呈现并强调主要特点或要点，但细节可能与要点无关、不恰当或不准确。

(B) 连贯及衔接方面：信息和分论点安排连贯，论证过程清楚，有效使用衔接手段，但句内或句间衔接有错误或显机械呆板，有时指代不清晰或不恰当。

(C) 词汇量方面：相对写作任务而言，所运用的词汇量充足，尝试运用非常见词汇但有时出现错误，拼写和构词出现一些错误，但不影响交流。

(D) 句式多样性和语法准确性方面：混合使用简单和复合句，语法和标点出现一些错误但基本不影响交流。

口语评分细则示例

同样，在雅思考试的口语部分，考官也是按四项标准分别评等级分：流利度和连贯性、词汇、句式丰富性和语法准确性以及语音。以一名口语获得6分的考生为例，这一分数所对应的口语水准应是：

(A) 流利度及连贯性方面：愿意进行详细描述，但有时因重复、自我更正或停顿而造成不连贯，运用不同的连接词和语篇标记，但有时不恰当。

(B) 词汇方面：尽管有时词汇运用不恰当，但词汇量足以详细表述主题，表意清楚，总体上能成功地变换措辞进行复述。

(C) 句式多样性及语法准确性方面：混合使用简单句式和复合句式，但不够灵活；使用复合句式时经常出错，但并不因此影响理解。

(D) 语音方面：总体能听懂，偶尔因发音错误对听者的理解造成负担。

评分受质量监控

据《IELTS评分标准、分数报告和解释》，所有雅思评分都由评卷官和考官在考试中心完成。所有评卷官必须事先接受培训，以确保其理解评分规定，并且证明其能够根据评分标准进行评分。评卷官每两年要重新接受测试，以确保其评分符合标准。每次考试都有系统监测，并对部分答卷进行二次评分。

笔记区

相关原文（摘自www.ielts.org）

Score processing, reporting and interpretation

All IELTS marking takes place at the test centre by trained markers and examiners. Markers are trained to understand the IELTS marking policy and are required to demonstrate that they are marking to standard before they are allowed to mark Listening and Reading papers. Markers are re-tested every two years to ensure that their marking remains up to standard. Systematic monitoring and double marking of a proportion of answer sheets are carried out at each administration.

Examiners for the Writing and Speaking modules are recruited and trained in line with agreed standards. They are required to demonstrate that they are marking to standard every two years in addition to on-going monitoring of their performance.

Candidates receive scores on a Band Scale from 1 to 9. A score is reported for each skill module of the test. The four individual module scores are averaged and rounded to produce an Overall Band Score. Overall Band Scores and Listening and Reading scores are presented as whole or half bands; Writing and Speaking band scores are reported in whole bands only.

Overall Band Score

Candidates receive a Test Report Form setting out their Overall Band Score and their scores on each of the four modules, Listening, Reading, Writing and Speaking. Each of the module scores is equally weighted. The Overall Band Score is calculated by taking the mean of the total of the four individual module scores.

Overall Band Scores are reported to the nearest whole or half band. For the avoidance of doubt, the following rounding convention applies; if the average across the four skills ends in .25, it is rounded up to the next half band, and if it ends in .75, it is rounded up to the next whole band.

Thus a candidate achieving 6.5 for Listening, 6.5 for Reading, 5.0 for Writing and 7.0 for Speaking would be awarded an Overall Band Score of 6.5 （25 ÷ 4 = 6.25 = Band 6.5）.

Likewise a candidate achieving 4.0 for Listening, 3.5 for Reading, 4.0 for Writing and 4.0 for Speaking would be awarded an Overall Band Score of 4.0 （15.5 ÷ 4 = 3.875 = Band 4.0）.

笔记区

On the other hand, a candidate achieving 6.5 for Listening, 6.0 for Reading, 6.0 for Writing and 6.0 for Speaking would be awarded band 6 (24.5 ÷ 4 = 6.125 = Band 6).

Listening and Reading

IELTS Listening and Reading papers contain 40 items and each correct item is awarded one mark; the maximum raw score a candidate can achieve on a paper is 40. Band scores ranging from Band 1 to Band 9 are awarded to candidates on the basis of their raw scores.

Although all IELTS test materials are pretested and trialled before being released as live tests, there are inevitably minor differences in the difficulty level across tests. In order to equate different test versions, the band score boundaries are set so that all candidates' results relate to the same scale of achievement. This means, for example, that the Band 6 boundary may be set at a slightly different raw score across versions.

The tables below indicate the mean raw scores achieved by candidates at various levels in each of the Listening, Academic Reading and General Training Reading modules during 2004 and they provide an indication of the number of marks required to achieve a particular band score.

Listening		Academic Reading		General Training Reading	
Band Score	Raw Score out of 40	Band Score	Raw Score out of 40	Band Score	Raw Score out of 40
5	16	5	15	4	15
6	23	6	23	5	23
7	30	7	30	6	30
8	35	8	35	7	34

The Academic and General Training papers are graded to the same scale. The distinction between the two modules is one of genre or discourse type. Academic papers may contain source texts featuring more difficult vocabulary or greater complexity of style. It is usual that, to secure a given band score, a greater number of questions must be answered correctly on a General Training Reading paper.

Writing and Speaking

When marking the Writing and Speaking modules examiners use detailed performance descriptors which describe written and spoken performance at each of the 9 IELTS bands.

笔 记 区

Writing

Examiners award a band score for each of four criterion areas: Task Achievement (for Task 1), Task Response (for Task 2), Coherence and Cohesion, Lexical Resource and Grammatical Range and Accuracy. The four criteria are equally weighted.

Speaking

Examiners award a band score for each of four criterion areas: Fluency and Coherence, Lexical Resource, Grammatical Range and Accuracy and Pronunciation. The four criteria are equally weighted.

笔 记 区

第一章　雅思阅读介绍篇

Ⅰ. 雅思阅读选材（Coverage）

无论是英语四、六级考试，还是托福、GRE考试，它们的选材都有各自的倾向性，雅思也不例外。熟悉选材，就能把握文章主要论题，积累相关背景知识。不过雅思选题非常广泛，包括世界范围的就业状况、教育状况、经济问题、语言学、考古学、生物学、种族、民族问题、女性歧视问题、环境保护及环境污染、人口爆炸及居住问题、城市化问题、地球灾难、地理现象、外星生物探讨、人类历史发展中的重要事件、重要人物及重要标志性产品等。

Ⅱ. 雅思阅读题型（Tasks）

雅思阅读题型之丰富堪称各大考试之最，共有9大题型，可分为主旨类和细节类两大类别。

主旨类：

1. 标题对应 *List of headings* that tests your ability to grasp the main idea of each paragraph.

Example 1:

Please choose the most suitable headings for paragraphs listed below.

***NB** There are more headings than paragraphs, so you will not use them all.*

List of headings

1. Types of intelligence
2. Emotional awareness
3. Defining emotional intelligence
4. Differences between IQ and EQ
5. EQ, more important than IQ
6. Handling interpersonal relationship
7. Some tips to improve emotional intelligence
8. Self-motivation
9. The significance of emotional intelligence
10. Managing one's emotions

笔 记 区

1. Paragraph A:
2. Paragraph B:
3. Paragraph C:
4. Paragraph D:
5. Paragraph E:

2. 最佳标题 *Best title* that tests your ability to grasp the gist of the whole passage.

Example 2:

Select the best title for the entire passage:

A. The tourist industry
B. Some economic benefits of tourism
C. The multiplier effect
D. How to improve tourism

3. 概述题 *Summary* that tests your ability to understand the main idea of a large area of the text and express the same idea in different ways.

Example 3:

Complete the summary below. Choose your answers from the list below the summary.

***NB** There are more words than spaces, so you will not use them all.*

Trust is a __1__ thing. Once __2__, it affords us tremendous freedom; but once trust is lost, it would impossible to __3__. Of course the truth is we never know who we can trust: those who were closest can __4__ us; and total strangers can come to our __5__. In the end, most people decide to trust only themselves—it really is the simplest way to keep from getting burned.

List of words

precious	earned	difficult	betray
ruined	fragile	show loyalty to	rescue
recover	side		

Excerpted from *Desperate Wives*

细节类：

1. 判断题 *TRUE/FALSE/NOT GIVEN or YES/NO/NOT GIVEN* that tests your ability to identify and understand detailed logical arguments or opinions in the passage.

笔记区

Example 4:

A.

Do the following statements agree with the information given in Reading Passage 1?

TRUE if the statement agrees with the information
FALSE if the statement contradicts the information
NOT GIVEN if there is no information on this

A prevalent attitude amongst many nurses in the group selected for study was that there was no reward or recognition for not utilizing the paid sick leave entitlement allowed them in their employment conditions.
If the nurses do not use their paid sick leave, they will get rewarded.

B.

Do the following statements agree with the information given in Reading Passage 1?

TRUE if the statement agrees with the views of the writer
FALSE if the statement contradicts the views of the writer
NOT GIVEN if it is impossible to say what the writer thinks about this

It was estimated that the leisure revolution would take place by the turn of the century with hours devoted to work falling to 25–30 per week. This reduction has failed to materialize.
At the turn of the last century, weekly work hours dropped to 25.

2. 配对题 *Matching* that tests your ability to locate specific information with its relevant features.

Example 5:

Match the theories with the following statements.

A. Behaviorism B. Humanism

1. dominates theory of humans' behavior before 1960s.
2. emphasizes the significance of cognitive learning.
3. maintains that rote learning is an effective way to memorize information.
4. suggests learning to know 'why' and 'how' is more important than knowing 'what' only.
5. implies the stimulus-response model is the key point in learning.

笔记区

3. 填空题*Gap-filling* that tests your ability to locate right information in a passage.

Example 6:

Complete the sentence below with words taken from the passage.
Use ***NO MORE THAN TWO WORDS*** *for each answer.*

1. The pages are then processed into photographic negatives and the film is used to produce aluminum printing plates ready for the presses.
   The pages are converted into...and...are made for use in the printing presses.
2. Dinosaur skulls are found in a great range of shapes and sizes, reflecting the different eating habits and lifestyles of a large and varied group of animals that dominated life on Earth for an extraordinary 165 million years.
   Dinosaurs had skulls of different shapes and sizes because of...and...
3. When two different masses of water meet, one will move beneath the other, depending on their relative densities in the subduction process. The densities are determined by temperature and salinity.
   The subduction process is the result of the difference in...and...
4. Fresh outbreaks of coral bleaching—which occurs when rising temperatures cause polyps to discard the tiny algae that gives reefs their colors and which is linked by some scientists to the greenhouse effect, are being recorded.
   Reefs contribute their various colors to...

4. 简答题 *Short-answer question* that tests your ability to locate the right information in a passage.

Example 7:

Answer the questions below using ***NO MORE THAN THREE WORDS*** *from the passage for each answer.*

Yet despite a positive treatment girls are much less likely to persist at a task following failure. Girls, moreover, are more likely than boys to attribute their failures to lack of ability, even on tasks where their ability exceeds that of boys. These paradoxical findings might at first seem to indicate an innate difference between boys and girls, but careful studies have identified environmental factors that can account for them.

What is the cause for the fact that girls regard themselves as incompetent for tasks?

笔记区

5. 图表题 *Table/Flow chart/Diagram* that tests your ability to locate and understand a process, a diagram or a table.

Example 8:

Complete the table below.

Write ***NO MORE THAN THREE WORDS*** *from the passage for each answer.*

Time	Location	Casualty
1788		830,000
	Quatemala	
1976		
		More than 5,000

6. 选择题 *Multiple choice* that tests your ability to identify main and supporting points and also to differentiate between them.

Example 9:

A.

The limbic system's structures are involved with many motivational behaviors such as obtaining food, drink and sex; with organizing emotional behaviors such as fear, anger and aggression; and with the storing of memory.

Which of the following functions is ***NOT*** *controlled by the limbic system?*

A. Eating

B. Learning a new word by heart

C. Breath and heart rate

D. Jealousy

B.

I never liked long walks, especially on chilly afternoons: dreadful to me was the coming home in the raw twilight, with nipped fingers and toes, and a heart saddened by the chidings of Bessie, the nurse, and humbled by the consciousness of my physical inferiority to Eliza, John and Georgiana Reed.

Excerpted from *Jane Eyre*

The author mentions a number of factors that she hated walks outdoors. Which ***THREE*** *of the following factors are mentioned?*

A. The weather was cold.

B. Her aunt always cursed her.

C. She was weaker and not so pretty as her cousins.

D. The journey was long.

E. The cousins sometimes bullied her.

F. The carer usually blamed her.

笔记区

Ⅲ. 雅思阅读评分标准（Band）

雅思阅读考试包括3篇文章，总长2,500~3,000字，考试时间1小时，需完成40道题。分为学术类（Academic）和移民类（General Training），题型相同，选材和评分标准略有差异。

等 级（A类）	答对题数	等 级（G类）	答对题数
9	40	9	40
8.5	38–39	8.5	39
8	36–37	8	38
7.5	32–35	7.5	37
7	29–31	7	35–36
6.5	26–28	6.5	30–34
6	23–25	6	26–29
5.5	19–22	5.5	22–25
5	16–18	5	18–21

笔 记 区

第二章　雅思阅读基础篇

Ⅰ. 词汇（Vocabulary）

快速准确的阅读对词汇的要求不仅限于它的意义，还包括它的词性、范畴、感情色彩、搭配、同义词等其他信息。很多情况下只需要掌握单词的词性、范畴和感情色彩，就能大致了解作者所要表达的信息。

参看下列来自《剑桥国际英语词典》的词条，看看能从中获得多少有关adverse的信息：

adverse /ˈædvɜːs, ədˈvɜs/ *adj.* [before *n*] going against something, or harmful

- *The match has been cancelled due to adverse* **weather conditions.**
- *They received a lot of adverse* **publicity/criticism** *about the changes.*
- *The advertising company responsible for the campaign says that they are surprised by the adverse public* **reaction** *to the poster.*
- *A lot of local people are worried about the adverse* **impact** *that the road building scheme may have on the environment.*
- *So far the drug is thought not to have any adverse* **effects.**

Excerpted from *Cambridge International Dictionary of English*

1. 词性（Part of Speech）

词性是单词在句中担任的角色，英语单词的词性分为名词、动词、形容词、副词、代词、冠词、连词、数词等。本节将讲述词性的判断、词性的功能及其运用。

- **如何判断名词和动词**

请说出下列划线部分的词性，并说明理由。

1. 身无彩凤双飞翼，心有灵犀一点通。
2. 春如旧。人空瘦。泪痕红浥鲛绡透。
3. 廉颇老矣，尚能饭否？

名词判断依据：

前面是否有冠词	前面是否有形容词	前面是否有介词
是否有复数标志	是否有所有格标志	词缀

动词判断依据：

前面是否有助动词	后面是否有名词	
是否有第三人称单数标志	是否有过去时标志	词缀

笔记区

Exercises A: ***Figure out the part of speech of the underlined part in each sentence.***

1. This <u>involves</u> dealing with emotions, like jealousy, resentment, anger, etc., that one may have difficulty accepting by, perhaps, giving oneself comfort food, or doing nice things when one is feeling low.
2. To <u>err</u> is human; to forgive, <u>divine</u>.
3. It is also considered positive for a company to provide <u>state-of-art</u> support for working parents with on-site day care, help for parents with sick children, and flexible hours whenever possible.
4. Fossilized <u>remains</u> of plants and animals also support the idea that continents move.
5. The consensus of academic opinion was that Australia had been <u>peopled</u> for less than 10,000 years.

Exercise B: ***Figure out all the NOUNs in the following sentences:***

1. Each leg ends in a pair of 'waling claws' that grasp vegetation, among other functions, but a third claw collaborates with associated spiny, elastic hairs to detach the leg from a sticky web strand.
2. There are occasions when giving a gift surpasses spoken communication, since the message it offers can cut through barriers of language and culture diversity.
3. The genetic inheritance a baby receives from its parents at the moment of conception fixes much of its later development, determining characteristics as varied as whether it will have blue eyes or suffer from a life-threatening illness such as cystic fibrosis.
4. An opposing view sees the three family divisions of labor styles as a reflection of the progressive changes couples make in response to changing life situations, rather than being an aspect of personality.
5. The conclusion last summer of a 10-year building program has seen the historic zinc-alum shacks and even older wooden sheds built at an early Antarctic base, on Heard Island in 1947, supplanted by vast, bright-colored buildings with bay-window views and ski-lodge décor.

- **词性的作用**

划分句子结构	寻找关键词
缩小选择范围	做题提示

Exercise C: ***Figure out the key words in the following items.***

1. Causes of volcanic eruption
2. Efforts to predict volcanic eruption
3. Volcanoes and the features of our planet

笔记区

4. Different types of volcanic eruption
5. International relief efforts
6. The unpredictability of volcanic eruptions

Exercise D: ***Complete the summary below. Choose your answers from the list below the summary.***

***NB** There are more words than spaces, so you will not use them all.*

Trust is a __1__ thing. Once __2__, it affords us tremendous freedom; but once trust is lost, it would be impossible to __3__. Of course the truth is we never know who we can trust: those who were closest can __4__ us; and total strangers can come to our __5__. In the end, most people decide to trust only themselves—it really is the simplest way to keep from getting burned.

List of words

precious	earned	difficult	betray
ruined	fragile	show loyalty to	rescue
recover	side		

Excerpted from *Desperate Wives*

Exercise E: ***Choose the correct headings for the paragraphs from the list of headings below.***

List of headings

A. Fire models for calculation

B. Difficulty in modeling

Paragraph 1. ____________________

Calculating this is not easy. Models used for the purpose have treated the fire as passive and stationary. But the movement of a fire is quite dynamic, and recent work by researchers, using a new model which takes into account a number of subtle facets suggests that the fire spreads much faster than earlier estimates had predicted.

Paragraph 2. ____________________

It's not easy trying to model accurately the movement of a fire, with a variety of influences such as the location, the content, the position of goods as well as the ventilation condition on the spot. For example, consider how air affects the direction of a fire.

笔记区

2. 词的感情色彩（Emotion）

单词分为褒义词、贬义词和中性词，体现在本义、程度、词根和文化等各方面。

Exercise F: ***Figure out the emotional aspect (favorable, unfavorable or neutral) of the underlined part in the following sentences.***

1. The convergence of these two growing trends—dropping out and logging on—exacerbates the serious consequences of a drop in political involvement and a rise in social isolation.
2. Here, too, the threat of unemployment has been looming on the horizon.
3. Thirty years after the fire he is still haunted by images of death and destruction.
4. There is grave concern over the use of such dams because of their adverse impact on health, their displacement of successful farmers and the severe limitations on their useful life due to siltation.
5. You have so many books.
6. Not 'thin' but 'slim' is the word to compliment a girl.
7. Leave him alone—such a drunkard.
8. She is, actually, not carefree, but careless.
9. You have no right to call my students 'stupid' or 'illiterate'; they are intelligent challenged.
10. The emphasis on individualism can cause discord in society, disagreements, and lack of harmony.
11. Keep all negative thoughts away from the interview and do not say anything derogatory about one's previous employer.
12. The major problems facing the world today are overpopulation, pollution, and starvation. The three blights are related.

3. 词义猜测

遇到生词要学会有根据地猜测（make intelligent guesses），可通过解释性单词、句式和标点、词根、句子的并列结构和上下文进行推测。

- **表示A=B的句式**

  A is B

  A refers to/means/represents/stands for B

  A is referred to as/is known as/is called B

  A is code/substitute for B

  定语从句/同位语从句

- **表示A=B的单词**

  A. In other words, B

笔记区

A, namely, B

A. i.e. B

A, that is, B

A or B, A/B

● **表示A=B的标点符号**

A, B, ...

A—B—...

A (B)

Exercises G: ***Figure out the meaning of the underlined part in the following sentences by using A=B pattern.***

1. A court interpreter is anyone who interprets in a civil or criminal court proceeding (eg. arraignment, motion, pretrial conference, preliminary hearing, deposition, trial) for a witness or defendant who speaks or understands little or no English.
2. Intellectual disability refers to a general slowness to learn and function within society, and the identification of intellectual disability is usually based on an assessment of a person's performance in a variety of tests.
3. The neglect syndrome refers to the failure of a patient to see objects or parts of the body on the side opposite the brain damage. Patients may dress only one side of their body and deny that opposite body parts are theirs.
4. The traditional telephone network consists of a pair of copper wires connecting the customer premises to a local exchange. This is known as the customer access network.
5. For instance 'YIKLA' was code for 'This is the life!'
6. British industry, in particular, has in recent decades often been criticized for its linguistic insularity—for its assumption that foreign buyers will be happy to communicate in English, and that awareness of other languages is not therefore a priority.
7. Another giant leap is occurring through the use of the Internet, the electronic network, that is ultimately likely to be the most revolutionary of all behavior-modifying technologies.
8. That seems to be the message from research conducted by Europanel, an association of research companies across 23 countries which monitor buying patterns using consumer panels.
9. As social beings, we need to be able to deal with other people which brings us to the next item on Goleman's list, namely: recognizing emotions in other people. This means, in effect, having or developing 'social radar', i.e. learning to read the weather systems-around-individuals or groups of people.
10. The thyreophorans, or 'shield bearers', also known as armoured dinosaurs, were

笔记区

quadrupeds with rows of protective bony spikes, studs, or plates along their backs and tails.

11. In all cases, someone has to act as a source of language data—an informant.
12. One of the most eminent of psychologists, Clark Hull, claimed that the essence of reasoning lies in the putting together of two 'behavior segments' in some novel way, never actually performed before, so as to reach a goal.
13. Though Aborigines might see themselves as indigenous (in the sense, as Josephine Flood explains, that they have no race history not associated with this continent) there is no doubt that they were in fact Australia's first migrants.
14. Leonardo da Vinci belongs to Renaissance—that period of rebirth, when after centuries of dormancy the souls of men awoke to the beauty and the wonder of the external world.
15. Palaeontologists believe that both dinosaurs and crocodiles evolved, in the later years of the Triassic Period (248–208 million years ago), from creatures called pseudosuchian thecodonts. Lizards, snakes and different types of thecodont are believed to have evolved earlier in the Triassic Period from reptiles known as eosuchians.

Exercise H: ***Figure out the meaning of the underlined part in the following sentences by using the word root.***

1. What is the task of a paleoseismologist?
2. The therapods, or 'beast feet', were bipedal, predatory carnivores.
3. Posterior pituitary—the rear portion of the pituitary regulates water and salt balance.
4. There are occasions when giving a gift surpasses spoken communication, since the message it offers can cut through barriers of language and culture diversity.
5. The classic example is the shy person, categorized by some people as arrogant and distant and by others as lively and friendly and very personable. How can two different groups make a definitive analysis of someone that is so strikingly contradictory?
6. Aphasia is partial or total loss of the ability to articulate ideas or comprehend spoken or written language, resulting from damage to the brain caused by injury or disease.

Exercise I: ***Figure out a pair of synonyms in the following sentences.***

Students who want to enter the University need more than just a conventional ID card—their identities must be authenticated by an electronic hand scanner. In some

笔记区

California housing estates, a key alone is insufficient to get someone in the door; his or her voiceprint must also be verified.

Exercise J: ***Figure out the meaning of the underlined part in the following sentences through the understanding of the context and making use of background information.***

1. Lack of insulin results in the more common form of diabetes, while too much cause hypoglycemia.
2. Under sympathetic, your skin will have goose bumps; while under parasympathetic, no goose bumps.
3. In France job advertisements flout the law openly by asking for applicants of a certain age.
4. Not being tangible, emotions are difficult to analyze and quantify, compounded by the fact that each area in the list above, does not operate in isolation.
5. Their finding gives teeth to the long-held prediction that freshwater runoff into the ocean would increase in the Arctic as a result of global warming.
6. In fact, the increase in population is phenomenal. In 1900, there were 1.2 billion people on the Earth. In 1950, there were 2.5 billion. By 2000, there were more than 6 billion people, and this number is likely to increase to 8 billion by 2030.
7. The prices are soaring; the government is taking every measure to check the inflation.
8. It is hard for people to appreciate how fast a fire can spread in a building.
9. Mind (you), I don't mind minding the children so long as they mind me.
10. We seem to have exhausted this topic of conversation.

4. 同义词转换(Synonyms)

形 式	文 章	问 题	转换原则
同义同形	subduction	subduction	Latin/Greek origin
同义相似形	profession	professional	词性转换
	original	old	同义词类
同义异形	women clothing	silk scarf, etc.	抽象与具体
	Nine out of ten people are... (refer to exercise K→)	... is common	paraphrase 言下之意

笔 记 区

Exercise K: ***Figure out whether the lady is accepting or refusing the invitation or compliment from the man.***

A:
HE: Can I buy you a drink?
SHE: Actually I'd rather have the money.

E:
HE: I think I could make you very happy.
SHE: Why? Are you leaving?

B:
HE: Your face must turn a few heads!
SHE: And your face must turn a few stomachs!!!

F:
HE: What would you say if I asked you to marry me?
SHE: Nothing. I can't talk and laugh at the same time!!!

C:
HE: Hi! Didn't we go on a date once? Or was it twice?
SHE: Must've been once. I never make the same mistake twice!!!

D:
HE: Go on. Don't be shy. Ask me out!
SHE: Okay, get out!!!

G:
HE: I'm a photographer. I've been looking for a face like yours!
SHE: I'm a plastic surgeon. I've been looking for a face like yours!!!

H:
Man: If I could see you naked, I'd die happy.
Woman: If I saw you naked, I'd probably die laughing.

Exercise L: ***Read the following poem and see how you understand it.***

The Pig

It was an evening in November,
As I very well remember,
I was strolling down the street in drunken pride,
But my knees were all aflutter,
And I landed in the gutter
And a pig came up and lay down by my side.

Yes, I lay there in the gutter
Thinking thoughts I could not utter,
When a colleen passing by did softly say,

"You can tell a man who boozes
By the company he chooses."
And the pig got up and slowly walked away.

Exercise M: ***Choose FOUR letters from A–G.***

The aims of psychological research include

A. treating ill patients with arthritis.

B. illustrating the reasons for violence.

C. helping people interact with natural environment.

D. telling us how people act when they are nervous.

E. making predictions about whether communicative teaching is better than audio-lingual teaching in English education.

F. improving learning environment for students to learn better.

G. describing ways to cure depression.

Passage:

Scientific research in general has four major goals: description, explanation, prediction and control. The first goal of psychological research is thus to describe behavior. The second goal is to explain behavior, which means to identify its causes. Successful explanation makes it possible to achieve the third goal—to predict behavior, for example, whether a particular therapeutic approach will help in the treatment of mentally ill patients. The fourth and final goal is control. If we understand certain behaviors and can predict when they will occur, then we are in a position to control the circumstances that cause them. If we can understand and predict depression, for example, we may be able to control it. Likewise, if we understand the process of learning sufficiently well, we can create conditions to improve the ability to learn.

Excerpted from *Psychology* by Kelly G. Shaver & Roger M. Tarpy

Exercise N: ***Look at the eight qualities A–H of 'good teachers' and match each quality to the statement with the same meaning.***

Good teachers

1. can adjust teaching materials to different learning situations.
2. facilitate students' understanding of the aims of the course.
3. are keen on developing the students as learners.
4. treat their students with dignity and concern.
5. continually improve their teaching by monitoring their skills.

笔 记 区

Good teachers...

A. are themselves good learners—resulting in teaching that is dynamic, reflective and constantly evolving as they learn more and more about teaching.

B. display enthusiasm for their subject and the desire to share it with their students.

C. recognise the importance of context and adjust their teaching accordingly.

D. encourage deep learning approaches and are concerned with developing their students' critical thinking skills, problem-solving skills and problem-approach behaviours.

E. demonstrate an ability to transform and extend knowledge, rather than merely transmit it.

F. recognise individual differences in their students and take advantage of these.

G. set clear goals, use valid assessment techniques and provide high-quality feedback to their students.

H. show respect for and interest in their students and sustain high expectations of them.

Exercise O: *TRUE/FALSE/NOT GIVEN*

North Americans use the word corn in a narrow meaning to refer to maize, whereas the British use it to refer to grain in general. Keats' Ruth standing 'amid the alien corn' is not standing in a field of maize.

Keats was from North America.

Simplification of words:

Simplified word	*Corresponding words in a passage*
about	approximately, around, or so, some
about	considering, in regard to, in terms of, respecting, on, with respect to
actually	as a matter of fact, effectually, in effect, in fact, practically, really, virtually
adjust to	adapt to, gear to, accommodate, go with, match, suit
against	opposing, averse, contradictory
at the same time	meanwhile, simultaneously, synchronously
attractive	alluring, fascinating, inducing, tempting,
be likely to	be tempted to, tend to, incline to, prone to
classify	assort, categorize, label
clue	clew, hint, implication
control	dominate, manage, monitor, supervise
destroy	damage, devastate, ruin, wreak/catastrophe, destruction, havoc, tragedy
do	be under way, carry out, commit, conduct, implement,
enough	adequate, ample, sufficient
evaluate	appraise, assess, judge
expect	anticipate, hope, long for, look forward to, wish

笔 记 区

good	fabulous, fantastic, marvelous, miraculous, terrific, wonderful
have	belong to, hold, own, possess, possession
important	critical, crucial, essential, fundamental, foremost, significant, vital, make a difference, matter, play a part
know	appreciate, be aware of, be conscious of, recognize, understand
mainly	basically, chiefly, essentially, primarily, principally
many	abundant, considerable, innumerous, numerous, substantial, a flood of, a good many, a great number/deal of, many a, a raft of, a wealth of
now	at present, presently, currently
obvious	apparent, clear, distinct, evident, manifest, overt
only	exclusively, merely, solely, no more than
plan	program, project, scheme, devise, plot
possible	potential, promising
relate to	associate with, connect to, correlate with, link with
send	convey, transmit
show	demonstrate, manifest, prove, reveal, unravel
take part in	be involved in, participate in
very	awfully, badly, considerably, disproportionately, excessively, extraordinarily, extremely, greatly, highly, radically, significantly

5. 易混淆点（Confusing Points）

- **表与事实不符的标志词：**

1. The private car ***is assumed to*** have widened our horizons and increased our mobility.
2. They ***purport*** to represent the wishes of the majority of parents at the school.
3. It was one of his ***so-called*** friends who supplied him with the drug that killed him.
4. Electronic technologies ***were to have*** heralded a paperless office.
5. You ***should have*** told me earlier you have got a new girl friend in New Zealand!
6. I ***had thought*** you were a dandy.

- **表绝对性的标志词：**

always	invariably	never	
all	none	every	only
completely	definitely	irrefutably	assuredly
undeniably	certainly	indisputably	without question

- **表二者选一的标志词：**

A instead of /rather than B　　A take the place of B

A in place of B　　A in preference to B

笔记区

A supplant B	Substitute A for B
Replace A with B	a move from A to B
A. Instead/rather, B	

• **表将来存在的形式：**

时态：	will, be going to, be to
虚拟语气：	could, would, might
时间状语：	on the horizon is.../ There are many years away before...
单词：	possible/potential/imminent/expect

Exercise P: ***TRUE/FALSE/NOT GIVEN***

1. Working hours are not expected to decrease, partly because the 24-hour society will need to be serviced; and secondly, because more people will be needed to keep the service/leisure industries running.

   The 24-hour society will have a negative effect on people's attitude to work.

2. The past 5 years alone have seen the leisure business expand by 25% with a change in emphasis to short domestic weekend breaks, and long-haul short breaks to exotic destinations in place of long holidays.

   Long holidays have taken the place of long-haul short breaks.

Exercise Q: ***Look at the list below of the uses of glass. According to the passage state whether these uses exist today, will exist in the future or are not mentioned by the writer.***

A. if the uses exist today
B. if the uses will exist in the future
C. if the uses are not mentioned by the writer

On the horizon are optical computers. These could store programs and process information by means of light-pulses from tiny lasers—rather than electrons.	1. optical computers
He now has a new commission—a glass sculpture for the headquarters building of a pizza company—for which his fee is half a million dollars.	2. sculptures
Although glass is rigid, and thus like a solid, the atoms are arranged in a random disordered fashion, characteristic of a liquid.	3. fashions
Glass as instant curtains is available now, but the cost is exorbitant.	4. curtains

笔记区

SUMMARY

semantil

1. semantic (语意) → 生词 义域

syntactic

2. syntactic (语法) → 生词词性

① 直接解释

主要是 解释 主要的词汇、难懂的概念

标志性连词："That's…… In other word…… or other……say namely…… or, similarly……

标点：；，·∠ (

4. 定语从句 同位语

根据内在逻辑关系来推断词意

1. 对比关系

标志性词：unlike, not, but, however, yet, dis ; while ; in contrast

2. 比较

similarly

标志性词：similarly, like, just as, too, also, the same as, as…as,

3. 因果关系

标志性词：because, since, for, such…that

4. 同义词的替代关系

标志性词：P27

③ 构词法（前缀，后缀，词根，复合词）

画出句中定、状语从句，画出枝叶 留主干，画出介词短语 把定语性从句看作一个整体，把非谓语动词结构看作一个整体，找出全句主、谓宾及主干以后确定句子的主要意思，句子主要针对推论或者什么，主体是什么发生了什么事。

笔记区

Ⅱ. 语法（Grammar）

与词汇相比较，语法更为重要。词汇无限，语法规则有限，若能从语法入手，不仅能顺利越过生词障碍，而且能更准确地把握文章的重点，更快获取所要的信息。本章将分别论述长句分割、句间关系、句子重心、主谓宾划分和难句分析等问题。

1. 长句分割

• 长句如何化繁为简

1. 标点： 逗号、分号、冒号等
2. 连词： and, but, or, rather than...
3. 从句标志： that, which, where, when...
4. 并列介词结构： from...from..., to...to..., either...or..., ...
5. 固定短语： so...that, from...to, assign...to, ...

Exercise A: ***Answer the questions in Italic type within 10 seconds.***

1. *How many skills are required in the society?*

   What is important is that the child develops the range of social skills—being able to express a preference, knowing how to take turns, being able to stand up for themselves, being able to get into a group, being able to make decisions, being able to share, having confidence to go off on their own. These all require careful nurturing. No one is telling parents not to think about their children's development. It is just that it is more important to think about a child's desire to chat and the importance of social behavior and play activity, than the actually more trivial markers of intellectual achievement such as being the first kid in the group to cut out a circle that looks like a circle.

2. *How many possible reasons are there accounting for intellectual disabilities?*

   For the majority of intellectual disabilities, there is no identifiable cause but there are some causes that are well documented. They include: brain damage at birth due to lack of oxygen—prolonged labour during childbirth; brain damage before birth due to factors such as rubella, drug or diet-related problems; damage after birth due to illnesses such as encephalitis or accidents; hereditary defects in the genes; abnormal chromosome count resulting in, for example, Down Syndrome.

Exercise B: ***Divide the following sentences into TWO parts.***

1. We cannot say definitely that the temperature rises are due to the greenhouse effect; the heating may be part of a 'natural' variability over a long time-scale that we have not yet recognized in our short 100 years of recording.
2. Of the two orders of dinosaurs, the Saurischia was the larger and the first to

笔记区

evolve. It is divided into two suborders: Therapoda, or therapods, and Sauropodomorpha, or sauropodomorphs.

3. Stone tools found in Kakadu have now been dated to at least 50,000 years, and camp sites as diverse as Lake Mungo in the Willandra lakes region of NSW and WA's upper Swan River have yield tools charcoal radiocarbon—dated to between 38,000 and 45,000 years.
4. While much work has been done on the development of power sources for water pumping, for many people in rural Africa the use of human energy remains the only practical option.
5. Expeditioners heading south were issued with pamphlets listing five-letter codes covering almost every conceivable situation so they could communicate with their families and still keep within strict 'word limits' during their year on base.
6. Combine the act of giving with some knowledge of and sensitivity to the culture of the recipient and you have an invaluable chance to earn respect and lay the foundations of a durable and mutually beneficial business relationship.
7. Most significantly, in dinosaurs, the pelvis and femur had evolved so that the hind limbs were held vertically beneath the body, rather than sprawling out to the sides like the limbs of a lizard.
8. The pulp and paper industry has not been badly affected by the electronic technologies that promised a paperless society but has been radically altered by the pressure from another front—a more environmentally conscious society driving an irreversible move towards cleaner industrial production.
9. The environmental effects were at the time either not understood, or regarded as an acceptable cost of economic prosperity in an increasingly import-oriented world economy.
10. That comes from years of exposure and familiarity with letters, from being read to, from playing with magnetic letters, drawing and fiddling with computers.
11. While staple foods such as maize and rice produced during the rainy season can be stored for consumption in the dry season, the same is not true of vegetables and fruit which are essential for good nutrition.
12. The beliefs of Vietnamese folk medicine associate illness with the absence of any of the three souls which maintain life, intelligence, and the senses, or of the nine spirits which collectively sustain the living body.
13. Traditional, egalitarian and collaborative styles are viewed by some as being dependent on female and male gender-role attitudes, both of self and partner.
14. An opposing view sees the three family divisions of labor styles as a reflection of the progressive changes couples make in response to changing life situations, rather than being an aspect of personality.
15. The conclusion last summer of a 10-year building program has seen the historic zinc-alum shacks and even older wooden sheds built at an early Antarctic base, on Heard Island in 1947, supplanted by vast, bright-colored buildings with bay-window views and ski-lodge decor.

笔 记 区

2. 句间关系

• 句与句、词与词的关系

句与句之间不是机械的排列，而是有序的排列，它们之间的关系可能是并列、递进、转折、因果、让步、条件、顺接等；同样的，词与词之间也存在这些关系。

因果关系：因A果B

A	account for/ be responsible for	B
	bring about/cause/engender/give rise to/induce/mean/trigger	
	contribute to /lead to / result in	
B	according to/due to/lie in	A
	be ascribed to/be attributed to	
	be based on/be guided by	
	depend/rely on	
	evolve from/come from	
	in the sense of/through	

***Example 1*:**

A report on young driver research prepared last year by Monash University's accident research center found that in 1990 and 1991, almost a third of the people killed in road crashes were drivers under 25, yet this age group represents only 14 per cent of the population.

若改为图示，则句中关系一目了然：

A report
□ — on ...
□ — prepared ...
□ — by ...
found that
□ — in ...
□ — almost a third of the people
• killed ...
□ — were drivers ...
□ — yet this age group represents ...

***Example 2*:**

Geological movements are not the only occurrences to trigger an earthquake. Human activity, most often the filling of reservoirs with extraordinarily large amounts of water, can also cause earthquakes. Lake Mead, on the Colorado River in the United States, was filled in 1935 and was the first example of an artificial lake being responsible for earthquake activity. Similarly, massive explosions, such as quarry blasting and nuclear tests can also wreak havoc.

Causes of earthquakes:

I. __1__

II. __2__

A __3__ for example __5__

B __4__ for example __6__ and __7__

Example 3:

Like lizards, dinosaurs are included in the class Reptilia, or reptiles, one of the five main classes of Vertebrata, animals with backbones.

Both dinosaurs and lizards are animals with backbones. (*TRUE/FALSE/NOT GIVEN*)

解题：

将生词用字母代替，得出Like a, b are included in the class c, or d, one of the five main classes of e, f. 进一步推出彼此关系：a/b < c=d < e=f, 考题问的是a & b < f, 关系一致，故答案为TRUE。

Exercise C: ***Use a word or phrase to create a link between the pairs of sentences. You should not try to make them into one sentence, but you need to make a bridge between them.***

Example:

I need to be in the right mood to study.

I find it difficult to study in a room which is not insulated from noise.

I need to be in the right mood to study. Moreover, I find it difficult to study in a room which is not insulated from noise.

1. The publishing industry has recently taken a number of technological leaps forward.
   The question remains as to whether technology will improve literary content.
2. Computers are widely seen in classrooms today.
   Children as young as five are learning to use them.
3. The fast food industry is facing considerable criticism from health professionals.
   Companies now often claim that their food is nutritious and full of healthy ingredients.
4. We are now in a position to order our groceries over the Internet.
   We can benefit from the extra leisure time this gives us.
5. It was disappointing that our football club lost in the final on Saturday.
   It didn't help that the captain tripped over and had to be taken off on a stretcher.
   Then, the referee gave a penalty kick to the other side as a result of the accident.

笔记区

Exercise D: ***Analyze the logic in the following sentences.***

Example 1: As our roads become more dangerous, more parents drive their children to more places, thus contributing to increased levels of danger for the remaining pedestrians.

More dangerous roads ↘
 more danger for pedestrians
more driving parents ↗

Example 2: As people work more, the appetite for leisure activities has grown to compensate for the greater stress in life.

More work → greater stress → growing appetite for leisure activities

1. Working hours are not expected to decrease, partly because the 24-hour society will need to be serviced; and secondly, because more people will be needed to keep the service/leisure industries running.

 ...A... ↘
 the same long working hours
 ...B... ↗

2. Dinosaur skulls are found in a great range of shapes and sizes, reflecting the different eating habits and lifestyles of a large and varied group of animals that dominated life on Earth for an extraordinary 165 million years.

 ...A... ↘
 different shapes and sizes of dinosaur skulls
 ...B... ↗

3. The reduction in children's freedom may also contribute to a weakening of the sense of local community. As fewer children and adults use the streets as pedestrians, these streets become less sociable places. There is less opportunity for children and adults to have the spontaneous exchanges that help to engender a feeling of community. This in itself may exacerbate fears associated with assault and molestation of children, because there are fewer adults available who know their neighbors' children, and who can look out for their safety.

 Fewer pedestrians → B → C → D → a weakening sense of community

4. When two different masses of water meet, one will move beneath the other, depending on their relative densities in the subduction process. The densities are determined by temperature and salinity.

 ...A... ↘
 C → subduction process
 ...B... ↗

5. Foods and medicine, also classified according to their reputed intrinsic nature as yin (cold) and yang (hot), may be taken therapeutically to correct the imbalance resulting from ill health, or to correct imbalance due to the overindulgence in a food manifestly excessively 'hot' or 'cold', or due to age or changed physiological status (for example, pregnancy).

 A + B + C + D → imbalance → corrected by foods and medicine

笔 记 区

6. When people get up, their blood pressure and heart rate go up and there are hormonal changes in their bodies; all these things can have an adverse effect on the blood system and increase the risk of a clot in the arteries which will cause a heart attack.

   Getting up → A + B go up → C → E in the blood system → F increase → may cause a heart attack

7. Even the most remote reefs are at risk of pollution from tourist resorts releasing sewage and ships dumping their rubbish. Tourists too are so numerous that at one popular reef, urine from swimmers, and droppings from fish they feed, have increased the nutrient level in the water so much that algal blooms flourish and threaten the very existence of the colorful corals.

   A + B → pollution

   C + D → nutrient level in the water increased → E → dying corals

8. When world grain prices are bad, farmers in Asia's uplands turn from rice to cash crops to supplement falling incomes, or clear larger areas of rainforest with catastrophic environmental consequences within just a few years. Cleared rainforest soils are highly erosive; even where they are not, they rapidly become acid and toxic under intense cultivation and plants die, forcing the clearing of everlarge areas.

   Bad grain price → A

   or B → highly erosive soils

   or C → D → plants die → E

9. At the same time, agricultural research worldwide has been contracting as governments, non-government bodies and private donors reduce funding because of domestic economic pressures. This means that at risk is the capacity to solve such problems as rice yield decline and research.

   A → reduce funding → B → C

10. You are unaware of what regulates your breathing, heart rate, hormone secretions, or body temperature. You're not concerned about these vital functions because they are usually controlled by a separate nerve system called the autonomic nerve system, which, in turn, is regulated by a master control center, the hypothalamus.

    A → B → C such as: D&E&F and G

3. 句子重心

与中文不同，英语中强调某个信息点可以不通过词义的加强，只要改变其位置就能起到强调的效果。知道了“常态”和“变态”的句式后，作者的重点就尽在掌握之中。

Can you figure out any difference between the following sentences? If you were the examiner, what question would you ask according to the five sentences?

On the farm, the goats grazed peacefully and were unaware of the approaching

笔记区

hunter.

Question: ____________________

The goats grazed peacefully on the farm and were unaware of the approaching hunter.

Question: ____________________

The goats grazed peacefully on the farm, unaware of the approaching hunter.

Question: ____________________

Grazing peacefully on the farm, the goats were unaware of the approaching hunter.

Question: ____________________

Since they grazed peacefully on the farm, the goats were unaware of the approaching hunter.

Question: ____________________

Conclusion:

4. 句子主干

- **如何确定句子的主谓宾(SVO)——排除定状补成分**

1. 舍弃逗号、破折号、括号之间的信息
2. 舍弃介宾结构
3. 舍弃从句结构
4. 舍弃非谓语成分(视具体情况，因为非谓语成分也可充当主语和宾语。)

Exercise E: ***Figure out the SVO in the following sentences within 5 minutes.***

1. All dinosaurs, whether large or small, quadrupedal or bipedal, fleet-footed or slow-moving, shared a common body plan.
2. Human activity, most often the filling of reservoirs with extraordinarily large amounts of water, can also cause earthquakes.
3. Tea, now an everyday beverage in many parts of the world, has over the centuries been an important part of rituals of hospitality both in the home and in wider society.
4. This ocean circulation, which brings warm waters northward and ships cooler water south, is thought to be responsible for the warming of northern Europe by several degrees.
5. Anyone who has experienced either the reduced volume of traffic in peak hour during school holidays, or the traffic jams near schools at the end of a school day, will not need convincing about these points.
6. One significant factor undermining agricultural economies of developing countries has been the farm trade war between the US and the EC.

笔记区

7. In recent surveys, when parents in some cities were asked about their own childhood experiences, the majority remembered having more, or far more, opportunities for going out on their own, compared with their own children today.
8. However, assuming the build-up of greenhouse gases is responsible, and that the warming will continue, scientists—and inhabitants of low-lying coastal areas—would like to know the extent of future sea level rises.
9. When airline pilot Percy Trezise began to explore the rock art galleries of Cape York Peninsula in the early 1960s—a hobby that was to obsess him for the next 30 years—the consensus of academic opinion was that Australia had been peopled for less than 10,000 years.
10. Given anything that resembles a well-rounded life—with adults and other children to listen to, talk to, to do things with—their minds will acquire naturally all the skills required for further learning.
11. Among the problems afflicting a burgeoning world population, overcrowding, poverty and environmental degradation are combining to put at risk the very essence of our survival—food.
12. Scientists are hoping that one day, with enough data and sufficiently powerful computers, they will be able to calculate, without actually setting fire to anything, the way a fire will spread in any given building.
13. However, undue reliance on such categories and the consequent 'pigeonholing' of individuals into one of the five categories can result in failure to provide the opportunities for each person to develop.
14. But the discovery, beginning two years ago, of a vast Aboriginal graveyard at Lake Victoria near the confluence of the Murray and Darling rivers has thrown even this into doubt.
15. Recent work by oceanographers, using a new model which takes into account a number of subtle facets of the sea—including vast and complex ocean currents—suggests that the rise in sea level may be less than some earlier estimates had predicted.
16. Antarctica's long dark winter evokes visions of early explorers barely surviving in huts, their huskies and sleds snowbound outside in the harshest conditions imaginable.
17. Evidence for this inconsistent level of performance comes from modern research and practice which have shown that with skilled training and opportunity for development, people with intellectual disability have much greater potential for acquiring skills and for participation in community life than previously had been thought possible.
18. Only Germany, with incentives to business to encourage the employment of older people, and France, with the introduction of legislation making it illegal to use age barriers in recruitment—or to make employees redundant because of their age—have done anything substantive to combat age discrimination.

笔记区

19. The origin of gyres lies in the fact that more heat from the Sun reaches the Equator than the Poles, and naturally heat tends to move from the former to the latter.
20. But the emergence of Emotional Intelligence as a theory suggests that the family situations and other social interactions where social skills were honed in the past are fast disappearing, so that people now sadly need to be re-skilled.
21. The two strongest predictors of whether children will learn to read easily and well at school are whether they have learned the names and the sounds of the letters of the alphabet before they start school.
22. The only Australian evidence which possibly indicates that counter-measures targeted specifically at young/novice drivers have been effective comes from evaluations of zero blood alcohol concentration legislation.

5. 重新组合

●疑难杂症

有些句子每个单词都能看懂，但就是不理解，究其原因，主要有两个：第一是缺乏相应的文化背景知识或专业知识（此类情况看不懂应放弃）；第二是句子为了强调、平衡等因素，各个成分的位置发生了变换，只要找出主谓宾重新排列或按中式思维重组即可。

Example:

Not even books wherewith to inform and train his mind were within his reach.

Even books

with which to inform and train his mind

were not within his reach.

Exercise F: ***Figure out the meaning of the following sentences.***

1. The sex ration will be favored which maximizes the number of descendants an individual will have.
2. Everybody includes too much, and nobody excludes too much.

6. 其他语法要点

●指代、比较级、数字

Exercise G: ***Figure out the specific information of the underlined part.***

1. Port cities become industrial, financial and service centers and political capitals because of their water connections and the urban concentration which arises there and later draws to it railways, highways and air routes.
2. A study by the European Federation for Transport and Environment found that car

笔记区

transport is seven times as costly as rail travel in terms of the external social costs it entails such as congestion, accidents, pollution, loss of cropland and natural habitats, depletion of oil resources, and so on.

3. Looking at a picture actively prevents children younger than nine from creating a mental image, and can make it difficult for older children.
4. Age laws merely act as a symbol of a commitment to change societal attitudes, and it is these that must be changed if we are to make progress.
5. They are immediately labeled by potential employers as difficult characters who would have problems fitting into a new organization and it is for these reasons rather than their age that they are rejected.
6. This involves dealing with emotions, like jealousy, resentment, anger, etc, that one may have difficulty accepting by, perhaps, giving oneself comfort food, or doing nice things when one is feeling low. Many people do this instinctively by buying chocolate or treating themselves; others are able to wrap themselves in positive thoughts or 'mother themselves'. There are, of course, many people who are incapable of doing this, and so need to be taught.
7. In wood, which is the source of about 90% of the world's paper production, fibers are bound together by lignin, which gives the unbleached pulp a brown color.
8. The destructive forces, which produce earthquakes, usually begin deep below the ground, along a fault in weaker areas of the earth's rocky outer shell, where sections of rock repeatedly slide past each other.

Exercise H: ***Answer the questions in Italic type.***

1. The Monash University report into young drivers concluded that younger drivers were more likely to take risks at night.
   It is concluded that compared with older drivers, younger drivers take more risks. (*TRUE/FALSE/NOT GIVEN*)
2. The reasons for these continuing changes are as numerous as the organizations experiencing them. (*Which two are in comparison?*)
3. When children were given words and pictures, those who seemed to ignore the pictures and pointed at the words learnt more words than the children who pointed at the pictures, but they still learnt fewer words than the children who had no illustrated stimuli at all.
   (*Please list the students according to their learning efficiency in a descending way.*)
4. Measurements have shown that the rate of heat transfer into the ocean by vertical diffusion is far lower in practice than the figures that many modelers have adopted.
   (*Which is the higher, the measured figure or modelers' assumption?*)
5. Research has shown that differences in capability are as wide within age groups as they are between them.

笔记区

(*Is age a definitive factor to one's capability?*)

6. Of all the things that humans do, none is more impressive and distinctively human than using language.

   The least special thing for humans is the use of language. (*TRUE/FALSE/NOT GIVEN*)

7. The hotel is the closest to Sydney Airport and is designed to provide the best available accommodation, food and beverage and meeting facilities in Sydney's southern suburbs.

   The hotel is the best one to provide accommodation, food and beverage in Sydney. (*TRUE/FALSE/NOT GIVEN*)

8. Paleontologists believe that both dinosaurs and crocodiles evolved, in the later years of the Triassic Period (c. 248–208 million years ago), from creatures called pseudosuchian thecodonts. Lizards, snakes and different types of thecodont are believed to have evolved earlier in the Triassic Period from reptiles known as eosuchians.

   Which evolved earliest, snakes, dinosaurs or crocodiles?

Exercise I: ***Answer the questions in Italic type or complete tables below.***

1. The first of the initiatives was an organizational structure with only 3 levels of management—compared to the traditional seven.

   How many more levels of management does the old organizational structure have?

2. Between 1990 and 1994 the proportion of consumers claiming to be unaware of or unconcerned about green issues fell from 18 to 10 percent but the number of green spenders among older people and manual workers has risen substantially.

   How many more people were concerned about environmental problems in 1994 compared with 1990?

3. AHI has set an expectation that employees will submit at least three suggestions for every one they receive from a customer.

   The ratio of a customer's suggestion to that of the employees' is...

4. Absence rates for the six months prior to the incentive scheme ranged from 3.69 percent to 4.32 percent. In the following six months they ranged between 2.87 percent and 3.96 percent. This represents a 20 percent improvement.

   The absence rates have decreased to...percent of the original.

5. Even the French, who are proud of their cuisine, are turning to the microwave. Latest Europanel figures show that 38% of French kitchens house a microwave, just under the figure of 40% in western Germany. In Britain, the figure is 57%.

   Which country ranks first in the use of microwaves?

6. Statistically, one-person households include single-parent households, the

笔记区

numbers of which are shooting up. The phenomenon is growing. Forty percent of Swedish homes are now one-person households, compared with 29% ten years earlier. In western Germany the figure is 35% (30% ten years ago), in the Netherlands 29% (16%), and in Ireland 21% (17%).

Which country boasted the highest increase rate in one-person households?

7. The Monash researchers also looked at United States road-crash information for 1989 on 6.6 million police-reported crashes involving fatalities, injuries and motor vehicle damage. The researchers looked at a sample of 44,000 crashes.

   How many records did the researchers examine, 6.6 million or 44,000?

8. Earthquakes can rip apart entire cities and outlying districts, as the 1995 disaster in Kobe, Japan showed. Seismologists, scientists who study earthquakes and related phenomena, have records dating back to 1556, from the Chinese province of Shensi, which indicate that earthquakes have been devastating our world for centuries. In that instance, a major earthquake is estimated to have killed nearly 830,000 people, while destroying whole towns and villages. More recently, a death toll of more than 66,000 was recorded in northern Peru in 1970, and 23,000 died in the Guatemala quake of 1976.

Date	Location	Casualty

9. Mintel's 1994 survey found that 13 percent of consumers are 'very dark green', nearly always buying environmentally friendly products, 28 percent are 'dark green', trying 'as far as possible' to buy such products, and 21 percent are 'pale green'—tending to buy green products if they see them. Another 26 percent are 'armchair greens'; they said they care about environmental issues but their concern does not affect their spending habits. Only 10 percent say they do not care about green issues.

   Match the items in the left column with those in the middle and the right ones.

13%	Dark green	Buy green products when they see them
21%	Non-green	Regard environmental issues important but rarely buy green products
26%	Pale green	Always buying green products
28%	Very dark green	Unaware of the environmental problems
10%	Armchair green	Buy green products as much as possible

笔 记 区

Ⅲ. 语篇（Discourse）

一句话，并非每个单词都要看懂；一篇文章，也无需每句话都看懂。英语文章的逻辑性和层次感决定了读者只要把握文章结构，就能舍次留主，明确作者重点、略过繁文缛节、减少干扰信息的影响。本章将论述英文论文结构、如何区分论点和论据、识别过渡段和过渡句以及把握文章的整体结构。

1. 论文结构

英文论文结构很简单——开头出论点、总分贯始终、结尾重申法。形象地说，它是一条鱼。

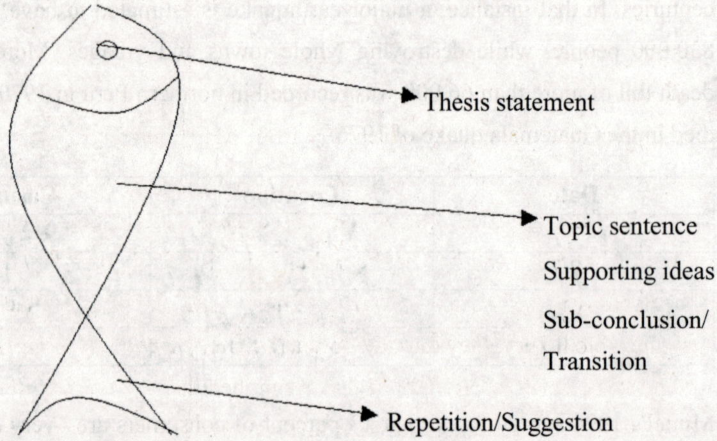

2. 区分论点和论据

Exercise A: ***Figure out the theses of the following paragraphs.***

1. The computer is assumed to have widened our horizons with a bombard of information. When we consider our children's knowledge, they can get more information and more ways of entertainment than they could without access to a computer. However, allowing their time dominated by computers has progressively eroded children's independent thinking ability. Children have lost much of their motivation to explore a question on their own but to depend on the information available online. In recent surveys, when parents in some cities were asked about their own childhood experiences, the majority remembered having more, or far more, opportunities to reflect on a question and discuss it with peers, compared with their own children today.
2. I don't know where I'm gonna go when the volcano blows—these words, suggested

笔记区

in a song by Jimmy Buffet in his 1979 Volcano album, probably reflect the concerns of many people living near active volcanoes. Volcanoes are beneficial to humans living on or near them. They produce fertile soil, and provide valuable minerals, water reservoirs, geothermal resources, and scenic beauty. But volcanoes can be very dangerous. Where can a person go to be safe from an erupting volcano? What types of volcanic hazards might they face? These questions are difficult to answer because there are many types of volcanic eruptions which produce different types of volcanic hazards.

3. Our research shows that no company can succeed today by trying to be all things to all people. It must instead find the unique value that it alone can deliver to a chosen market. We have identified three distinct value discipline, so called because each discipline produces a different kind of customer value. Choosing one discipline to master does not mean that a company abandons the other two, only that it picks a dimension of value on which to stake its market reputation over the long term.
4. Undoubtedly the desire for food has been, and still is, one of the main causes of great political events. But man differs from other animals in one very important respect, and that is that he has desires which are, so to speak, infinite, which can never be fully gratified and which would keep him restless even in Paradise. When the Abrabs, who had been used to living sparingly on a few dates, acquired the riches of the Eastern Roman Empire and dwelt in palaces of almost unbelievable luxury, they did not, on that account, become inactive. Hunger could no longer be a motive, for Greek slaves supplied them with exquisite viands at the slightest nod. But other desires kept them active: four in particular, which we can label acquisitiveness, rivalry, vanity and love of power.

Adapted from *On Human Nature and Politics* by Bertrand Russell

Exercise B: ***Figure out the topic sentences of the following paragraphs.***

1. Read a poem more than once. A good poem will no more yield its full meaning on a single reading than will a Beethoven symphony on a single hearing. One does not listen to a good piece of music once and forget it; one does not look at a good painting once and throw it away; a poem is not like a newspaper to be hastily read and cast into wastebasket. It is to be hung on the wall of one's mind.
2. Companies pursuing product leadership continually push products into the realm of the unknown, the untried, or the highly desirable. Reaching that goal requires that they challenge themselves in three ways. First, they must be creative. More than anything else, being creative means recognizing and embracing ideas that may originate anywhere—inside the company or out. Second, they must commercialize their ideas quickly. To do so, all their business and management processes are

笔记区

engineered for speed. Third and most important, they must relentlessly pursue ways to leapfrog their own latest product or service. If anyone is going to render their technology obsolete, they prefer to do it themselves. Product leaders do not stop for self-congratulation. They are too busy raising the bar.

3. The value of snobbery in general, its humanistic 'point', consists in its power to stimulate activity. A society with plenty of snobberies is like a dog with plenty of fleas: it is not likely to become comatose. Every snobbery demands of its devotees unceasing efforts, a succession of sacrifices. The society-snob must be perpetually lion-hunting; the modernity-snob can never rest from trying to be up-to-date. Swiss doctors and the Best that has been thought or said must be the daily and nightly preoccupation of all the snobs respectively of disease and culture.

Excerpted from *Selected Snobbery* by Aldous Huxley

论点与分论点所处的位置

Thesis statement	Topic sentence
1. 强转折词之后的内容	
2. what / how/ why 疑问句(及其答句)	
3. 第一段最后一句	3. 本段第一句
4. 结合文章题目检验	4. 上段最后一句

3. 论据的特征

Exercise C: *Answer the questions below.*

1. There are very significant time and money costs for parents associated with transporting their children to school, sport and to other locations. Research in the United Kingdom estimated that this cost, in 1990, was between 10 billion and 20 billion pounds.

When parents drive their children to school

A. children are more keen to play sport.

B. the costs are significant.

C. it reduces parents' free time.

D. traffic jams are a problem.

2. Instead, many deaths and injuries result from falling objects and collapsing buildings, while fire resulting from broken gas or fallen power lines is another danger. The Kobe earthquake in January 1995 lasted only 20 seconds, yet resulted in a death toll of over 5,000 and injured approximately 26,000 people. Fires burnt out of control for several days after the earthquake, which was followed by hundreds of after-shocks. Because of fears of damage to gas pipelines and any

笔记区

leaks being potentially disastrous, inhabitants endured freezing winter conditions.

Why does the author referred to Kobe here?

3. There is a danger in paying too much heed to seemingly high risk zones and erecting less stable buildings solely because of their being in a low risk zone. Prior to the earthquake, Kobe was not regarded as at serious risk, but after the disaster, investigation of the damage revealed that nearly all deaths occurred in small buildings that shattered rather than twisted when stressed.

Less stable buildings are built in ... risk zones. A. high B. low

4. 识别过渡段与过渡句

过渡段与过渡句的特征

位置：

关键词：

显著特征：

Exercise D: ***Figure out the main idea of Section A and Section B within 10 seconds respectively. Finish the choices.***

Gift

Section A

Gifts are a fundamental element of culture and our lives as social creature: a bar of chocolate on Valentine; a rosy carnation on Mother's Day or a bottle of Chardonnay for a party, though small, can convey a wealth of meaning about your gratitude and appreciation as well as the importance you place upon the relationship. There are occasions when giving a gift surpasses spoken communication, since the message it offers can cut through barriers of language and culture diversity. Combine the act of giving with knowledge of the culture, and you have an invaluable chance to lay the foundations of a durable relationship.

For all countries, take account of climate. A pack of preserved *tofu* can be ruined by extremely hot or humid climates, possibly causing the receiver considerable anguish. Consider the products that are abundant in the country concerned and try for something uncommon there. Think about the level of language skills: a book in English may be at best useless, at worst embarrassing, to a person with limited English. Inform yourself as much as possible about local customs, rules and etiquette, especially to do with wrapping, presenting, superstitions, taboos and importantly, customs and quarantine regulations. The following is a brief account of the etiquette of gift-giving in some countries of Asia and the Middle East.

笔记区

Section B

Hong Kong Chinese appreciate greeting cards, though obviously they will not refuse small tokens of friendship in the form of gift.

Books with plenty of illustrations are most appreciated in Indonesia. Inappropriate items are alcohol, products made from pigs and warm clothing. Ties and cuff links are not commonly worn.

In Iran, short-sleeved shirts and any visual representation of naked people, are highly inappropriate. Don't bother with ties, videos or records. As in all Islamic countries, there is a strict taboo on any pork products.

Respecting the Arab tradition, gifts should endeavour to praise the recipient in Iraq and should always be in an order that can be reasonably reciprocated.

Avoid certain colour combinations: red, white and black (colours of the Nazi flag); red, green and black (the Palestinian flag) in Israel.

Gifts are normally exchanged at the beginning of meetings with Japanese and should be given and received with both hands. It is seen as impolite to give an unwrapped gift. The emphasis should be on high quality, though not necessarily expensive, items. When in Jordan, it is preferable, but not vital, to avoid green in packaging. Do not give books, videos that mention Israel. Normal Arab customs apply, so no alcohol, pork, women's clothing, etc.

Again, the exchange should be made with both hands in Korea. Do not use red ink to write the names of the recipients.

Laos has virtually no cultural taboo items. It would be difficult to offend with virtually any gift.

Business contacts in the People's Republic of China are keen recipients of good Scotch whisky and American cigarettes, to the point where it is almost obligatory to take some along when you go there.

Do not open gifts in the presence of the giver in Philippines. Not recommended are items alluding to religion.

For Thailand, gifts should not be wrapped or packaged in black. Modest gifts, like ties, scarves and key rings, are much appreciated. Traditionally, sharp objects like knives or even letter openers are not given as gifts.

No special gift-giving customs in Vietnam, but liquor and wine can be problematic, for reasons pertaining to Vietnamese tastes rather than morality or religion.

笔 记 区

Multiple Choices:

1. When giving a gift to a person in Indonesia, the giver should

   A. give ties or cufflinks.

   B. give a bottle of wine or beer.

   C. give a book with many pictures.

   D. give warm clothing.

2. When giving gifts to a person in Iran

   A. items made from pigs are often appreciated.

   B. videos and records are popular.

   C. short-sleeved shirts should be avoided.

   D. certain colour combinations should be avoided.

3. When giving gifts to a Japanese person

   A. you should give a gift with one hand and receive a gift with the other.

   B. you should not give an unwrapped gift.

   C. the quality of the gift is not important.

   D. the gift should be expensive.

4. When giving a gift to a person in Laos

   A. the gift should be a cultural taboo.

   B. the gift might easily offend the receiver.

   C. almost any gift will be acceptable.

   D. gifts are not well-received.

5. When giving a gift to a person in China

   A. cigarettes are an excellent choice.

   B. cigarettes are taboo.

   C. gifts are generally not opened in the presence of the giver.

   D. gifts are generally reciprocated.

6. When giving a gift to a person in Vietnam, alcohol should be avoided because

   A. Vietnamese morality forbids it.

   B. Vietnamese religion forbids it.

   C. Vietnamese law forbids it.

   D. Vietnamese people don't like the taste.

5. 文章整体结构

Exercise E: ***Figure out the logic of the whole passage by using the passage, the questions, or the title only.***

笔记区

Example 1

Road Technology since the Romans

Between 43 AD and 81 AD Roman Britain acquired a 6,000 km network of technically advanced, hard wearing and straight highways linking towns of importance. Today Britain's motorway system is only half that length. The basic Roman philosophy of building a road to cope with different types and volumes of vehicles and using local materials where possible still applies today.

Roman roads were cambered with ditches on either side and built on embankments to give them a properly drained base. A surfacing layer of small stones was used over gravel or larger stones, although some Roman roads were covered with large paving flags, which is where term 'pavement' originates.

Once the Romans left Britain, its roads fell into ruin through lack of maintenance. They became run down, dusty highways in the summer and quagmires in the winter. It seems that the next milestone in the history of roads was not until the 18th and 19th centuries, with the advent of the Turnpike Trust. This raised cash for necessary maintenance in local areas to cope with the increasing numbers of wheeled vehicles, coaches and carriages wishing to travel at faster speeds.

In 1816 John McAdam observed that it was the native soil that supported the weight of traffic which, when dry, would carry any weight without sinking. He advised that the native soil be made dry and a covering impenetrable to rain be placed over it. However, road maintenance was not given much priority due to the popularity of the railways, until the motor car superseded the horse and cart. Cars, however, accentuated the problem of dust, described by the medical journal 'The Lancet' in 1907 as 'the greatest' modern plague.

Like so many other scientific advances, the solution came by accident. Tar mixed with stone had been used in footpaths in certain parts of Britain in 1832, and tarred gravel was applied to roads in Nottingham in 1869, but the biggest breakthrough came in 1901. A surveyor called E. Purnell Hooley was visiting Denby Iron Works near Derby when he noticed a dust-free length of road produced by a burst tar barrel. The resulting pool of tar had been covered with ironworks slag. Hooley experimented with blending hot slag and tar as a byproduct from the coal industry and in 1902 patented the process produced by a company known as Tar MacAdam syndicate Ltd. The company's name was later changed to Tarmac.

Nowadays, blacktop materials are made up of bitumen from oil which is blended with rock, gravel or slag. A number of varieties have evolved for different uses in road construction, including hot-rolled asphalt for surfacing major roads, dense bitumen macadam for lower layers of a road and open-textured macadam. Modern surfaces are bituminous-bound, graded stone supplied as a premix. Binders themselves have

笔记区

undergone technical developments. They are customized, ranging from soft to very hard to suit the traffic flow.

To accommodate higher traffic levels, either the thickness of the road must be increased or the materials improved. Hence the introduction within the last 10 years of heavy duty macadam in the road base which is three times as stiff as the dense bitumen and aggregate mix.

Alternatively, the structural design can be changed. For example, on an experimental reconstruction section of the M6 at Bescot, West Midlands, the heavy duty 'upside-down design' was introduced in the 1980s. Here, rolled asphalt overlays a thinner than normal road-base macadam, over a second rolled asphalt layer, all of which lie on a sub-base which is again thinner than normal. This structure is thought to perform well due to the lower rolled asphalt layer being more resistant to deformation and inhibiting cracking at the bottom of the road base.

Another innovative idea is the use of geotextiles. In research geotextiles are being placed between the sub-grade soil and a drainage layer beneath the sub-base. The sub-grade material is often clay and in the absence of the geotextile could, over time, clog the sub-base and reduce its efficiency as a drainage layer. But geotextiles can also have structural uses, and could provide improved resistance to cracking and rutting in roads.

The logic ____________

Example 2

New Rules for the Chemical Logistics

The logic ____________

Example 3

Questions 1–3

1. Among the following media, which one had the superior popularity in the past?
   A. Radio
   B. Books
   C. TV
   D. Internet

2. Most people were attracted by soap series because
   A. They were difficult to get
   B. They were exotic and rare
   C. They were featured by light humor
   D. They attested to the modernity of art

笔 记 区

3. According to the passage, the phrase ‘couch potato’ refers someone who

   A. is very wealthy

   B. is indulged in watching TV

   C. extremely favors a couch

   D. likes nothing but potatoes

Questions 4–8

As the most popular medium, the distinguished characteristic of computers is that they are more ___4___ than books, more ___5___ than television, more ___6___ than movies, more ___7___ than radio. In a word, they are ___8___.

The logic ______________

Example 4

Nomadic Bedouin are well known for traditions of hospitality in the desert. According to Middle Eastern tradition, guests are served both tea and coffee from pots kept ready on the fires of guest tents where men of the family and male visitors gather. Cups of ‘bitter’ cardamom coffee and glasses of sugared tea should be constantly refilled by the host.

For over a thousand years, Arab traders have been bringing Islamic culture, including tea drinking, to northern and western Africa. Techniques of tea preparation and the ceremonial involved have been adapted. In West African countries, such as Senegal and The Gambia, it is fashionable for young men to gather in small groups to brew Chinese ‘gunpowder’ tea. The tea is boiled with large amounts of sugar for a long time.

Tea drinking in India remains an important part of daily life. There, tea made entirely with milk is popular. ‘Chai’ is made by boiling milk and adding tea, sugar and some spices. This form of tea making has crossed the Indian Ocean and is also popular in East Africa, where tea is considered best when it is either very milky or made with water only. Curiously, this ‘milk or water’ formula has been carried over to the preparation of instant coffee, which is served in cafes as either black, or sprinkled on a cup of hot milk.

In Britain, coffee drinking, particularly in the informal atmosphere of coffee shops, is currently in vogue. Yet, the convention of afternoon tea lingers. At conferences, it remains common practice to serve coffee in the morning and tea in the afternoon. Contemporary China, too, remains true to its long tradition. There are as yet no signs of coffee at such occasions.

The logic ______________

笔 记 区

Example 5

Title: Worrying about Entering an Aging Society?

The logic ______________

Example 6

Title: Refer to Exercise D: Gift

The logic ______________

Example 7

Love and Marriage

Love is holding hands in the street; Marriage is holding arguments in the street.	Love is losing your appetite; Marriage is losing your figure.
Love is a dinner for two in your favorite restaurant; Marriage is Chinese take-out.	Love is sweet nothings but in the ear; Marriage is sweet nothings but in the bank.
Love is cuddling on a sofa; Marriage is deciding on a sofa.	Love is a flickering flame; Marriage is flickering television.
Love is a romantic drive; Marriage is a tarmac drive.	Love is one drink and two straws; Marriage is 'Don't you think you have had enough!'

The logic ______________

Example 8

The Value of Studying A Foreign Language at an Early Age

The logic ______________

Example 9

Some Misconceptions about Aboriginal Australia

In the early 1960s, the consensus of academic opinion was that Australia had been peopled for less than 10,000 years. Stone tools found in Kakadu have now been dated to at least 50,000 years, and camp sites as diverse as lake Mungo in the Willandra lakes region of NSW and WA's upper Swan River have yield tools charcoal

笔记区

radiocarbon-dated to between 38,000 and 45,000 years. They are indisputable evidence of the great antiquity of Aboriginal culture.

Thirty years ago, the first Australians were still thought of as a backward race. Trezise recalls in his book Dream Road, that there was much sage discussion on whether they were even capable of abstract thought. Since then, reawakened interest in and growing knowledge of Australia's Aboriginal heritage has demonstrated that this is a complex, subtle and rich culture.

The closer we look at Australian prehistory, the more it continues to confound our assumptions. Until recently, the authoritative view was that the population of Australia in 1788 was probably somewhere between 250,000 and 500,000. But the discovery, beginning two years ago, of a vast Aboriginal graveyard at Lake Victoria near the confluence of the Murray and Darling rivers has thrown even this into doubt. At least 10,000 skeletons are buried in the sands of lake Victoria, possibly as many as 40,000. Archaeologist Dr Colin Pardoe of the SA museum says the idea of 300,000 or so people in Australia before white settlement must be radically re-evaluated. 'I believe that we should be thinking 10 times that', he told science writer Julian Cribb recently.

Though Aborigines might see themselves as indigenous, there is no doubt that they were in fact Australia's first migrants. Their springboard was provided by the last ice age, or Pleistocene period, during which so much water was locked up on land that the ocean level dropped perhaps 150m. There was never a complete land bridge to South East Asia, but Arnhem Land was linked to Papua New Guinea for most of the past 100,000 years. This would have been one of the easiest routes for ice-age immigrants moving south.

Exercise F

1. ***Figure out the main idea of Paragraphs A and C in the above passage.***
   4 mis + conception + s

   Paragraph 1: ________________________

   Paragraph 2: Culture: complex or backward

   Paragraph 3: ________________________

   Paragraph 4: Origin: immigrant or indigenous

2. ***Figure out the topic sentence in each paragraph going with the title.***

   Paragraph 1: The consensus of academic opinion was that...

   Paragraph 2: ________________________

   Paragraph 3: ________________________

   Paragraph 4: ________________________

笔记区

Exercise G: ***Figure out the outline of the following passage.***

Common Faults and Eye Movement

There are a number of bad habits which poor readers adopt. Most of these involve using extra body movement in the reading process. In efficient reading, the muscles of the eye should make the only external movement. Of course there must be vigorous mental activity, but extra movements, such as pointing with the finger or moving the lips, do not help reading and often slow it down.

A fault that is often seen when students are trying to concentrate is pointing to the words with a finger, pencil or ruler. While marking the line might be helpful for beginning readers, it is certainly unnecessary for normal readers. Besides slowing down the reader, pointing at lines or words tends to cause the student to focus his attention on the wrong thing. The important thing to concentrate on while reading is not the location of the words on the page but the idea that the author is trying to communicate.

Another common fault easily observed is head movement. The belief that this head movement aids reading is pure nonsense. Eye muscles are quite capable of shifting the eyes from word to word, and they need no help from neck muscles. Often students are quite unaware that they are moving their heads while reading and they need to be reminded by the teacher not to do it.

Vocalization is another fault. Some poor readers think it necessary to pronounce aloud each word as it is read. The chief disadvantage of pronouncing words while you read them is that it tends to tie reading speed to speaking speed, and the silent reading of most normal readers is nearly twice as fast as their speaking. Usually this fault can be eliminated in older students by their own conscious effort, possibly with the aid of a few reminders from the teacher.

Subvocalization is the most difficult of all types of vocalization, where there is no body movement. But an inner type of speech persists: within the student's mind he is saying each word to himself, clearly pronouncing each word and then listening to himself, as it were. This fault is difficult, but not impossible, to cure. Probably the main reason for this problem is the nature of written language. English is written in an alphabet: a set of symbols which stand for speech-sounds. The speech-sounds in turn stand for an idea or thought. But it is not necessary to say or hear the word in order to get its meaning. It is quite possible to look at the printed word and get the idea directly. Students should practice grasping quickly the ideas presented on a printed page, and not reading aloud without error.

笔记区

When the eyes are reading a line of print they make a series of short jerky movements along the line, stopping after every one or two words for a very brief pause. The eyes do not, as some people erroneously believe, make a smooth even movement along the line. Each time the eye stops it sees a certain span of material and this span is called the 'span of recognition'. The span of recognition for most readers is a little over one word. When eye movements are photographed and recorded on a moving strip of film it can be shown that good readers do actually see two or three words in a fixation, while poor readers see one word or less per fixation.

One more reading fault the students might see while observing another reading or become conscious of in their own reading is the making of 'regressions'. A regression is a backward movement along a line of print. All readers make regressions, but good readers make very few and bad readers make a large number. Possibly this bad habit was started by the student's reading material not being properly graded for him. Forcing him to read too difficult material has engendered the habit of making regressions. To cure this habit the student should be given ample amounts of easy reading.

	Fault	Cause	Solution
1			
2			
3			
4			
5			
6			

Exercise H: ***Analyze the structure of the writing by Bertrand Russell and pay attention to the thesis, the topic sentences, the transitions, the ways to list examples and the balance within a sentence.***

What I Have Lived for

Three passions, simple but overwhelmingly strong, have governed my life: the longing for love, the search for knowledge, and unbearable pity for the suffering of mankind. These passions, like great winds, have blown me hither and thither, in a wayward course, over a great ocean of anguish, reaching to the very verge of despair. I have sought love, first, because it brings ecstasy—ecstasy so great that I would often have sacrificed all the rest of life for a few hours of this joy. I have sought it, next, because it relieves loneliness—that terrible loneliness in which one shivering consciousness looks over the rim of the world into the cold unfathomable lifeless abyss. I have sought it finally, because in the union of love I have seen, in a mystic miniature, the prefiguring vision of the heaven that saints and poets have imagined.

笔记区

This is what I sought, and though it might seem too good for human life, this is what—at last—I have found.

With equal passion I have sought knowledge. I have wished to understand the hearts of men. I have wished to know why the stars shine. And I have tried to apprehend the Pythagorean power by which number holds sway above the flux. A little of this, but not much, I have achieved.

Love and knowledge, so far as they were possible, led upward toward the heavens. But always pity brought me back to earth. Echoes of cries of pain reverberate in my heart. Children in famine, victims tortured by oppressors, helpless old people a burden to their sons, and the whole world of loneliness, poverty, and pain make a mockery of what human life should be. I long to alleviate this evil, but I cannot, and I too suffer.

This has been my life. I have found it worth living, and would gladly live it again if the chance were offered me.

Exercise I: ***Read the passage and finish the following two tasks.***

Vocabulary Change

Borrowing is a way of adding new vocabulary items to a language. Speakers of a language often have contact with speakers of other language. If a speaker of one of these languages does not have a readily available word for something in the world and a speaker of the other language does, the first speaker often borrows the word from the second speaker. The first settlers in North America had contact with the Indians who had already developed names for places and things peculiar to the North American continent. Consequently, the settlers borrowed such words as Massachusetts, Wisconsin, Michigan, Illinois, Chicago, and Mississippi, to mention a few place—names only.

Another large group of words came into English as a result of contact through invasion, in this case the Norman Conquest of England in 1066. Various kinds of words were borrowed into English: for matters of government like crown, country, duke, court, and prince; for matters of law like judge, jury, crime, accuse, marry, and prove; for matters of war like battle, arms, soldier, siege, danger and march; and for matters of religion like angel, saint, pray, save, blame, virtue, and vice. Then, too, today we find interesting pairs of words such as cow and beef, sheep and mutton, calf and veal, and pig and pork in which the first item, the name of the animal, is Germanic in origin and the second item, the meat of the animal, is a borrowing from French. Perhaps the occurrence of such pairs reflects a society in which the

笔记区

conquered Englishmen raised the animals for the table of the conquering Norman.

Several points can be made about the Normal Conquest. First, the borrowings from French do not show much, if any, cultural superiority in the invaders. Secondly, although the Normans were conquerors, they eventually gave up their French to become speakers of English, just as their ancestors had eventually given up their Germanic language when they invaded France. Thirdly, the borrowings do not show the same intimate relationships between the conquered and conqueror as the borrowings that resulted from the earlier Danish invasions of the ninth and tenth centuries, when 'everyday' words such as egg, sky, gate, skin, skirt, skill, skull, scatter, sister, law, weak, give, take, call and hit, and particularly the pronouns they, them, and their and the verb are were borrowed from the Danish invaders.

The kinds of contact speakers have with each other may often be judged from the particular items that are borrowed. For example, English has borrowed numerous words from French having to do with clothing, cosmetics and luxury goods, like ensemble, lingerie, suede, perfume, rouge, champagne and deluxe. From German have come words associated with food like hamburger and delicatessen. From Italian have come musical words like piano, opera, solo, sonata, soprano, trombone and serenade. From various Indian languages have come words for once exotic dress items like bandanna, sari, bangle, and pajama. And from Arabic have come some interesting words beginning with al-(the Arabic determiner): alcohol, alchemy, almanac and algebra.

Of course, Latin and Greek have provided English with the richest resource for borrowing more formal learned items. Large numbers of words have been borrowed into English from both languages, particularly leaned polysyllabic words. Numerous doublets also exist in English, that is, words that have been borrowed twice, once directly from Latin, and the second time through another language, most often French.

Latin	English	French	English
magister	magistrate	maitre	master
securus	secure	sur	sure

North American English shows a wide contact with other languages in its borrowings: French, Spanish, German, Dutch, American Indian and various African languages.

At different times speakers of certain languages have shown noticeable resistance to borrowing words, and they have preferred either to exploit native resources or to resort to loan translations instead. Such an English word as superman is a loan translation of the ubermensch just as marriage of convenience is a loan translation of

笔记区

the French marriage de convenance and it goes without saying of the French ca va sans dire.

Borrowings are also assimilated to different degrees. Sometimes a borrowing is pronounced in a decidedly foreign way for a while, but it is usually soon treated according to native sound patterns if it occurs frequently. In English, words such as garage, salon, masseur, ghoul and hickory, borrowed from a variety of foreign languages, are pronounced according to the sound system of English and not according to the phonological rules of the source language.

One process involves narrowing the meaning of word so that the word achieves a more restricted meaning over the course of time. Meat now means a particular kind of food, not food in general, as it does in the following quotation from the King James version of 'Genesis': 'And God said, Behold, I have given you eery herb bearing seed, which is upon the face of the earth, and every tree, in which is the fruit of a tree yielding seed; to you it shall be for meat.' Likewise, deer now refers to a particular kind of animal, not animal in general, as it did in Shakespeare's words 'But mice and rats and such small deer have been Tom's food for seven long years.' Worm now refers to a particular kind of crawling creature, not any crawling creature, although some of the original more general meaning is contained still in slowworm, blindworm, and glowworm. Fowl and hound refer to a particular kind of bird and dog and wife, to a particular kind of woman. However, in the case of the last word we can note a more general meaning in midwife, wife of Bath, and perhaps housewife. Finally, North Americans use the word corn in a narrow meaning to refer to maize, whereas the British use it to refer grain in general. Keats' Ruth standing 'amid the alien corn' is not standing in a field of maize.

The opposite process is widening of meaning. In this process a word achieves a more general meaning. The words bird and dog once referred to specific types of birds and dogs, not to the species in general. The word virtue described a characteristic associated with men, but not with women, just as only women could be said to be hysterical, since men were not possessed of wombs (hystera being the Greek word for 'uterus'). The word sensible once meant 'sensitive,' as it still does in French, and alibi referred to the fact that a person was elsewhere when something happened, not that he had some kind of excuse for something.

1. *Figure out the outline of the passage with **ONE WORD ONLY.***

   Threes ways of vocabulary change

   I. __(1)__

   i. Two __(4)__ to borrow words from other languages

   ii. __(5)__ features of Norman Conquest

   iii. __(6)__ of words borrowed from other languages

笔记区

iv. Words from ___(7)___ and ___(8)___

v. Wide ___(9)___ between North American English and other languages

vi. ___(10)___ to borrowing words

vii. ___(11)___ of borrowing words

II. ___(2)___

III. ___(3)___

2. *English has borrowed a variety of words from other languages. However, we may still figure out the origin of some words by their nature. Complete the table below with* ***NO MORE THAN THREE WORDS.***

Origin	Class	Words
	cosmetics	
German		
		piano
		sari
		alcohol
Latin and Greek		
		them

Exercise J: *Read the following passage and figure out its outline.*

How Market Leaders Keep Their Edge

Our research shows that no company can succeed today by trying to be all things to all people. It must instead find the unique value that it alone can deliver to a chosen market. We have identified three distinct value disciplines, so called because each discipline produces a different kind of customer value. Choosing one discipline to master does not mean that a company abandons the other two, only that it picks a dimension of value on which to stake its market reputation over the long term.

The first value discipline we call operational excellence. Companies that pursue this are not primarily product or service innovators, nor do they cultivate deep, one-to-one relationships with customers. Instead, operationally excellent companies provide middle-of-the-market products at the best price with the least inconvenience. Their proposition to customers is simple: low price or hassle-free service, or both.

The second value discipline we call product leadership. Its practitioners concentrate on offering products that push performance boundaries. Their proposition to customers is an offer of the best product period. Moreover, product leaders do not build their positions with just one innovation; they continue to innovate year after year, product cycle after product cycle. Johnson & Johnson, for instance, is a product leader in the medical equipment field. With Nike, the superior value does not reside just in its athletic footwear, but also in the comfort customers can take from knowing that whatever product they buy from Nike will represent the hottest style and technology on the market. For these product leaders, competition is not about price or customer service (though those can't be ignored), it's about product performance.

The third value discipline we have named customer intimacy. In adherents focus on delivering not what the market wants but what specific customers want. Customer-intimate companies do not pursue one-time transactions; they cultivate relationships. They specialize in satisfying unique needs, which often only they recognize, through a close relationship with—and intimate knowledge of—the customer. Their proposition to the customer: We have the best solution for you and we provide all the support you need to achieve optimum results, or value, or both, from whatever products you buy. Long-distance telephone carrier Cable & Wireless, for example, practices customer intimacy with a vengeance, achieving success in a highly competitive market by consistently going the extra mile for its selectively chosen small-business customers.

Questions 1–8

The following is a list of features of the disciplines.

A. if the feature is specific to the first discipline

B. if the feature is specific to the second discipline

C. if the feature is specific to the third discipline

D. if it is not mentioned in the passage

1. Investing a large sum of fund in R&D
2. Providing products of superior quality
3. Fostering one-to-one relationships with customers
4. Following an operating model to buy large quantities and negotiate better prices
5. Developing a new style and sticking to it throughout the year
6. Representing the state-of-art technology on the market
7. Aiming to be a trouble shooter for customers
8. Devoting a lot to advertising and promotion

第三章　雅思阅读实战篇

掌握每个细节后，真正要快速准确地把握一篇文章还需要有效的阅读方法和步骤。对于篇幅相当长的文章，阅读时不可能字斟句酌，建议阅读步骤如下：

1. 看标题
2. 浏览所有问题
3. 通读全文：首段—每段首末句—末段
4. 看路标词
5. 看定位词
6. 看插图
7. 看题目要求
8. 看范例
9. 分析问题和记忆

1. 看标题

目的：文章主旨 + 结构 + 全文关键词

Exercise A: ***Look at the following titles and see what you can get.***

1. Rising Seas
2. Human-powered Pumps for African Farmers
3. Principles of Fiber Opticals
4. Holism of Education
5. Paper Money
6. Numeration
7. Give Up Six Words and Change Your Life
8. The Nature and Aims of Archaeology
9. Obtaining Linguistic Data
10. Visual Symbols and the Blind

2. 浏览所有问题

目的：题型 + 阅读重点 + 关键词 + 暗示 + 难度系数

要求：1分钟

Exercise B: ***Go through the following questions within 1 minute and see what you have got in your mind.***

Questions 1–7

Use the information in the text to match the people (listed A–E) with the opinions (listed 1–7) below. Write the appropriate letters (A–E) in boxes 1–7 on your answer sheet. Some people match more than one opinion.

A. Dr. Broca
B. Dr. Brinkman
C. Geschwind and Galaburda
D. Charles Moore
E. Professor Turner

笔 记 区

Example	*Answer*
Monkeys do not show a species specific preference for left or right-handedness.	B

1. Human beings started to show a preference for right-handedness when they first developed language.
2. Society is prejudiced against left-handed people.
3. Boys are more likely to be left-handed.
4. After a stroke, left-handed people recover their speech more quickly than right-handed people.
5. People who suffer strokes on the left side of the brain usually lose their power of speech.
6. The two sides of the brain develop different functions before birth.
7. Asymmetry is a common feature of the human body.

Questions 8–10

Using the information in the passage, complete the table below. Write your answers in boxes 8–10 on your answer sheet.

	Percentage of children
One parent left-handed One parent right-handed	8 ____
Both parents left-handed	9 ____
Both parents right-handed	10 ____

Question 11

*Choose the correct letter, **A, B, C** or **D**.*

11. A study of monkeys has shown that

    A. monkeys are not usually right-handed.

    B. monkeys display a capacity for speech.

    C. monkey brains are smaller than human brains.

    D. monkey brains are asymmetric.

Exercise C: ***Go through the following questions within 1 minute and see what you have got in your mind.***

Questions 1–6

Do the following statements agree with the information given in Reading Passage 1? In boxes 1–6 on your answer sheet write

TRUE	if the statement agrees with the information
FALSE	if the statement contradicts the information
NOT GIVEN	if there is no information on this

笔记区

1. Modern official athletic records date from about 1900.
2. There was little improvement in athletic performance before the twentieth century.
3. Performance has improved most greatly in events requiring an intensive burst of energy.
4. Improvements in athletic performance can be fully explained by genetics.
5. The parents of top athletes have often been successful athletes themselves.
6. The growing international importance of athletics means that gifted professional sportsmen would attract more attention.

Questions 7–10

Complete the sentences below with words taken from Reading Passage 1. Use ***ONE WORD*** *for each answer. Write your answers in boxes 7–10 on your answer sheet.*

7. According to Professor Yessis, American runners are relying for their current success on ________________.
8. Yessis describes a training approach from the former Soviet Union that aims to develop an athlete's ________________.
9. Yessis links an inadequate diet to ________________.
10. Yessis claims that the key to setting new records is better ________________.

Questions 11–13

Choose the correct letter, ***A, B, C*** *or* ***D.*** *Write your answers in boxes 11–13 on your answer sheet.*

11. Biomechanics films are proving particularly useful because they enable trainers to
    A. highlight areas for improvement in athletes.
    B. assess the fitness levels of athletes.
    C. select top athletes.
    D. predict the success of athletes.

12. Biomechanics specialists used theoretical models to
    A. soften the Fosbury flop.
    B. create the Fosbury flop.
    C. correct the Fosbury flop.
    D. explain the Fosbury flop.

13. John S. Raglin believes our current knowledge of athletics is
    A. mistaken.
    B. basic.
    C. diverse.
    D. theoretical.

3. 通读全文:看首段——首末句——末段

目的:文章主旨和段落大意

要求:3分钟,读懂大意

笔记区

Exercise D: ***Read the following passage within 1 minute and finish the choice.***

Animal Talk

Like people, other living creatures can communicate. However, animal communication is sometimes sound communication and sometimes action communication.

A good example of action communication is the honeybee. Scientists have watched the activities of bees for a long time. One bee starts out from a beehive, the bees' home. The bee goes out to look for flowers. It finds flowers and then flies back to the hive. At the hive, the returning bee seems to move around in a dance. Other bees seem to watch. Then these bees fly out of the hive—straight to the same flowers. The first bee has somehow given information to the other bees. The bees communicated through action.

Sound communication is more common among animals. Whales in the ocean seem to 'sing' to one another. Scientists have listened to whale songs with underwater microphones. They know that each whale has its own song. Scientists can recognize some whales by their songs. So far, however, scientists do not understand what the whales are saying.

Many animals—such as wild dogs, gorillas, lions, and tigers—live together in groups like families. The members of the 'family' communicate with one another about proper behavior in the group. Their communication is sometimes a sound, sometimes an action, sometimes both. For example, a young wild dog will lie down in front of an older, more important dog. The young dog is communicating through the action.

Mother lions and tigers make gentle sounds to call their babies. They use other sounds to warn the young animals about danger. The songs of birds also carry messages. In one song they may be calling to their mates. In another song they may be saying, 'This is my garden. Stay out.'

Some animals seem to want to talk to human beings. For example, dolphins in the ocean often swim very close to people. They make high squeaky little sounds to the people. Are they trying to talk? Animals are talking with one another. Perhaps someday we can learn their languages, and we can talk with them too.

The main idea of the timed reading is

A. all creatures make sounds.

B. animals seem to communicate with one another.

C. all communication is sound.

笔记区

Exercise E: ***Read the following passage within 1 minute and finish the choice.***

Health, Ethics, and Vegetarians

Claire has been a vegetarian for years. She stopped eating meat because of how she felt. As she told her doctor, she always felt tired. Her doctor found that her blood cholesterol was high. Therefore, her doctor suggested that she cut down on meat, especially red meat. Claire decided to 'go all the way.' She bought a vegetarian cookbook and stopped eating meat. She still eats eggs and cheese occasionally now, however, most of her food consists of vegetables, fruits, and grains. Claire balances her diet to get all of the necessary vitamins, minerals, proteins, and carbohydrates. Claire became a vegetarian to improve her health.

Nancy is an animal lover. Nancy grew up on a farm where there were cows and chickens. As she grew older, she started to reduce the amount of meat that she ate. One day she realized that she had stopped eating meat altogether. It had never seemed right to her that animals were raised to be killed for food.

When Aaron was a student, he was on a strict budget the little money that he had for food, he spent on rice, inexpensive vegetables, and spices. He learned to be a very good cook. Now Aaron is a successful engineer, but he still eats simple foods, and no meat. Aaron became a vegetarian from economic necessity; he is a vegetarian today by choice.

Twenty years ago, Kim's doctor told her that she had arthritis. Her bone joints (shoulders, knees, elbows, fingers) were red and sore. Her doctor told her that there was no cure, but that some people felt better if they stopped eating meat, potatoes, tomatoes, eggplant, and sugary foods. Kim tried these suggestions, and for twenty years she has avoided arthritis pain. Kim became a vegetarian to control the disease.

Simon is an environmentalist. He knows that the Earth can produce food for many people, but the amount of food is finite (limited). He knows that the population is increasing rapidly, but land for growing food is not increasing at all. He knows that it takes sixteen kilograms of grain to make one kilogram of meat; he thinks about the fifteen kilograms of grain that are wasted if he eats meat. 'Somewhere,' he says, 'someone is starving, dying from lack of food. How can I enjoy a thick steak?' Simon's ethics—his ideas about what is right and wrong—make him a vegetarian.

The main idea of this reading is that

A. people become vegetarians for different reasons.

B. meat is harmful to one's health.

C. people become vegetarians because they want to be good to animals.

笔记区

Exercise F: *Read the following passage within 1 minute and finish the choice.*

More Sensitive Than Machines, More Aware Than People

After every major earthquake there are reports of strange animal behavior. Birds of many kinds have acted strangely before the earthquake. Chickens do not fly up to roost on a pole or branch; they stay on the ground. Pigeons and crows fly in unusual patterns. Canaries and parakeets stop singing in their cages. Normally quiet dogs start to bark; noisy dogs fall silent. Fish that normally stay deep in the water swim near the surface of the water in large schools. Snakes come out of their holes. Is this behavior related to earthquakes? Can scientists use animal behavior to predict earthquakes?

Scientists are not likely to start focusing on animal behavior as a way of predicting earthquakes. There are too many animals and too many ways that they behave. Instead, scientists will look for the causes of these changes in animal behavior. Perhaps people can sense what the birds, the fish, the dogs, and the snakes are sensing (feeling).

The Kobe earthquake in Japan happened on January 17, 1995. A lot of water in that area is bottled for sale. Therefore, there were supplies of dated water in bottles. Scientists studied this water. Between October and January 10, the water showed a sharp increase in chlorine and sulfates. Another study focused on radon in the water. Between October and the end of December, the amount of radon increased fourfold. There was another dramatic increase of radon on January 7. On January 8, the radon level was ten times higher than the October level. Then the radon began to decrease. A week later, disaster struck. Perhaps some animals are sensitive to the changes in these gases.

Just before the Loma Prieta earthquake, seismologist at Stanford University, noted a burst of magnetic noise. Some physicists began experiments with squeezing dry rocks. They found that the rocks generated electricity just as they crumbled. Because earthquakes squeeze rocks, the researchers set up equipment to monitor earthquake-prone zones. Their results seem to support the conclusion that animals sense electric current.

In California, researchers have ‘heard’ the groans and rumbles of faults for several years. Now they are beginning to understand that a sound from one fault gets ‘answers’ from other nearby faults. These noises are evidence of changes in the Earth’s crust, and geologists may learn to understand their messages. Perhaps animals are able to detect these sounds and know that something is going to happen.

The main idea of this reading is that

A. animals have a number of interesting behavior patterns.

B. scientists are trying to find out what animals are sensing before an earthquake.

C. earthquakes may be predicted by different kinds of signals in the Earth.

笔 记 区

4. 看路标词

目的：重要考点

路标词：

A. 强转折词：but, however, in fact ...

B. 表顺接：next, A lead to B, combine A with B ...

C. 表并列：too, also, another, new, similarly, likewise ...

D. 表递进：in addition to, additionally, furthermore ...

Exercise G: ***Read the following 'Dear John Letter' and discuss with fellow students how you feel about the 'But.'***

Dear Ricky,

For the past 17 years, you have been my best friend. You have seen me through difficult times, happy times and just about every phase of my life. You have always been here when I've needed you and I counted on you at all times.

But, I can no longer continue our relationship. The distance between us is just too great. Please return the picture of me that I sent to you.

Love,

Becky

The Marine, with hurt feelings, asked his fellow Marines for any snapshots they could spare of their girlfriends, sisters, ex-girlfriends, aunts, cousins, etc. There were 57 photos in that envelope... along with this note:

Dear Becky,

I'm so sorry, but I can't quite remember who you are. Please take your picture from the pile, and send the rest back to me.

Take Care,

Ricky

笔记区

5. 看定位词（Eye-catching words）

目的：快速准确定位

定位词：

A. 大写字母

B. 数字

C. 标点符号

D. 特殊形式

E. 单位符号

F. 特长/特难单词

Exercise H: ***Read the following passage and underline all the eye-catching words.***

When a volcano erupts it will sometimes eject material such as rock fragments into the atmosphere. This material is known as tephra. The largest pieces of tephra (greater than 64 mm) are called blocks and bombs. Blocks and bombs are normally shot ballistically from the volcano. Blocks and bombs as large as 8–30 tons have fallen as far away as 1 km from their source (Bryant, 1991). Small blocks and bombs have been known to travel as far away as 20–80 km (Scott, 1989)! Some of these blocks and bombs can have velocities of 75–200 m/s (Bryant, 1991). Smaller ejecta such as lapilli (2–64 mm) and ash (<2 mm) which are convected upward by the heat of the eruption will fall out farther from the volcano. Most particles greater than a millimeter in size will fall out within 30 minutes of the time they are erupted (W.I. Rose personal communication). The smallest particles which are less than .01 mm can stay in the atmosphere for two or three years after a volcanic eruption. Sometimes these particles produce fantastic sunsets such as was seen after the eruptions of Krakatau in 1883 and Pinatubo in 1991. Some scientists believe that these particles may contribute to global warming.

6. 看插图

目的：寻找答案 + 验证答案

Exercise I: ***Read the following passage and complete the table.***

In 1952 the neurophysiologist Nathaniel Kleitman and one of his students, Eugene Aserinsky, studied the rolling movements of the eyes which occur early in sleep. As the volunteers began to fall asleep, the electrodes detected the slow rolling eye movements which could be seen easily through their eyelids. Soon after, the volunteers fell deeper into sleep and their eyes became still. An hour or so later, to the great surprise of Aserinsky, the pen recorders showed that the eyes were moving

笔记区

again. This time they were not just swinging from side to side but were darting back and forth (see the figure). These rapid eye movements continued for some time and then the eyes came to rest again.

These phases of rapid eye movement (R.E.M.) occur every ninety minutes or so and represent a distinct and important stage of sleep. The huge slow waves of normal sleep are replaced by a higher frequency pattern closer to the brainwaves of the normal waking state. In this state of 'paradoxical sleep,' most of the muscles of the body are paralysed, cut off from the restless activity of the brain by inhibitory signals from a tiny region deep in the brainstem. The only responses to the brain activity are the eye movements and the occasional twitching of fingers or the grinding of the teeth.

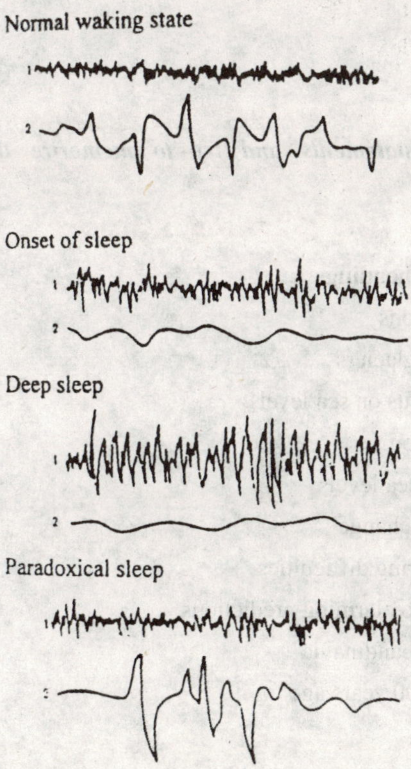

These signals were picked up with electrodes stuck to the scalp and face of a volunteer. In each case the upper trace 1 shows the electroencephalogram, which reflects the activity in the cerebral cortex, while the trace 2 below shows the movements of the eyes.

Complete the table within 10 minutes.

State	Brainwaves	Eyes	Body
Waking	1	/	/
Onset of sleep	Slower	2	/
3	4	5	/
Paradoxical sleep	As waking	6	7

笔记区

7. 看题目要求

目的：做什么 + 怎么做 + 定位提示

Exercise J: ***Read the direction and underline useful information.***

Look at paragraphs C, D and E. Using the information in the passage, complete the flow chart below. Write your answers in boxes 32–35 on your answer sheet. Use ***ONE OR TWO WORDS*** *for each answer.*

8. 看范例

目的：答题模式 + 暗示

9. 分析问题和记忆

目的：关键词 + 大致定位 + 规模效应

Exercise K: ***Analyze the following statements and try to memorize the information as much as possible.***

List of headings

i. Contrary indications
ii. Europe's Alpine glaciers
iii. Growing consensus on sea level
iv. Ice cap observation
v. Causes of rising sea levels
vi. Panel on climate change
vii. Sea level monitoring difficulties
viii. Group response to alarming predictions
ix. Stockholm and Scandinavia
x. The world 130,000 years ago

Exercise L: ***Analyze the following statements and try to memorize the information as much as possible.***

1. The high points and low points of life have a predictable plan according to this article.
2. A person's memory is greatest when he/she is about 45.
3. The peak for vocabulary is 30.
4. You are more likely to commit suicide if you are married than divorced.
5. People are most pessimistic when they are in their twenties.
6. Creative people produce high level work throughout their lives.

笔记区

7. Although there is a predictable life plan that people share, there are exceptions to the plan.
8. Adolescence is the happiest period of life.

Exercise M: ***Analyze the following choices of matching and try to memorize the information as much as possible.***

1. Passive smoking
2. Compared with a non-smoker, a smoker
3. The American Medical Association

A. includes reviews of studies in its reports.
B. argues for stronger action against smoking in public places.
C. is one of the two most preventable causes of death.
D. is more likely to be at risk from passive smoking diseases.
E. is more harmful to non-smokers than to smokers.
F. is less likely to be at risk of contracting lung cancer.
G. is more likely to be at risk of contracting various cancers.
H. opposes smoking and publishes research on the subject.
I. is just as harmful to smokers as it is to non-smokers.
J. reduces the quantity of blood flowing around the body.

Exercise N: ***Analyze the following summary and try to memorize the information as much as possible.***

How do the birds find their way on their enormously long journeys? The young birds are not taught the road by their __1__, because often the parents fly off first. We have no __2__ how the birds find their way, particularly as many of them fly __3__ night, when landmarks could hardly be __4__. And other birds migrate over the sea, where there are no __5__ at all. A certain kind of plover, for __6__, nests in Canada. At the end of the summer these birds __7__ from Canada to South America; they fly 2,500 miles, non-stop, over the ocean. Not only is this very long flight an extraordinary feat of endurance, but there are no landmarks on the ocean to __8__ the birds.

Exercise O: ***Analyze the following statements and try to memorize the information as much as possible.***

1. According to British research, a mere twelve percent of vehicles tested produced over fifty percent of total pollution produced by the sample group.
2. It is currently possible to measure the pollution coming from individual vehicles whilst they are moving.
3. Residents of Los Angeles are now tending to reduce the yearly distances they

笔记区

travel by car.

4. Car-pooling has steadily become more popular in Los Angeles in recent years.
5. Charging drivers for entering certain parts of the city has been successfully done in Cambridge, England.

Exercise P: ***Analyze the following statements and try to memorize the information as much as possible.***

1. Besides planets and their moons, there are also asteroids and comets in the solar system.
2. The Milky Way and Galaxy are the same thing.
3. The Sun is the only star in the solar system.
4. The Sun converts its mass into energy by atomic reaction.
5. The planet Mercury has two other names called by man: the morning star and evening star.

Exercise Q: ***Analyze the following statements and try to memorize the information as much as possible.***

1. The pull of gravity is greater than that of water.
2. Water is able to dissolve more substances than any other liquid.
3. At its beginning the Earth was more likely to support life than any other planet.
4. The human body is made up of 80% water.

Exercise R: ***Analyze the following statements and try to memorize the information as much as possible.***

According to the passage, decide which of the following statements is ***NOT*** *true.*

A. Interstate highways could provide a special service in the war time.
B. In deciding the location of interstate highways, people's transportation patterns and their desires were ignored.
C. The era of building of the interstate highway system came to an end when Frank Turner was alive.
D. Frank Turner couldn't understand why people did not support the interstate highways.
E. Many people enjoy the benefits of the interstate highway system without consciously realizing the fact.

笔记区

SUMMARY

笔记区

第四章　雅思阅读补充习题

Ⅰ. 段落大意的把握

Exercise A: ***Read the following paragraphs and find out the topic of each paragraph.***

A. It will not take a long time to retrain a slow reader.
B. Slow readers fail to realize their full potential.
C. Fast readers understand and remember better than slow readers.
D. Rapid readers can relax and enjoy their reading.
E. Readers feel no strain when they read at a slow speed.
F. Rapid readers read different materials at different rate.
G. Most people can read fast.
H. More practice is required to increase reading speed.
I. Rapid reading is applicable to both easy and difficult material.
J. Brain and eye muscles can be trained to get information more quickly.

1. Fast readers are alert, active and efficient readers. Vast researches as well as records kept by speed-reading teachers prove the faster, the better understanding the readers will develop. On the other hand, slow readers tend to be passive and unskilled. Their comprehension or understanding is often low because they work too far below their potential to remain alert and interested. As a result, their minds wander.

2. Research and the records of hundreds of teachers show that anyone with average intelligence (and good sight) can read and understand simple material at 800–1,200 words per minute. The brain can absorb more rapidly than one can send material to it. A habit of lazy, passive reading has produced slow readers. Eye muscles will respond to training. One needs a mental 'set' to absorb material quickly.

3. It is true that efficient readers do not read everything at the same rate. They vary speed and techniques according to the difficulty of the material and their purpose for reading it. They will find, however, that as their basic rate improves, their rate for other materials will also improve. Their rapid, medium, and slow rates will all increase. Thus, a well-trained reader may be reading difficult material twice as fast as a nontrained reader reads easy material. Remember: rapid readers can read as slowly as they choose and as fast as they choose.

笔记区

4. Once rapid reading has become a habit, readers enjoy and savor style just as much as they did before at slower speeds. It takes time to make rapid reading a habit. But, once the habit has been formed, readers feel no more strain than they did at their old slower rates.

5. It has been proved many times in school and reading clinics that readers can double or triple their rates in thirty to sixty days. The increase depends upon the amount of daily practice time.

(Words:316)

Exercise B: ***Read the following passage and find out the main idea of each paragraph.***

A. Deteriorating quality of people
B. Substitution of 'cheese food' for traditional cheese
C. Quantity goes before quality
D. The role of science in vegetable production
E. Less tasteful food in America
F. Role of economics in cheese production
G. Inferior copy of cheese
H. The relationship between bland food and obesity
I. The economic reason for failure to enjoy fresh vegetables
J. The effect of 'deep freezing' on foods

Man Is What He Eats

1. Over the years, I have come to feel that way about what science has done to food. What America eats is handsomely packages; it is usually clean and pure; it is excellently preserved. The only trouble with this is: year by year it grows less food to eat. It appeals increasingly to the eye. But who eats with his eyes?

2. Take cheese, for instance. Here and there, in big cities, small stores specialize in cheese. At such places, one can buy at least some of the first-rate cheeses that we used to eat—such as those we had with pie and macaroni. Long ago, this cheese began to be supplanted by a material called 'cheese foods'. Some cheese foods are fairly edible; but no one comes within miles of the old kinds—for flavor.

3. What happened? Science—or what is called science—stepped in. The old-fashioned cheeses didn't ship well enough. They crumbled, became moldy, and dried out. 'Scientific marketing' then took effect. In food, as in many other things, the 'scientific marketers' regard quality as secondary as long as they can sell most persons anyhow.

笔记区

4. Economics entered. It is possible to turn out in quantity a bland, impersonal, practically imperishable substance more or less resembling, say cheese—at lower cost than cheese. Chain groceries shut out the independent stores and 'standardization' became a principal means of cutting cost.

5. Imitations also came into the cheese business. There are American duplications of most of the celebrated European cheeses, mass-produced and cheaper by far than imports. They would cause European food-lovers to gag and guffaw—but generally, the imitations are all that's available in the supermarkets. People buy them and eat them.

6. For years, I could not figure out what had happened to vegetables. I knew, of course, that most vegetables, to be enjoyed in their full deliciousness, must be picked fresh and cooked at once. Our vegetables, however, come to us through a long chain of command. There are merchants of several sorts—wholesalers before the retailers, commission men, and so on—with the result that what were once edible products become, in transit, mere wilted leaves and withered tubers.

7. It is only lately that I have found how much science of genetics is involved. Agronomists and the like have taken to breeding all sorts of vegetables and fruits—changing their original nature. This sounds wonderful and often is insane. For the scientists have not as a rule taken any interest whatsoever in the taste of the things they've tampered with!

8. I wonder if this blandness of our diet doesn't explain why so many of us are overweight and even dangerously so. When things had flavor, we knew what we were eating all the while—and it satisfied us. But, of the average tinned or glass-packed strawberry jam, you need half a cupful to get the idea of what you're eating.

9. It is, however, 'deep freezing' that has really rung down the curtain on American cookery. Nothing is improved by the process. Most foods, cooked or uncooked, are destroyed in the deep freeze for all people of sense and sensibility. The essential oils that make peas peas—and cabbage cabbage—must undergo fission and fusion in freezers. Anyhow, they vanish. Some meats turn to leather. Others to wood pulp.

10. We are abandoning quality—even, to some extent, the quality of people. The 'best' is becoming too good for us. We are suckling ourselves on machine-made mediocrity. It is bad for our souls, our minds, and our digestion. It is the way our wiser and calmer forebears fed, not people, but hogs: as much as possible and as fast as possible, with no standard of quality. Therefore, I call, here, for rebellion.

Adapted from *Science Has Spoiled My Supper* by Philip Wylie

（Words：636）

笔记区

Exercise C: ***Read the following passage and find out the main idea of each paragraph.***

A. Fear to lose people's attention
B. Inescapable from TV
C. Hours spent on TV
D. Emphasis on concentration
E. Advantage of following TV's lead
F. Desire for effortless work
G. What we have paid for TV?
H. Failure to focus one's attention
I. Reason for people's short attention span
J. Inefficient communication brought by TV
K. Nature of TV news
L. Boring and dismissible TV news
M. Discouraged thinking
N. Attraction of TV
O. Oversimplification in decision-making

1. It is difficult to escape the influence of television. If you fit the statistical averages, by the age of 20 you will have been exposed to at least 20,000 hours of television. You can add 10,000 hours for each decade you have lived after the age of 20. The only things Americans do more than watching television are work and sleep.

2. The trouble with television is that it discourages concentration. Almost anything interesting and rewarding in life requires some constructive, consistently applied effort. The dullest, the least gifted of us can achieve things that seem miraculous to those who never concentrate on anything. But television encourages us to apply no effort. It sells us instant gratification. It diverts us only to divert, to make the time pass without pain.

3. Television's variety becomes a narcotic, not a stimulus. Its serial, kaleidoscopic exposures force us to follow its lead. The viewer is on a perpetual guided tour: 30 minutes at the museum, 30 at cathedral, 30 for a drink, then back on the bus to the next attraction—except on television, typically, the spans allotted are on the order of minutes or seconds, and the chosen delights are more often car crashes and people killing one another. In short, a lot of television usurps one of the most precious of all human gifts, the ability to focus your attention yourself, rather than just passively surrender it.

4. Capturing your attention—and holding it—is the prime motive of most television programming and enhances its role as a profitable advertising vehicle. Programmers live in constant fear of losing anyone's attention—anyone's. The

笔记区

surest way to avoid doing so is to keep everything brief, not to strain the attention of anyone but instead to provide constant stimulation through variety, novelty, action and movement. Quite simply, television operates on the appeal to the short attention span.

5. In the case of news, this practice results in inefficient communication. I question how much of television's nightly news effort is really absorbable and understandable. Much of it is what has been aptly described as 'machine-gunning with scraps.' I think the technique fights coherence. I think it tends to make things ultimately boring and dismissible (unless they are accompanied by horrifying pictures) because almost anything is boring and dismissible if you know almost nothing about it.

6. TV's appeal to the short attention span is not only inefficient communication but decivilizing as well. Consider the casual assumptions that television tends to cultivate: that complexity must be avoided, that verbal precision is an anachronism. It may be old-fashioned, but I was taught that thought is words, arranged in grammatically precise ways.

7. Everything about this nation—the structure of the society, its forms of family organization, its economy, its place in the world—has become more complex, not less. Yet its dominating communications instrument, its principal form of national linkage, is one that sells neat resolutions to human problems that usually have no neat resolutions. It is all symbolized in my mind by the hugely successful art form that television has made central to the culture, the 30-second commercial: the tiny drama of the earnest housewife who finds happiness in choosing the right toothpaste.

8. When before in human history has so much humanity collectively surrendered so much of its leisure to one toy, one mass diversion? When before has virtually an entire nation surrendered itself wholesale to a medium for selling? This society is being forced-fed with trivial fare, and I fear that the effects on our habits of mind, our language, our tolerance for effort, and our appetite for complexity are only dimly perceived.

Adapted from *The Trouble with Television* by Robert MacNeil

(Words: 610)

Exercise D: ***Each item represents one different type of transaction between nations. Match the news item to the transaction types.***

Example	*Answer*
News item **1**	**a**

笔 记 区

News item 2:
News item 3:
News item 4:
News item 5:
News item 6:
News item 7:
News item 8:
News item 9:
News item 10:
News item 11:
News item 12:
News item 13:
News item 14:

List of headings

A. Official visits
B. Sister cities
C. Setting up a diplomatic office
D. Restoring diplomatic relations
E. Establishing diplomatic relations
F. Recalling an ambassador
G. Pledging support
H. Withholding support
I. Denial of an allegation
J. Holding negotiations
K. Signing an agreement
L. Lodging a protest
M. Issuing an ultimatum
N. Expulsion of diplomats

List of headings (Alternatives)

a. Fishing row
b. Japanese visit
c. Diplomats expelled from Italy
d. Thai-Lao talk
e. Iran warns U.S.
f. W. German consulate inaugurated in Shanghai
g. Australia and SDI
h. Hangzhou and Boston become sister-cities
i. France, Iran ties
j. U.S. pledges assistance to Aquino
k. Indonesia denies pact with China
l. Protocol signed
m. Australia raps French nuke testn
n. Vanuatu establishes relations with China

News items

1. Paris-France said on Sunday it was recalling its ambassador in Ottawa after 4 French politicians and 17 islanders were arrested on charges of fishing illegally in Canadian waters. The French Foreign Ministry said in a statement the decision to recall Ambassador Philippe Husson to Paris for consultations had been taken because of a "worsening of the French-Canadian dispute over fishing." Canadian fisheries officials boarded the trawler Croix de Lorraine, from the small French-held islands of St-Pierre-Miquelon south of Newfoundland, last Thursday after the crew attempted to fish in Canadian waters.

2. Shanghai (Xinhua)—The Consulate-General of the Federal Republic of Germany in Shanghai was inaugurated yesterday.

3. As a special envoy of the Prime Minister of Japan, Masayoshi Ito, Chairman of the Executive Board of the Liberal Democratic Party of Japan, is scheduled to

笔记区

visit China this month, a Chinese Foreign Ministry spokesperson announced yesterday.

4. An agreement to establish sister-city relations between Hangzhou, capital of Zhejiang Province, and the U.S. city of Boston, Massachusetts, was signed last Saturday by Hangzhou Mayor and Boston Mayor.

5. Jakarta—Indonesia has denied a report it has reached agreement with China to normalize diplomatic relations, which were suspended more than 20 years ago, Foreign Minister Ali Alatas was quoted as saying, 'The report was speculative and not based on fact,' the newspaper suara Pembaruan quoted Alatas as saying on Monday.

6. Sofia—China and Bulgaria on Wednesday agreed on technological exchanges and research co-operation in vegetable cultivation. At the 21st session of the China-Bulgaria Scientific and Technological Co-operation Committee, the two sides also identified the fields of exchanges in agriculture and in light, textile, machinery and coal industries. A protocol was signed.

7. Rome—The Italian government expelled a Soviet and an Indian Diplomat on Tuesday after accusing them of spying, a reliable source said here yesterday. The Foreign Ministry declined immediate comment, but denied unconfirmed reports that a second Soviet Diplomat had also been expelled.

8. Paris—Iran's Naval Commander-in-Chief threatened on Thursday to order his forces into action against U.S. navy units patrolling in the gulf if they 'get in the way,' the Iranian News Agency reported in a dispatch monitored here. 'We will take resolute action if the presence of U.S. ships clearly threatens our interests,' said Captain Mohammed, Hossein Malekzadgan.

9. Canberra—The Australian government has again made a strong protest to France against a new French nuclear test at Mururoaatoll in the South Pacific. Prime Minister and Foreign Minister, who made separate visits to Paris earlier this year, both protested at the highest level of the French government against the continued French nuclear testing in the Pacific.

10. Canberra—Australia confirmed yesterday it would not endorse U.S. President Ronald Reagan's Strategic Defence Initiative or 'Star Wars' Research Programme. Foreign Minister Bill Hayden reaffirmed Australia's position to U.S. Defence Secretary Caspar Weinberger on the last full day of a three-day visit.

11. Manila—U.S. Defence Secretary Caspar Weinberger assured Philippine President Corazon Aquino yesterday that the Reagan Administration would assist her

笔记区

government with economic aid.

12. Paris—France's newly-appointed Socialist Prime Minister Michel Rocard said he intended to restore France's diplomatic relations with Iran after a 10-month break in line with the previous government's commitments. Rocard made the announcement at the end of a weekly cabinet meeting.

13. Vientiane, Laos—Thai and Laotian army chiefs began talks yesterday to improve relations, two days after their forces withdrew from bloody battlefields in a disputed border area. Thailand's General Chaovalit Yongchaiyuth, held talks with Laos' General Sisavat Keobounphan a few hours after arriving in Vientiane as head of the highest-level Thai delegation to Laos in nine years. The two officers last week negotiated a ceasefire in one of the bloodiest border clashes since 1975.

14. The government of the PRC and the government of the Republic of Vanuatu, formerly the New Hebrides, are to establish diplomatic relations at ambassador level. A communique was signed in Port Vila by Ambassador Extraordinary and Plenipotentiary of China and Prime Minister and Minister of Foreign Affairs of Vanuatu. (Words: 677)

Exercise E: ***Analyze the structure of the following summary and complete it.***

At the beginning of the nineteenth century the only __1__ roles for women were __2__, there was virtually nothing for them to do except stay at home or hire out as maids, governess, and, before long, teachers. Women were not allowed to own __3__ —in most cases, not even the clothes they wore. A working wife was not allowed to her __4__ but was required to turn them over to her __5__. In the case of separation or __6__, a woman had no legal __7__ on her husband and was not allowed to keep the children. She had no __8__ status, which meant that she was not permitted to bring __9__ or to give testimony in courts. Often, she was not __10__ to inherit property or to __11__ a will. She was barred from public office and __12__ from public life generally. For the most part, women __13__ opportunities for education, vocational training, and professional employment. The national consensus was that women __14__ in the home, and __15__ efforts were made to see that they stayed there.

List of words

property	domestic	suit	permitted
excluded	lacked	belonged	determined
husband	wages	acceptable	claims
legal	make	divorce	

笔记区

Exercise F: ***Complete the summary of the passage using the words from the list.***

The first __1__ in helping the patient is to accept and __2__ his illness. The cause of symptoms must be found, and measures to relieve them and to __3__ recurrence must be taken. Thorough examinations are __4__. Although the __5__ may suspect that the illness is __6__ to emotional rather than physical causes, he must search carefully for any evidence of __7__ disease. It is not unknown for an illness considered __8__ to be later diagnosed as cancer or some other __9__ the thorough search for physical causes of the symptoms helps to gain the patient's __10__. He knows that his condition and __11__ are being taken seriously. If no organic basis for his complaints is found, he usually will find this news easier to accept when he knows he has had a __12__ examination.

Finding no physical cause for the disorder points the way to understanding the patient's condition. What is the cause? Is it __13__ stress? If so, what kind? What are the problems which are __14__ the patient?

List of words

acknowledge	disease	thorough	prevent
psychosomatic	welfare	confidence	points
essential	upsetting	symptoms	physician
emotional	due	step	physical

Exercise G: ***Complete the summary of the passage using the words from the list.***

As a nation, we are starting to realize that we cannot __1__ the solid waste dilemma just by finding new places to put trash. Across the country, many individuals, __2__ and businesses have found __3__ ways to reduce and better manage their trash through a coordinated mix of practices that includes source reduction.

Simply put, source reduction is waste __4__. It includes many actions that reduce the __5__ amount and harmfulness of waste created. Source reduction can conserve __6__, reduce pollution, and help cut waste disposal and handling costs (it avoids the costs of __7__, land filling, and combustion).

Source reduction is a basic solution to too much garbage: less __8__ means less of a waste problem. Because source reduction actually prevents the __9__ of waste in the first __10__, it comes before other __11__ that deal with trash after it is already generated. After source reduction, recycling is the preferred waste management option because it reduces the __12__ of waste going to landfills and conserves resources.

笔记区

List of words

increase	measures	waste	creative
recycling	disposal	communities	place
solve	amount	resources	prevention

Exercise H: ***Analyze the structure of the following passage and complete the summary.***

On Monday August 29, Hurricane Katrina ravaged New Orleans, Louisiana and Mississippi, leaving a trail of destruction in her wake. It will be some time until the full toll of this hurricane can be assessed, but the devastating human and environmental impacts are already obvious.

Katrina was the most feared of all meteorological events, a major hurricane making landfall in a highly-populated low-lying region. In the wake of this devastation, many have questioned whether global warming may have contributed to this disaster. Could New Orleans be the first major U.S. city ravaged by human-caused climate change?

The correct answer is that there is no way to prove that Katrina either was, or was not, affected by global warming. For a single event, regardless of how extreme, such attribution is fundamentally impossible. We only have one Earth, and it will follow only one of an infinite number of possible weather sequences. It is impossible to know whether or not this event would have taken place if we had not increased the concentration of greenhouse gases in the atmosphere as much as we have. Weather events will always result from a combination of deterministic factors (including greenhouse gas forcing or slow natural climate cycles) and stochastic factors (pure chance).

Due to this semi-random nature of weather, it is wrong to blame any one event such as Katrina specifically on global warming—and of course it is just as indefensible to blame Katrina on a long-term natural cycle in the climate.

Adapted from *Is There a Connection?* by Stefan Rahmstorf

(Words: 249)

Questions 1–4

Hurricane Katrina ravaged three states, leaving __1__ impacts on humans and environment. Though most people are questioning whether it has anything with global warming, the answer is not clear because weather events always results from __2__ and __3__. Therefore, it is unfair to contribute the disaster either to global warming or __4__ in the climate.

笔记区

Ⅱ. 细节的寻找与对应

Exercise A: ***Find out all the figures in the passage as quickly as possible.***

If the World Were a Village of 100 People

If we could shrink the earth's population to a village of precisely 100 people, with all the existing human ratios remaining the same, it would look something like the following:

There would be: 57 Asians, 21 Europeans, 14 from the Western Hemisphere, both north and south, 8 Africans.

There would be: 52 females and 48 males.

There would be: 70 non-white and 30 white.

There would be: 70 non-Christian and 30 Christian.

There would be: 89 heterosexual and 11 homosexual.

6 people would possess 59% of the entire world's wealth and all 6 would be from the United States.

80 would live in substandard housing; 70 would be unable to read; 50 would suffer from malnutrition; 1 would be near death; 1 would be near birth.

1 (yes, only 1) would have a college education; 1 would own a computer.

When one considers our world from such a compressed perspective, the need for acceptance, understanding and education becomes glaringly apparent. The following is also something to ponder:

If you woke up this morning with more health than illness, you are more blessed than the million who will not survive this week. If you have never experienced the danger of battle, the loneliness of imprisonment, the agony of torture, or the pangs of starvation, you are ahead of 500 million people in the world.

If you have food in the refrigerator, clothes on your back, a root overhead and a place to sleep, you are richer than 75% of this world.

If you have money in the bank, in your wallet, and spare change in dish someplace, you are among the top 8% of the world's.

If your parents are still alive and still married, you are very rare, even in the United States and Canada.

Someone once said: what goes around comes around. So

Work like you don't need the money.

Love like you've never been hurt.

Dance like nobody's watching.

Sing like nobody's listening.

Live like it's Heaven on Earth.

(Words: 340)

笔 记 区

Exercise B: ***Crimes have their own cycle. Match the crimes with their peak time.***

A. January
B. July
C. May
D. June
E. Night
F. Weekend

1. Murder
2. Rape
3. Violent attack
4. Burglary
5. Dog bites
6. Suicides

The Crime of the Month

Crime has its own cycles, a magazine reported some years ago. Police records that were studied for five years from over 2,400 cities and towns show a surprising link between changes in the season and crime patterns.

The pattern of crime has varied very little over a long period of years. Murder reaches its high during July and August, as do rape and other violent attacks. Murder, moreover, is more than seasonal: it is a weekend crime. It is also a nighttime crime: 62 percent of murders are committed between 6 p.m. and 6 a.m.

Unlike the summer high in crimes of bodily harm, burglary has a different cycle. You are most likely to be robbed between 6 p.m. and 2 a.m. on a Saturday night in December, January, or February. The most uncriminal month of all? May—except for one strange statistic. More dog bites are reported in this month than in any other month of the year.

Apparently our intellectual seasonal cycles are completely different from our criminal tendencies. Professor Huntington, of the Foundation for the Study of Cycles, made extensive studies to discover the seasons when people read serious books, attend scientific meetings, make the highest scores on examinations, and propose the most changes to patents. In all instances, he found a spring peak and an autumn peak separated by a summer low. On the other hand, Professor Hungtington's studies indicated that June in the peak month for suicides and admissions to mental hospitals. June is also a peak month for marriage.

Possibly, soaring thermometers and high humidity bring on our strange and terrifying summer actions, but police officials are not sure. 'There is, of course, no proof of a connection between humidity and murder,' they say. 'Why murder's high time

笔 记 区

should come in the summertime we really don't know.'

(Words: 308)

Exercise C: ***Read the following passage and put the statements in the appropriate headings.***

Youth Violence: Fact Sheet

Youth violence is an important public health problem that results in deaths and injuries.

The following statistics provide an overview of youth violence in the United States.

- In 2003, 5,570 young people with ages 10 to 24 were murdered on average of 15 each day. Of these victims, 82% were killed with firearms (CDC 2006).
- In 2004, more than 750,000 young people with ages 10 to 24 were treated in emergency departments for injuries sustained due to violence (CDC 2006).
- An estimated 30% of 6th to 10th graders in the United States were involved in bullying as a bully, a target of bullying, or both (Nansel et al. 2001).

Consequences

- Direct and indirect costs of youth violence (e.g., medical, lost productivity, quality of life) exceed $158 billion every year (Children's Safety Network Economics & Data Analysis Resource Center 2000).
- In addition to causing injury and death, youth violence affects communities by increasing the cost of health care, reducing productivity, decreasing property values, and disrupting social services (Mercy et al. 2002).

Groups at Risk

- Among 10 to 24 year olds, homicide is the leading cause of death for African Americans, the second leading cause of death for Hispanics, and the third leading cause of death for American Indians, Alaska Natives, and Asian/Pacific Islanders (CDC 2006).
- Of the 5,570 homicides reported in 2003 among 10 to 24 year olds, 86% were males and 14% were females (CDC 2005).
- Male students are more likely to be involved in a physical fight than female students (41% vs. 25%; CDC 2004).

Risk Factors

Research on youth violence has increased our understanding of factors that make some populations more vulnerable to victimization and perpetration. Research

笔记区

associates the following risk factors with perpetration of youth violence (DHHS 2001; Lipsey and Derzon 1998; Resnick et al. 2004):

Individual Risk Factors

- History of violent victimization or involvement
- Attention deficits, hyperactivity, or learning disorders
- History of early aggressive behavior
- Involvement with drugs, alcohol, or tobacco
- Low IQ
- Poor behavioral control
- Deficits in social cognitive or information-processing abilities
- High emotional distress
- History of treatment for emotional problems
- Antisocial beliefs and attitudes
- Exposure to violence and conflict in the family

Family Risk Factors

- Authoritarian childrearing attitudes
- Harsh, lax, or inconsistent disciplinary practices
- Low parental involvement
- Low emotional attachment to parents or caregivers
- Low parental education and income
- Parental substance abuse or criminality
- Poor family functioning
- Poor monitoring and supervision of children

Peer/School Risk Factors

- Association with delinquent peers
- Involvement in gangs
- Social rejection by peers
- Lack of involvement in conventional activities
- Poor academic performance
- Low commitment to school and school failure

Community Risk Factors

- Diminished economic opportunities
- High concentrations of poor residents
- High level of transiency
- High level of family disruption
- Low levels of community participation
- Socially disorganized neighborhoods

笔 记 区

Protective Factors

Protective factors buffer young people from risks of becoming violent. These factors exist at various levels. To date, protective factors have not been studied as extensively or rigorously as risk factors. However, identifying and understanding protective factors are equally as important as researching risk factors.

Most research is preliminary. Studies propose the following protective factors (DHHS 2001; Resnick et al. 2004):

Individual Protective Factors

- Intolerant attitude toward deviance
- High IQ or high grade point average
- Positive social orientation
- Religiosity

Family Protective Factors

- Connectedness to family or adults outside of the family
- Ability to discuss problems with parents
- Frequent shared activities with parents
- Consistent presence of parent during at least one of the following: when awakening, when arriving home from school, at evening mealtime, and when going to bed
- Involvement in social activities

Peer/School Protective Factors

- Commitment to school
- Involvement in social activities

Adapted from *http://www.cdc.gov/ncipc/factsheets/yvfacts.htm*

(Words: 653)

Questions 1–10

There are many risk factors accounting for adolescents' violent behavior.

A. if the risk is an individual factor;

B. if the risk is a family factor;

C. if the risk is a school factor;

D. if the risk is a community factor.

1. Lack of community activities
2. Low intelligence
3. Undesirable performance in study
4. Failure to control one's behavior
5. Exposure to violence in the family
6. Rejection by fellow students

笔记区

7. Ignorance to children's development
8. Low income
9. Making friends with delinquent peers
10. Aggressive behavior in childhood

Ⅲ. 分类与过程

Exercise A: ***Complete the descriptions with the information of the charts.***

Questions 1–7

What are teenagers doing during their waking hours? The responses suggest __1__ major kinds of activity. Given the amount of time spent in school, a significant portion of the teenager's time is devoted to __2__. It is worth noting, however, that although nearly 20% of the adolescent's time is spent in the __3__, only 12% is spent doing __4__. Teenagers spend about one-third of their time in what the researchers call __5__ activities—errands, eating, personal care and grooming—with almost one-third of time, or 8.8% of total time, devoted to __6__ and eating. Without the responsibilities of career and family, the adolescent can devote more than 40% of the waking time to __7__ activities, primarily socializing with peers.

Questions 8–12

As shown in the figure, the results of the study suggest that adolescents spend their time in __8__ different social worlds. One of these, in which they spend more than one-third of their waking time, is the __9__. The second social world of the adolescent is the __10__, where one must follow uniform rules or pay a penalty. More than a quarter of the adolescent's time is spent in __11__ other than home and school. In what may be a uniquely American phenomenon, a significant fraction of this time—nearly 4% of the teenager's total waking activity—is spent in an __12__.

Questions 13–15

There is no better indicator of the psychological changes that occur during adolescence—especially the search for identity—than the data showing with whom adolescents spend their time. As shown in the figure, more than one-quarter of the teenager's time is spent __13__. This matches the popular view of teenagers as withdrawn or not communicating with other members of their families. But it contradicts the equally common notion that teenagers are highly dependent on interactions with peers. And despite the typical parent's complaint that all teenagers do at home is eating and sleeping, nearly 20% of their time is spent in the company of other __14__. Finally, almost 30% of the time is spent with __15__.

笔 记 区

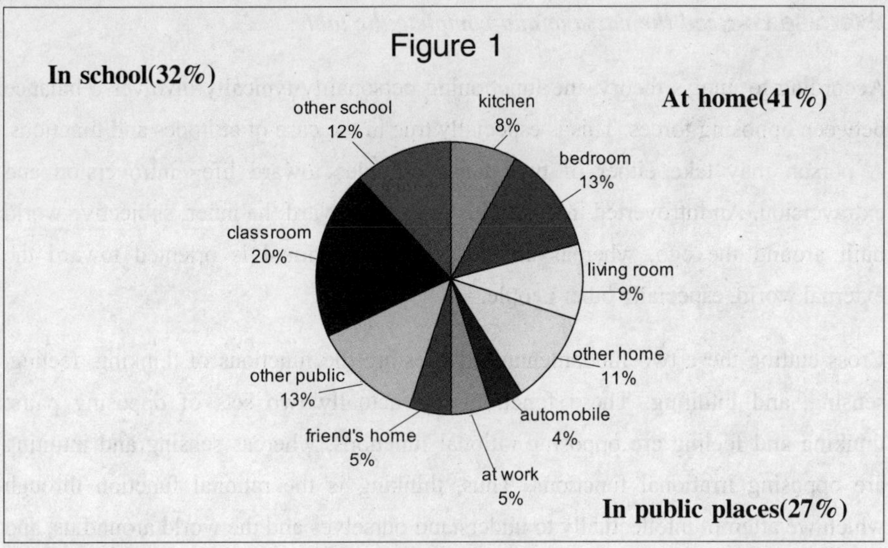

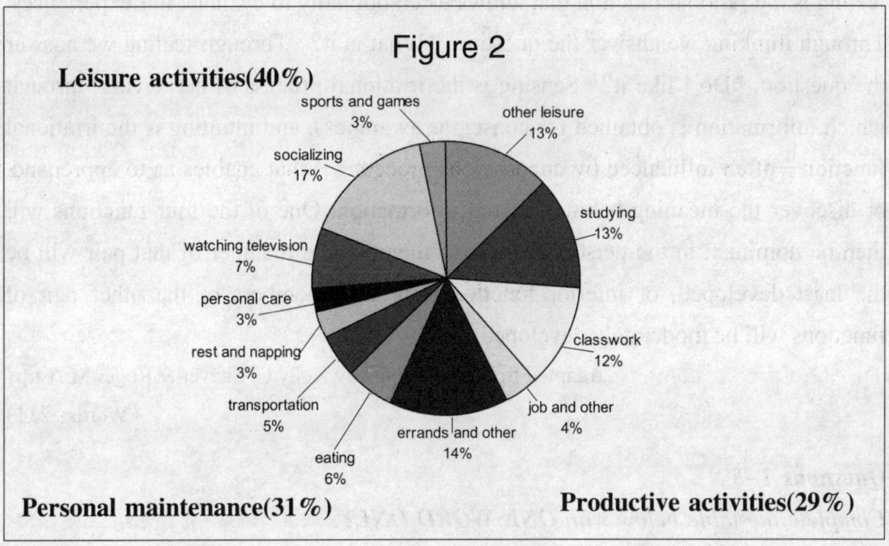

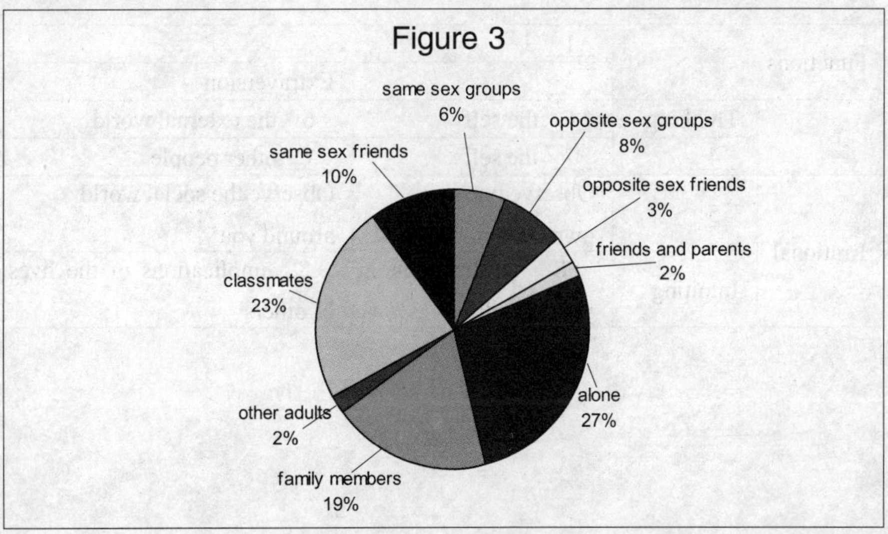

Source of the above three figures: *Being Adolescent* by Csikszentmihalyi & Larson

笔记区

Exercise B: ***Read the passage and complete the table.***

According to Jung's theory, the functioning personality typically involves a balance between opposing forces. This is especially true in the case of attitudes and functions. A person may take either of two major attitudes toward life—introversion and extraversion. An introverted individual is oriented toward the inner, subjective world built around the ego, whereas an extraverted individual is oriented toward the external world, especially other people.

Cross-cutting these two fundamental attitudes are the functions of thinking, feeling, sensing, and intuiting. These functions are actually two sets of opposing pairs: thinking and feeling are opposing rational functions, whereas sensing and intuiting are opposing irrational functions. Thus, thinking is the rational function through which we attempt intellectually to understand ourselves and the world around us, and feeling is the rational function that allows us emotionally to evaluate our experiences. Through thinking we answer the question, 'What is it?' Through feeling we answer the question, 'Do I like it?' Sensing is the irrational process of perceiving, through which information is obtained for conscious awareness, and intuiting is the irrational function—often influenced by unconscious processes—that enables us to apprehend, or discover the meaning behind sensory information. One of the four functions will then be dominant in the person's behavior; the opposite member of that pair will be the least developed, or inferior function. The two members of the other pair of functions will be moderately developed.

Adapted from *Psychology* by Kelly G. Shaver & Roger M. Tarpy

(Words：234)

Questions 1–8

Complete the table below with ***ONE WORD ONLY****.*

<table>
<tr><td colspan="2" rowspan="2">Functions</td><td colspan="2">___1___</td></tr>
<tr><td>___2___</td><td>Extraversion</td></tr>
<tr><td rowspan="2">___3___</td><td>Thinking</td><td>___6___ the self</td><td>___6___ the external world</td></tr>
<tr><td>___4___</td><td>___7___ the self</td><td>___7___ other people</td></tr>
<tr><td rowspan="2">Irrational</td><td>___5___</td><td>Observe one's own behavior</td><td>Observe the social world around you</td></tr>
<tr><td>Intuiting</td><td>___8___ implications in your own life</td><td>___8___ implications of the lives of others</td></tr>
</table>

Exercise C: ***Read the passage and complete the chart.***

In his classic psychology text, William James (1892) distinguished between the self as an object of reflection (the *Me*) and the self as a conscious agent (the *I*). This distinction remains valid today. The figure illustrates the structure of the self, with some of the subdivisions identified by James.

The *Me* is the sum total of all that a person can call his or her own. It is further subdivided into the material self, the spiritual self, and various social selves. The material self is a single entity consisting of one's physical being and possessions. The spiritual self is also a single entity, incorporating psychological faculties such as personality traits, verbal skills, social perceptions and attitudes. In contrast, there are numerous social selves, which vary for each category of people who recognize you as an individual. Thus, you might have one self that you reveal to your parents, one that you present to your close friends, one that you take with you to your job, and one that you offer to your professor.

Rather than being a collection of elements, the *I* is the ongoing process of consciousness: the thinker, the knower, the pure ego. It can reflect on the contents of the *Me*, but it is separate from them. It can direct the individual's purposive behavior, but it is separate from that behavior.

Adapted from *Psychology* by Kelly G. Shaver & Roger M. Tarpy

(Words: 224)

Questions 1–7

Complete the chart below with the choices in the list.

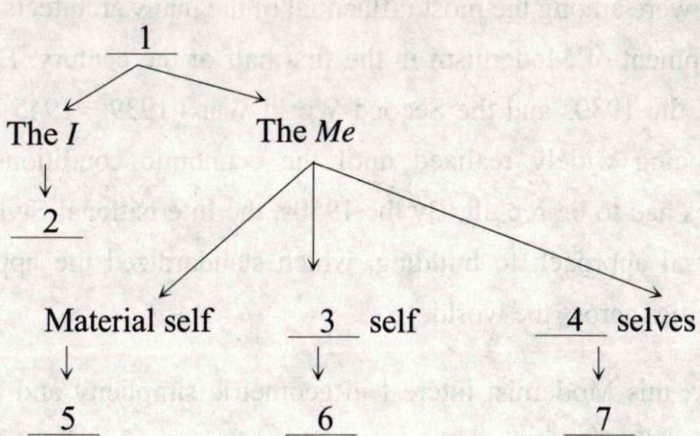

List of choices

A. Social
B. Attitudes
C. Physical beings
D. Self
E. Spiritual
F. Consciousness
G. Object of reflection
H. For different people in life
I. Psychological

笔记区

Exercise D: ***Read the passage and complete the table.***

The use of an architectural style cannot be said to start or finish on a specific date; neither is it possible to say exactly what characterizes a particular movement. But the origins of what is now generally known as modern architecture can be traced back to the social and technological changes of the 18th and 19th centuries.

Instead of using timber, stone and traditional building techniques, architects began to explore ways of creating buildings by using the latest technology and materials such as steel, glass and concrete strengthened steel bars, known as reinforced concrete. Technological advances also helped bring about the decline of rural industries and an increase in urban populations as people moved to the towns to work in the new factories. Such rapid and uncontrolled growth helped to turn parts of cities into slums. By the 1920s architects throughout Europe were reacting against the conditions created by industrialization. A new style of architecture emerged to reflect more idealistic notions for the future. It was made possible by new materials and construction techniques and was known as Modernism.

By the 1930s many buildings emerging from this movement were designed in the International Style. This was largely characterized by the bold use of new materials and simple, geometric forms, often with white walls supported by stilt-like pillars. These were stripped of unnecessary decoration that would detract from their primary purpose—to be used or lived in.

Walter Gropius, Charles Jeanneret (better known as Le Corbusier) and Ludwig Mies van der Rohe were among the most influential of the many architects who contributed to the development of Modernism in the first half of the century. But the economic depression of the 1930s and the Second World War (1939—1945) prevented their ideas from being widely realized until the economic conditions improved and war-torn cities had to be rebuilt. By the 1950s, the International Style had developed into a universal approach to building, which standardized the appearance of new buildings in cities across the world.

Unfortunately, this Modernist interest in geometric simplicity and function became exploited for profit. The rediscovery of quick-and-easy-to-handle reinforced concrete and an improved ability to prefabricate building sections meant that builders could meet the budgets of commissioning authorities and handle a renewed demand for development quickly and cheaply. But this led to many badly designed buildings which discredited the original aims of Modernism.

Influenced by Le Corbusier's ideas on town planning, every large British city built

笔记区

multi-storey housing estates in the 1960s. Mass-produced, low-cost high-rises seemed to offer a solution to the problem of housing a growing inner-city population. But far from meeting human needs, the new estates often proved to be windswept deserts lacking essential social facilities and services. Many of these buildings were poorly designed and constructed and have since been demolished.

By the 1970s, a new respect for the place of buildings within the existing townscape arose. Preserving historic buildings or keeping only their facades (or fronts) grew common. Architects also began to make more use of building styles and materials that were traditional to the area. The architectural style usually referred to as High-tech was also emerging. It celebrated scientific and engineering achievements by openly parading the sophisticated techniques used in construction. Such buildings are commonly made of metal and glass; examples are Stansted Airport and the Lloyd's Building in London.

Disillusionment at the failure of many of the poor imitations of Modernist architecture led to interest in various styles and ideas from the past and present. By the 1980s' the coexistence of different styles of architecture in the same building became known as Post-Modernism. Other architects looked back to the classical tradition. The trend in architecture now favours smaller scale building design that reflects a growing public awareness of environmental issues such as energy efficiency.

(Words: 631)

Questions 1–7

Complete the table below with ***NO MORE THAN THREE WORDS.***

PERIOD	STYLE OF PERIOD	BUILDING MATERIALS	CHARACTERISTICS
before 18th century	traditional	___1___	
1920's	introduction of ___2___	steel, glass and concrete	exploration of latest technology
1930s–1950s	___3___		geometric forms
1960s	decline of Modernism	prefabricated sections	___4___
1970s	end of Modernist era	traditional materials	___5___ of historic buildings
1970s	beginning of ___6___ era	metal and glass	sophisticated techniques paraded
1980s	Post-Modernism		___7___

笔记区

Exercise E: ***Put the following jumbled sentences into the correct order.***

A. Full on the neck to tighten the triangle.

B. Put the tie round your neck with the wide end on the right. (The wide end should be twice as long as the narrow end.)

C. Adjust by pulling at the hanging ends.

D. Thread this wide end down through the knot.

E. Bring the wide end across the front of the narrow end. Bring it back up and through the loop.

F. You should now have a 2 part triangle knot. Pull this tight.

G. Bring it up through the back of the loop.

H. Bring this wide end round again—down to the left, across behind the hanging narrow end, up to the right and back through the loop.

I. Wrap the wide side from right to left across the front of the knot.

Exercise F: ***Read the passage and complete the flow chart.***

There are technical limitations to the amount of paper which can be recycled and some paper products cannot be collected for re-use. These include paper in the form of books and permanent records, photographic paper and paper which is badly contaminated. The four most common sources of paper for recycling are factories and retail stores which gather large amounts of packaging material in which goods are delivered, also offices which have unwanted business documents and computer output, paper converters and printers and lastly households which discard newspapers and packaging material. The paper manufacturer pays a price for the paper and may also incur the collection cost.

Once collected, the paper has to be sorted by hand by people trained to recognize various types of paper. This is necessary because some types of paper can only be made from particular kinds of recycled fibre. The sorted paper then has to be repulped or mixed with water and broken down into its individual fibres. This mixture is called stock and may contain a wide variety of contaminating materials, particularly if it is made from mixed waste paper which has had little sorting. Various machinery is used to remove other materials from the stock. After passing through the repulping process, the fibres from printed waste paper are grey in colour because the printing ink has soaked into the individual fibres. This recycled material can only be used in products where the grey colour is not acceptable, and the fibres must be de-inked. This involves adding chemicals such as caustic soda or other alkalis, soaps and detergents, water-hardening agents such as calcium chloride, frothing agents and

笔记区

bleaching agents. Before the recycled fibres can be made into paper they must be refined or treated in such a way that they bond together.

(Words: 296)

Questions 1–5

*Complete the flow chart below with **ONE OR TWO WORDS** from the passage.*

Waste paper collected from: → The paper is then ____2____

Factories

Retail stores

____1____

Paper converters and printers

Households

↓

and ____3____

By adding water

↓

Chemicals are added in order to ____4____ → The fibres are then ____5____

Exercise G: ***Read the information below and answer questions.***

Classic Tours—Coach Break Information

Luggage

We ask you to keep luggage down to one medium-sized suitcase per person, but a small holdall can also be taken on board the coach.

Seat Allocation

Requests for particular seats can be made on most coach breaks when booking, but since allocations are made on a first come first served basis, early booking is advisable. When bookings are made with us you will be offered the best seats that are available on the coach at that time.

Travel Documents

When you have paid your deposit we will send to you all the necessary documents and labels, so that you receive them in good time before the coach break departure date. Certain documents, for example, air or boat tickets, may have to be retained and your driver of courier will then issue them to you at the relevant point.

Special Diets

If you require a special diet you must inform us at the time of booking with a copy of the diet. This will be notified to the hotel or hotels on your coach break, but on certain coach breaks the hotels used are tourist class and whilst offering value for money

笔记区

within the price range, they may not have the full facilities to cope with special diets. Any extra costs incurred must be paid to the hotel by yourself before departure from the hotel.

Accommodation

Many of our coach breaks now include, within the price, accommodation with private facilities, and this will be indicated on the coach break page. Other coach breaks have a limited number of rooms with private facilities which, subject to availability, can be reserved and guaranteed at the time of booking—the supplementary charge shown in the price panel will be added to your account.

On any coach break there are only a limited number of single rooms. When a single room is available it may be subject to a supplementary charge and this will be shown on the brochure page.

Entertainment

Some of our hotels arrange additional entertainment which could include music, dancing, film shows, etc. The nature and frequency of the entertainment presented are at the discretion of the hotel and therefore not guaranteed and could be withdrawn if there is a lack of demand or insufficient numbers in the hotel.

(Words: 383)

Questions 1–6

1. If you want to sit at the front of the coach
   A. ask when you get on the coach.
   B. arrive early on the departure date.
   C. book your seat well in advance.
   D. avoid travelling at peak times.

2. Your air tickets
   A. will be sent to your departure point.
   B. must be collected before leaving.
   C. will be enclosed with other documents.
   D. may be held by your coach driver.

3. If you need a special diet you should
   A. inform the hotel when you arrive.
   B. pay extra with the booking.
   C. tell the coach company.
   D. book tourist class.

4. It may be necessary to pay extra for
   A. a bathroom.

笔记区

B. boat tickets.

C. additional luggage.

D. entertainment.

5. Entertainment is available

A. at all hotels.

B. if there is the demand.

C. upon request.

D. for an additional cost.

6. With every booking Classic Tours guarantee you will be able to

A. request high quality meals.

B. take hand luggage on the coach.

C. use your own personal bathroom.

D. see a film if you want to.

Ⅳ. 长句分析

Exercise A: ***Practice with Facts and Non-Facts.***

Hidden Persuader

In 1957, James Vicary, an American market researcher, thought of using a special movie projector, a tachistoscope [ta-KISS-ta-SCOPE], as an advertising instrument. He knew that the tachistoscope can flash a message on a movie screen at 1/3000 of a second. He also knew that people were able to read such a fast message, but they did not know it—they didn't even know that the message was there. Vicary arranged a six-week study. During those six weeks, messages suggesting that people buy popcorn and soft drinks were flashed on the screen while the movie was going on. Sales for that period showed a 60 percent increase in popcorn sales and a 20 percent increase in soft drink sales. Vicary proved that the tachistoscope could influence people in a theater. No one complained about the messages on the screen until the results of the study were published.

(Words：148)

*Indicate which statements are facts by writing F in the blank and which ones are inferences or judgments (your own or the writer's) by writing **NF** in the blank.*

1. ______ One three-thousandth of a second is a very short time.
2. ______ James Vicary was interested in advertising as part of his job.
3. ______ The tachistoscope was invented before 1958.
4. ______ Popcorn and soft drinks are sold in movie theaters.

笔 记 区

5. ______ People can read a message that is flashed on a movie screen for 1/3000 of a second.
6. ______ The people in the movie theater did not know that the tachistoscope was being used.
7. ______ Because people are influenced without knowing it, the tachistoscope is a bad machine.
8. ______ People respond to suggestions.
9. ______ Movie-theater owners should not have slowed the use of the tachistoscope.
10. ______ The tachistoscope increased sales of popcorn more than sales of soft drinks.
11. ______ People prefer popcorn to soft drinks.
12. ______ People do not like to be tricked.

Exercise B: *TRUE/FALSE/NOT GIVEN*

Technical and Further Education

Australia's Technical and Further Education (TAFE) sector is a nationally recognised government system of vocational education and training and is the major provider of the skills required by the Australian workforce.

TAFE is the largest of the tertiary education sectors in Australia. It accounts for approximately 70 percent of post-secondary education enrolments. There are 232 major TAFE colleges in Australia.

Although each state and territory administers its own system of TAFE, the qualifications they award are transferable throughout Australia. Although TAFE colleges cannot award tertiary-level degree, some TAFE courses permit TAFE graduates to be admitted with advanced standing into degree courses offered by universities.

TAFE courses provide initial and further education at professional, para-professional, post-trade, trade and operative level. TAFE courses are developed in collaboration with industry and the community to ensure the most up-to-date education and training is provided.

Private post-secondary institutions

These private institutions are like TAFE colleges because they teach special skills for jobs but each one of them usually specializes in courses for one industry.

There are many private institutions in Australia offering a wide range of courses: English language (ELICOS, see Chapter 6), secretarial studies, data processing, pilot training, business and management, recreational courses and religious studies. (Other

笔记区

courses offered by private post-secondary institutions are listed in Chapter 7, *Special Studies.*)

If you successfully complete these courses you receive a qualification called a 'certificate' or 'diploma.' These are widely recognised by professional associations and industries in Australia, and are sometimes recognised by higher education institutions for credit. Before you undertake a courses at a private post-secondary institution you should check that the certificate or diploma offered is appropriate for your particular purpose because some private institutions offer courses which are not recognised. If you want to enter a higher education institution from a private post-secondary institution, you should ask the higher education institution whether they accept the qualification before you start your course.

(Words: 323)

Questions 1–6

1. There are more people studying in TAFE colleges than in any other kind of higher education institution.
2. TAFE qualifications are accepted anywhere in Australia.
3. Some TAFE colleges offer university degrees.
4. Each TAFE college specializes in teaching skills for working within one specific industry.
5. The next chapter deals with English language courses.
6. Certificates or diplomas from all private post-secondary institutions are recognized everywhere in Australia.

Exercise C: *TRUE/FALSE/NOT GIVEN*

The Australian political scene is dominated by two major parties that have quite different political agendas. However, the policies of the Australian Labor Party and the Liberal Party have become much more difficult to tell apart in recent years. In fact, it would be true to say that both parties consist of conservative, moderate and radical elements, and therefore the general public is often perplexed about which party to vote for. Nonetheless, it is usual to find that an Australian will lean towards supporting one of these two parties and remain faithful to that party for life.

The Labor Party was formed early in the twentieth century to safeguard the interests of the common working man and to give the trade unions political representation in Parliament. The Party has always had strong connections with the unions, and supports the concept of a welfare society in which people who are less fortunate than others are financially, and otherwise, assisted in their quest for a more equitable slice of the economic pie. The problem is that such socialist political agendas are

笔记区

extremely expensive to implement and maintain, especially in a country that, although comparatively wealthy, is vast and with a small working and hence taxpaying population base. Welfare societies tend towards bankruptcy unless government spending is kept in check. The Liberal Party, on the other hand, argues that the best way to ensure a fair division of wealth in the country is to allow more freedom to create it. This, in turn, means more opportunities, jobs created etc., and therefore more wealth available to all. Just how the poor are to share in the distribution of this wealth (beyond being given, at least in theory, the opportunity to create it) is, however, less well understood. Practice, of course, may make nonsense of even the best theoretical intentions, and often the less politically powerful are badly catered for under governments implementing 'free-for-all' policies.

It is no wonder that given the two major choices offered to them, Australian voters are increasingly turning their attention to the smaller political parties, which claim to offer a more balanced swag of policies, often based around one major current issue. Thus, for instance, at the last election there was the No Aircraft Noise Party, popular in city areas, and the Green Party, which is almost solely concerned with environmental issues.

(Words: 391)

Questions 1–10

1. Policies as support of the concept of a welfare society are costly.
2. Australians usually vote for the party they supported early in life.
3. The Labor Party was formed by the trade unions.
4. Radical groups are only found within the Labor Party.
5. The Liberal Party was formed after the Labor Party.
6. Welfare-based societies invariably become bankrupt.
7. According to the author, theories do not always work in practice.
8. Some Australian voters are confused about who to vote for.
9. The No Aircraft Noise Party is only popular in the city.
10. The smaller parties are only concerned about the environment.

Exercise D: *TRUE/FALSE/NOT GIVEN*

Nowadays, without a qualification from a reputable school or university, the odds of landing that plum job advertised in the paper are considerably shortened. Moreover, one's present level of education could fall well short of future career requirements.

It is no secret that competition is the driving force behind the need to obtain increasingly higher qualifications. In the majority of cases, the urge to upgrade is no

笔记区

longer the result of an insatiable thirst for knowledge. The pressure is coming from within the workplace to compete with ever more qualified job applicants, and in many occupations one must now battle with colleagues in the reshuffle for the position one already holds.

Striving to become better educated is hardly a new concept. Wealthy parents have always been willing to spend the vast amounts of extra money necessary to send their children to schools with a perceived educational edge. Working adults have long attended night schools and refresher courses. Competition for employment has been around since the curse of working for a living began. Is the present situation so very different to that of the past?

The difference now is that the push is universal and from without as well as within. A student at secondary school receiving low grades is no longer as easily accepted by his or her peers as was once the case. Similarly, in the workplace, unless employees are engaged in part-time study, they may be frowned upon by their employers and peers and have difficulty even standing still. In fact, in these cases, the expectation is for careers to go backwards and earning capacity to take an appreciable nosedive.

At first glance, the situation would seem to be laudable: a positive response to the exhortation by a former Prime Minister, Bob Hawke, for Australia to become the 'clever country'. Yet there are serious ramifications according to at least one educational psychologist. Dr. Brendan Gatsby has caused some controversy in academic circles by suggesting that a bias towards what he terms 'paper' excellence might cause more problems than it is supposed to solve. Gatsby raises a number of issues that affect the individual as well as society in general.

Firstly, he believes the extra workload involved is resulting in abnormally high stress levels in both students at secondary school and adults studying after working hours. Secondly, skills which might be more relevant to the undertaking of a sought after job are being overlooked by employers interviewing candidates without qualifications on paper. These two areas of concern for the individual are causing physical and emotional stress respectively.

Gatsby also argues that there are attitudinal changes within society to the exalted role education now plays in determining how the spoils of working life are distributed. Individuals of all ages are being driven by social pressures to achieve academic success solely for monetary considerations instead of for the joy of enlightenment. There is the danger that some universities are becoming degree factories with an attendant drop in standards. Furthermore, our education system may be rewarding doggedness above creativity, the very thing Australians have been encouraged to

笔记区

avoid. But the most undesirable effect of this academic paper chase, Gatsby says, is the disadvantage that 'user-pays' higher education confers on the poor, who invariably lose out to the more financially favoured.

Naturally, although there is agreement that learning can cause stress, Gatsby's comments regarding university standards have been roundly criticised as alarmist by most educationists who point out that, by any standard of measurement, Australia's education system overall, at both secondary and tertiary levels, is equal to that of any in the world.

(Words: 601)

Questions 1–8

F 1. It is impossible these days to get a good job without a qualification from a respected institution.

F 2. Most people who upgrade their qualifications do so for the joy of learning.

T 3. In some jobs, the position you hold must be reapplied for.

N 4. Some parents spend extra on their children's education because of the prestige attached to certain schools.

T 5. According to the text, students who performed badly at school used to be accepted by their classmates.

N 6. Employees who do not undertake extra study may find their salary decreased by employers.

T 7. Australians appear to have responded to the call by a former Prime Minister to become better qualified.

T 8. Australia's education system is equal to any in the world in the opinion of most educationists.

Exercise E: *TRUE/FALSE/NOT GIVEN*

Weapon to Fight against Viruses

Viruses are deceptive little buggers, mutating often to dodge their hosts' immune defenses. Plants fight back using a weapon called RNA interference (RNAi), which rips apart the viral machinery. Now, a new study shows that fruit flies employ the same defense—the first example of animals using this antiviral strategy. According to a related study, the genes behind this resistance are evolving rapidly to keep up with an ever-changing adversary.

For most creatures, RNA is just the middle man that helps a gene make a protein. But many viruses can get by on RNA alone. When they invade a cell, their RNA infiltrates the host's genetic machinery, tricking it into making viral proteins. Scientists knew that all cells can shred unwanted RNA using RNAi, but they had

笔记区

never observed living animals using this strategy to defend against viruses.

Fruit flies were the logical place to check, since it is relatively easy to disable their genes. Microbiologist Shou-Wei Ding of the University of California, Riverside, and colleagues took flies that were missing one of the three main RNAi genes (dcr-2, ago-2 and r2d2), and infected them with two types of virus. The mutant flies died much more rapidly than did normal flies, the team reports 24 March in *Science*, evidence that the RNAi mechanism is at least one of the fly's defenses against viruses.

Complementing these results, a different study, published 21 March in *Current Biology*, found that the fruit fly RNAi mechanism is constantly adapting to new viral strategies. A team led by evolutionary biologist Darren Obbard of the University of Edinburgh, United Kingdom, compared more than 8,000 genes across three fruit fly species and found the three main RNAi genes were among the most variable. From the data, the authors calculate that these genes have been evolving faster than 97% of the fruit fly genome. Of course, virus genes are evolving quickly as well. 'Each side invents a new weapon,' Obbard says, 'making it an ongoing arms race.'

Because humans have similar RNAi genes, these two papers suggest that humans may also use RNAi to ward off viruses, says plant virologist David Baulcombe of the Sainsbury Laboratory in the U.K. If so, Ding imagines that future drug treatments might target the proteins that viruses use to foil RNAi.

Adapted from *Defense! —The fruit fly uses RNA interference to ward off viral invaders*

by Michael Schirber

(Words: 383)

Questions 1–8

1. Viruses are deceptive buggers to destroy their hosts' immune defenses.
2. RNA interference is a useful weapon to fight against viruses.
3. Fruit flies is the only example of animals using RNAi as an antiviral strategy.
4. Unlike viruses, most creatures can get by on RNA only.
5. All the cells can get rid of unwanted RNA using RNAi.
6. Fruit flies have three main RNAi genes.
7. RNAi mechanism is the most powerful defense against viruses for fruit flies.
8. RNAi genes in fruit flies have been evolving faster than virus genes.

笔 记 区

V. 定位训练

Exercise A: ***Cover the right column and figure out what the icon is standing for; go through the whole table within 1 minute; and finish the questions without looking back.***

Common icons

Icon	
a	a. No cigarette smoking is allowed
b	b. Subway
c	c. Mechanic available for car repair
d	d. Bicycle path
e	e. Information here
f	f. Police cars at a police station
g	g. Traffic goes around the circle here
h	h. Train station
i	i. Bus stop
j	j. Hotel or bed and breakfast
k	k. Restaurant
l	l. Parking
m	m. Facilities for handicapped persons

Questions 1–5

1. Which three symbols show public transportation? (Write the letters of the symbols.)

____

2. Which two symbols are most interesting to tired and hungry travelers?

____

3. Which two symbols are letters of the alphabet?

____

4. One of the symbols is a 'not allowed' symbol. Which one is it?

____

5. Which sign will you watch for if your car isn't working well?

____

Exercise B: ***Find out the specific information required.***

Planet Earth is truly a beautiful place. Nature lovers value the diversity, the variety. It's true: this world of ours is filled with unusual and interesting sites. Most people know about spectacular places like the Himalayan Mountains, the Grand Canyon, Victoria Falls, the Pyramids of Giza in Egypt, Hawaii, the Alps, and Fujiyama (Mount Fuji). In fact, there are places of beauty in every country, in every part of the world.

The many varieties of people are part of the beauty of our planet. The world is made up of people from all races and people of many cultures. The dark-skinned people from parts of Africa and the Middle East, the pale northern Europeans, the small Asian people, and the Native Americans—each group has distinctive features. Each group has a unique kind of beauty. If a person could look at all the members of the human family, what a variety she would see: the young, the old, the tall, and the short; hair in colors of brown, red, gold, silver, white, and black; and eyes in colors from blue and green to nearly dark. In addition, each group of people has a culture of its own, too. To be able to live together in peace and harmony is yet another kind of beauty.

The world is alive with colors, too. There's a rainbow of colors in the feathers of birds and in the flowers and leaves of plants. From the deep navy blue of Lake Baikal in Siberia to the azure blue of Crater Lake in Oregon, from the golden white froth of Horseshoe Falls in Niagara Falls, Ontario, to the silver of the Plata River in Argentina, and from the green of the rain forests on Kalimantan (the island of Borneo) to the gem-like quality of green Lake Irazu in Costa Rica, Earth is a colorful, spectacular place.

The variety of life forms makes the planet rich in beauty. Biodiversity is beautiful. The oceans and seas are filled with life: the jellyfish floating in the water, the coral reefs, the brightly colored fish, and the dolphins, seals and whales. In the Southern Hemisphere, Australia is home to animals that live no other place on Earth: the kangaroo, the platypus, the fuzzy koala, and the noisy kookaburra in the Australian gum tree. Africa has striped zebras, spotted cheetahs, and bright pink flamingos. In Central America the rain forests are alive with parrots, toucahs, and quetzals-birds of many colors.

The world is also a place of incredibly wondrous shapes. The frozen waterfall of travertine (stone) at Hamam Meskoutine in Algeria, the turquoise colored waters of the limestone pools flowing down the mountainside at Pamukkale in Turkey, the white limestone cliffs of Dover, the basalt crystals (another kind of rock) of the Giant's Causeway in Northern Ireland, and the karst dome-rock formations (hills of a kind of limestone) of Kweilin in China—each of them has a unique quality that makes the world a more beautiful place. Even the great open grasslands of the Pampas, the veldt, the steppes, and the great prairies add something to Earth's charm.

(Words: 517)

Questions 1–7

1. Words for four kinds of rock in paragraph 5:

____

2. The names of three kinds of birds in paragraph 4:

____

笔记区

3. The names of four great grasslands in paragraph 5:

___

4. The names of three mountains or groups of mountains (mountain ranges) in paragraph 1:

___

5. Three specific colors of blue are mentioned in paragraphs 3 and 5. What are they?

___

6. Names of Australian animals in paragraph 4:

___

7. Names of two waterfalls in paragraphs 1 and 3:

___

Exercise C: ***Arrange the constellation in an order starting from Aries and ending with Pieces and figure out the features of each constellation. Additionally, figure out the missing constellation.***

1. Leo is self-expression seeking confidence, ease, and honor in the social world. The house where your Leo rules is where you will be challenged to 'shine'; to apply the posivitive, creative qualities of your sun sign, and find a sense of inner peace. *July 23rd–August 22nd*

2. Aries is fiery-will in actions, pioneering energy, new growth seeking to emerge. The house where your Aries rules is where you will be challenged to grow and learn; where new things will keep emerging. Here you throw yourself into physical activity. *March 21st–April 19th*

3. Gemini is abstract curiosity seeking to dorm a picture of the world, and to communicate those perceptions to others. The house where your Gemini rules is where you will be challenged to learn by following your curiosity, where communication will be important, and where you will be able to see both sides of an issue. *May 21st–June 20th*

4. Scorpions are the most sexual of the signs in terms of cravings and desires. Never satisfied with just one love, constantly needing to get another notch on their belts. Scorpions are sly and have a bit of a dare-devil streak in them, definitely the most risque of all the signs. Never tell a scorpion a secret—they won't keep it! *October 23rd–November 21st*

5. Cancer is healing, nurturing, and sensitivity seeking psychological understanding, emotional self-expression, and the capacity to heal others. The house where your Cancer rules is where you will be challenged to create a 'safe place' in which to grow emotionally. Here you have deep feelings, and tend to be super-sensitive and

笔记区

defensive. *June 21st–July 22nd*

6. Pisces is mystical dreaminess, warmth, and healing compassion seeking self-transcendence. The house where your Pisces rules is where you will be challenged to discern between illumination and illusion. Here is a doorway, either to higher spiritual knowledge or to escape through day-dreaming or self-indulgence. It's difficult to learn to trust and follow your intuition, and you will feel as if you are acting blindly. *February 19th–March 20th*

7. Libra is balance, harmony, and love of beauty seeking self-completion. The house where your Libra rules is where you will be challenged to find balance. Here you ability to see both sides of any issue can lead to difficulty making choices. *September 23rd–October 22nd*

8. Aquarius is eccentricity and radical individuality seeking freedom of the soul and communication with the group mind. The house where your Aquarius rules is where you will be challenged to seek new knowledge in order to break down old ideas. Here you are very much ahead of your time. *January 20th–February 18th*

9. Sagittarius is an expansion quest to discover truth and the interconnectedness of all things. The house where your Sagittarius rules is where you will be challenged to expand your experiences. You are philosophical about the affairs of this house and generous with its gifts. *November 22nd–December 21st*

10. Taurus is deliberation and determination seeking practical productivity in this world. The house where your Taurus rules is where you will be challenged to be practical and productive. You hand on to the things of this house for security. *April 20th–May 20th*

11. Capricorns are very career-orientated people. They are ambitious and have opinions about everything. They do sometimes tend to have a bit of a doom and gloom persona, always seeing the down side of things first. Some Capricorns are narrow-minded in their thinking but only because they want to do what they think is the very best thing to do. *December 22nd–January 19th*

(Words：602)

Exercise D: *Test your logic!*

Directions: *There are 11 facts listed below for this logic puzzle. After reading them, help the waitress who is serving the table to figure out the answer to this question:*

WHO ordered the cola, cheeseburger with pickles and French fries?

1. 6 friends went to a hamburger drive-in and decided to eat inside the restaurant.

笔 记 区

2. The friends sat in a booth, 3 people on each side of the table.
3. They ordered 6 different means.
4. Jack sat next to Jill.
5. Jill sat opposite the boy who sat next to Betty.
6. Archie ordered cola, a plain hamburger and French fries and sat across from Jane.
7. The boy who had the vanilla milk shake and two hot dogs sat across from Betty.
8. The girl who ordered the diet cola, fish sandwich, and onion rings sat between Archie and Reggie.
9. Reggie didn't order a diet cola, grilled chicken sandwich, and French fries or a cola and taco salad.
10. The girl who ordered the diet cola, grilled chicken sandwich and French fries sat across from Archie.
11. The girl who sat next to Jack had a cola and taco salad.

Exercise E: *Let's give ourselves a big treat!*

Directions: *ALL the words in the list below are hidden in this grid of letters. The words are in straight lines that are oriented diagonally, horizontally, or vertically. Some words will share letters when they cross each other. Also, the letters for some words may be in reverse order. For example, 'ekahs' is 'shake' spelled backwards. Have fun and see how many words you can find!*

BIG MAC; BURGER; CATSUP; CHEESE; COKE; COOKIE; FRIES; GOLDEN ARCHES; HAPPY MEAL; ICED TEA; LETTUCE; MCDONALD'S; MUSTARD; PICKLE; SALAD; SESAME SEED BUN; SHAKE; WENDY'S; WHOPPER

B	M	C	D	F	C	H	E	E	S	E
M	U	S	T	A	R	D	O	D	E	K
N	A	R	M	E	L	I	L	D	S	O
S	S	G	G	E	C	A	E	Y	A	C
D	I	R	O	E	N	U	D	S	M	V
B	A	E	L	O	R	N	T	S	E	N
O	B	V	D	E	E	E	H	T	S	R
I	F	C	E	W	I	E	A	N	E	E
C	M	I	N	T	N	I	P	P	E	L
E	D	I	A	A	H	K	P	W	D	K
D	K	H	R	E	R	O	Y	E	B	C
T	C	A	C	O	H	O	M	W	U	I
E	S	A	H	W	R	C	E	A	N	P
A	E	S	E	S	A	L	A	D	S	A
C	A	T	S	U	P	C	L	R	E	D

Ⅵ. 综合训练

Exercise: ***You should spend about 20 minutes on Questions 1–13 which are based on Reading Passage below.***

I Don't Know Where I'm Gonna Go When the Volcano Blows

A. These words, suggested in a song by Jimmy Buffet in his 1979 Volcano album, probably reflect the concerns of many people living near active volcanoes. Volcanoes are beneficial to humans living on or near them. They produce fertile soil, and provide valuable minerals, water reservoirs, geothermal resources, and scenic beauty. But volcanoes can be very dangerous. Where can a person go to be safe from an erupting volcano? What types of volcanic hazards might they face? These questions are difficult to answer because there are many types of volcanic eruptions which produce different types of volcanic hazards.

B. When Mount St. Helens erupted on May 18, 1980, red hot lava did not spew out of the volcano and pour down its flanks. This perception of a volcanic eruption is a common one and is probably due in part to pictures seen on television or in books of the beautiful lava flows and lava fountains in Hawaii. The type of eruptions in Hawaii is known as Hawaiian volcanism and is far less dangerous than the eruptions produced by Mount St. Helens. It is important to know what type of an eruption a volcano is most likely to produce so that the types of hazards produced by such an eruption can be identified. Knowledge of these types of hazards will help determine where a person would need to go to be safe during a volcanic eruption.

C. Volcanic eruptions can be placed into two general categories: those that are explosive, such as at Mount St. Helens, and those that are effusive, such as in Hawaii. The most active volcano in the world, Kilauea Volcano on the big island of Hawaii, is generally a non-explosive volcano (though there have been occasions when it erupted explosively). Eruptions from it normally result in gently flowing lava flows, spatter cones, and lava fountains. Another type of non-explosive volcanism is flood basalts. Lava flows from this type of eruption are extruded from fissures and cover vast areas. These non-explosive eruptions are the least dangerous type of volcanic eruption since people rarely get killed by them (Francis, 1993). However, they are devastating and may have global consequences.

D. Many eruptions are explosive in nature. They produce fragmental rocks from erupting lava and surrounding country rock. Some eruptions are highly explosive and produce fine volcanic ash that rises many kilometers into the atmosphere in

笔记区

enormous eruption columns. Explosive activity also causes widespread ash fall, pyroclastic flows, debris avalanches, landslides, pyroclastic surges, and lahars. Explosivity is usually the result of gases expanding within a viscous lava. Another mechanism for explosions at volcanoes occurs when surface water or ground water enters a magma chamber. These eruptions are likely when a volcano occurs in a wet area or in the sea.

E. Earthquakes related to volcanic activity may produce hazards which include ground cracks, ground deformation, and damage to manmade structures. There are two general categories of earthquakes that can occur at a volcano: volcano-tectonic earthquakes and long period earthquakes.

F. Earthquakes produced by stress changes in solid rock due to the injection or withdrawal of magma (molton rock) are called volcano-tectonic earthquakes (Chouet, 1993). These earthquakes can cause land to subside and can produce large ground cracks. These earthquakes can occur as rock is moving to fill in spaces where magma is no longer present. Volcano-tectonic earthquakes don't indicate that the volcano will be erupting but can occur at anytime.

G. The second category of volcanic earthquakes are long period earthquakes which are produced by the injection of magma into surrounding rock. These earthquakes are a result of pressure changes during the unsteady transport of the magma. When magma injection is sustained a lot of earthquakes are produced (Chouet, 1993). This type of activity indicates that a volcano is about to erupt. Scientists use seismographs to record the signal from these earthquakes. This signal is known as volcanic tremor.

H. People living near an erupting volcano are very aware of volcanic earthquakes. Their houses will shake and windows rattle from the numerous earthquakes that occur each day before and during a volcanic eruption. Residents in Pompeii felt earthquakes daily before Vesuvius erupted in A.D. 79 but continued to go about their daily routines (Francis, 1993). When Mount Pinatubo in the Philipines erupted in 1991, nerves were rattled as much as windows by volcanic earthquakes.

I. Earthquakes exhibiting volcanic tremor warn of an impending eruption so that people can be evacuated to areas of safety. The volcanic tremor signal has been used successfully to predict the 1980 eruptions of Mount St. Helens and the 1991 eruption of Pinatubo. Volcano-tectonic earthquakes can cause damage to manmade structures and landsliding. To prevent damage from being done, structures should be built according to earthquake standards, building foundations should be constructed on firm ground and not unconsolidated material which may

笔记区

amplify earthquake intensity, and buildings should be constructed on stable slopes in areas of low hazard potential.

Adapted from www.geo.mtu.edu/ volcanoes/hazards/primer

(Words: 832)

Questions 1–5

Choose the most suitable headings for the paragraphs from the list of headings below. Paragraph A has been done for you as an example.

NB *There are more headings than paragraphs, so you will not use all of them. You may use any heading more than once.*

Example	***Answer***
Paragraph A	VI

List of headings

Ⅰ. Explosive volcanic eruptions

Ⅱ. Difference between Mount St. Helens and Hawaii volcanoes

Ⅲ. Alertness to volcanic earthquakes

Ⅳ. Awareness of Pompeii people of Vesuvius eruption

Ⅴ. Types of volcanic eruptions

Ⅵ. Advantages and dangers of volcanoes

Ⅶ. Disasters caused by explosive volcanic eruptions

Ⅷ. Features of volcano-tectonic earthquakes

Ⅸ. Tips for constructing manmade structures against the earthquake damage

Ⅹ. Damages to manmade structures

1. Paragraph C:
2. Paragraph D:
3. Paragraph F:
4. Paragraph H:
5. Paragraph I:

Questions 6–8

*Write **NO MORE THAN THREE WORDS** for each answer.*

6. What type of volcanic eruption is least devastating?
7. What two materials mainly account for the explosive volcanic eruption?
8. Which type of earthquake can indicate a possible occurrence of a volcano eruption?

笔 记 区

Questions 9–13

Complete the summary below. Choose **NO MORE THAN TWO WORDS** *from the passage for each answer.*

Among the hazards caused by volcanic eruptions, volcanic earthquakes may produce damage to __9__ and manmade structures. Two types of earthquakes can occur at a volcano. Volcano-tectonic earthquakes are produced by the movement of __10__, which in turn results in the changes of stress. They can cause land-sliding and huge __11__ in ground. The other type called long period earthquakes are caused by the __12__ of the magma and people can predict a volcanic eruption by sensing their __13__.

SUMMARY

笔 记 区

第五章　雅思考试扩充阅读

Directions: *Read the following passages (1 –14) and finish the following choices within 10 minutes for each.*

1. Finding the Lost Freedom

The private car is assumed to have widened our *horizons* and increased our mobility. When we consider our children's *mobility*, they can be driven to more places and more distant places than they could visit without *access* to a motor vehicle. However, allowing our cities to be *dominated* by cars has progressively *eroded* children's independent mobility. Children have lost much of their freedom to explore their own neighbourhood or city without adult supervision. In recent surveys, when parents in some cities were asked about their own childhood experiences, the majority remembered having more, or far more, opportunities for going out on their own, compared with their own children today. They had more freedom to explore their own environment.

Children's independent access to their local streets may be important for their own personal, mental and psychological development. Allowing them to get to know their own neighbourhood and community gives them a 'sense of place'. This depends on 'active exploration,' which is not provided for when children are passengers in cars. Such children may see more, but learn less. Not only is it important that children be able to get to local play areas by themselves, but walking and cycling journeys to school and to other destinations provide *genuine* play activities in themselves.

There are very significant time and money costs for parents associated with transporting their children to school, sport and to other locations. Research in the United Kingdom estimated that this cost, in 1990, was between 10 billion and 20 billion pounds.

The reduction in children's freedom may also contribute to a weakening of the sense of local community. As fewer children and adults use the streets as pedestrians, these streets become less sociable places. There is less opportunity for children and adults to have the *spontaneous* exchanges that help to *engender* a feeling of community. This in itself may *exacerbate* fears associated with assault and *molestation* of children, because there are fewer adults available who know their neighbours' children, and who can look out for their safety.

The extra traffic involved in transporting children results in increased traffic *congestion*, pollution and accident risk. As our roads become more dangerous, more parents drive their children to more places, thus contributing to increased levels of danger for the remaining pedestrians. Anyone who has experienced either the reduced

笔 记 区

volume of traffic in peak hour during school holidays, or the traffic jams near schools at the end of a school day, will not need convincing about these points. Thus, there are also important environmental implications of children's loss of freedom.

As individuals, parents strive to provide the best upbringing they can for their children. However, in doing so, e.g. by driving their children to sport, school or recreation, parents may be contributing to a more dangerous environment for children generally. The idea that 'streets are for cars and back yards and playgrounds are for children' is a strongly held belief, and parents have little choice as individuals but to keep their children off the streets if they want to protect their safety.

In many parts of Dutch cities, and some traffic-calmed *precincts* in Germany, residential streets are now places where cars must give way to pedestrians. In these areas, residents are accepting the view that the function of streets is not solely to provide mobility for cars. Streets may also be for social interaction, walking, cycling and playing. One of the most important aspects of these European cities, in terms of giving cities back to children, has been a range of 'traffic calming' initiatives, aiming at reducing the volume and speed of traffic. These initiatives have had complex interactive effects, leading to a sense that children have been able to 'recapture' their local neighbourhood, and more importantly, that they have been able to do this in safety. Recent research has demonstrated that children in many German cities have significantly higher levels of freedom to travel to places in their own neighbourhood or city than children in other cities in the world.

Modifying cities in order to enhance children's freedom will not only benefit children. Such cities will become more environmentally sustainable, as well as more sociable and more livable for all city residents. Perhaps it will be our concern for our children's welfare that convinces us that we need to challenge the dominance of the car in our cities.

(Words:732)

Glossary:

horizon: 地平线、知识面
mobility: 机动性、灵活性 (mobile)
access: 入口、使用途径 a means or the right of entering
dominate: 支配 control by power
erode: 侵蚀、腐蚀 wear away
genuine: 真实的、真正的 authentic
spontaneous: 自发的、自然产生的 self-generated
engender: 造成 bring into existence
exacerbate: 恶化、加剧 aggravate

笔 记 区

molestation: 骚扰
congestion: 堵塞
precinct: 管辖区、范围 district

Reading Comprehension:

1. One of the benefits of car use is
   A. it helps children's independent mobility.
   B. it allows children to be driven to more places.
   C. it allows cities to be dominated by cars.
   D. it helps the economy.
2. One of the problems of car use is
   A. it makes drivers selfish.
   B. it gives children too much freedom.
   C. it makes children lazy.
   D. it reduces children's freedom to explore their own neighbourhood.
3. When parents drive their children to school
   A. children are more keen to play sport.
   B. the costs are significant.
   C. it reduces parents' free time.
   D. traffic jams are a problem.
4. If children can explore their own neighbourhood
   A. they will develop a 'sense of place.'
   B. they will not want to use cars.
   C. they will become more fit.
   D. they will make new friends.
5. If fewer children and adults use the streets, then
   A. shops and services are harmed.
   B. assaults on children increase.
   C. children and adults find it hard to get to know each other.
   D. children become less independent.
6. Because of the extra traffic
   A. noise levels increase.
   B. danger levels for pedestrians increase.
   C. there are more traffic jams during school holidays.
   D. there is more pressure on people to buy cars.
7. As individuals, parents try to
   A. encourage their children to play more sports.
   B. bring up their children well.
   C. care about the environment.
   D. use their cars wherever possible.

笔记区

8. In some areas of Germany
   A. cars have been banned.
   B. streets have been closed to cars.
   C. cars must give way to pedestrians.
   D. children must walk to school.
9. 'Traffic calming' measures have
   A. angered local drivers.
   B. made the streets quieter.
   C. made it difficult for children to get to school.
   D. allowed children to get to know their neighbourhood.
10. Measures to make cities safer for children also have the effect that
   A. the city becomes more sociable.
   B. schools attract more pupils.
   C. car prices drop.
   D. child molestation decreases.

参考译文：

找回失去的自由

1）人们认为，私家车拓宽了我们的视野，增加了我们的灵活性。当考虑我们孩子的活动范围时，与没有汽车时相比，我们可以驾车送他们去更多、更远的地方。不过，任由我们的城市被小汽车占据，将使孩子们渐渐丧失自主能动性。孩子们失去了很多不在成人监督下探索居住的小区或城市的自由。最近在一些城市进行的调查中，当被问及童年时代的经历时，大多数家长都记得他们拥有比自己的孩子更多，或者多得多的单独出去的机会。他们享有更大的去探索周围环境的自由。

2）孩子独自到当地的街道上对他们的身体、精神和心理发展都很重要。让孩子们了解邻近地区或社区会培养他们的"地方感"。这有赖于"积极的探索"，这是待在小汽车里的孩子所无法体会到的(这样的孩子可能见识的更多，但学到的更少)。不仅是孩子们能够自己到当地的游乐区很重要，步行或骑车去学校或其他地方则更是孩子们真正的娱乐活动。

3）父母驾车送孩子们去学校、运动场所和其他地方会花费很多时间和金钱。据1990年英国所做的研究估计，这需要花费100～200亿英镑。

4）孩子们自由度的减少还削弱了当地的社区感。由于现在步行的成人和孩子比以前少了，所以街道变得没有以前"友好"了。成人和孩子们进行自发交流的机会也少了，而正是这种交流使人们产生社区感。这本身就使家长更加担心孩子遭受袭击和骚扰，因为熟悉邻居孩子并能保护孩子安全的大人少了。

笔记区

5) 家长接送孩子增加了交通堵塞、污染以及交通事故的危险。随着道路变得更危险，更多的家长驾车送孩子去更多的地方，因此对其他的行人造成了更大的危险。凡经历过学校假期高峰时段交通量骤减或放学时学校附近交通堵塞的人，对此都深有体会。所以，孩子们失去自由对环境也有着重大的影响。

6) 作为个人，家长们尽力为孩子提供最好的生活条件。不过这样做的时候(如驾车送孩子去运动、去学校或娱乐场所)，通常家长们有可能导致孩子所处的环境更加危险。“街道是汽车的天下；后院和操场才是孩子们的地方”，这是人们根深蒂固的想法；而作为个人，家长几乎没有选择。为了确保孩子的安全，他们只能让孩子们远离街道。

7) 在荷兰很多城市和德国一些“宁静”区域的居民区街道上，汽车必须给行人让路。在这些地方，居民们正在形成这样的观点：街道不仅是车辆的交通通道，它还是人们社交、行走、骑车和玩耍的地方。就欧洲城市将城市还给孩子们这点而言，其中最重要的一方面是出现了一系列旨在减少交通量，降低汽车行驶速度的“改善交通”提案。这些提案已经产生了复杂的互动效应，让人们感到孩子们能够“夺回”他们居住的小区；更重要的是孩子们这么做的时候很安全。最近的研究表明，与世界上其他城市的孩子相比，很多德国城市里的孩子能够更自由地去周围地区游玩。

8) 为了给孩子们更多的自由而改造城市，受益的不仅仅是孩子。这样的城市环境更加可持续发展，而且城市中的所有居民也会交往更加密切、居住更加舒适。可能对孩子健康的关心使我们相信有必要挑战汽车在城市中的主导地位。

背景知识：

八十年代，美国城市规划及建筑学界开始出现“新都市主义”(New Urbanism)的思潮，使居住人群具有社区感、地域感、安全感。新都市主义强调“街”的多功能性，它是人们进行社会交往的场所，是儿童玩耍的地方，是步行与自行车交通的通道以及住宅入口的门前道路。新都市主义主张“接触”街道，通过提供街道的各种活动，使街道变得有吸引力，甚至鼓励汽车停在街道上，不仅使人行与车行有一种缓冲，而且鼓励步行活动和创造活泼的气氛。

http://www.c-snd.com/mag/news_detail.asp?news_id=330&qihao=%2017

2. How to Raise a Bright Child

Teachers and other specialists in early childhood education *recognise* that children develop at different rates. Given anything that resembles a well-rounded life—with adults and other children to listen to, talk to, to do things with—their minds will *acquire* naturally all the skills required for further learning.

Take, for example, reading. The two strongest predictors of whether children will

笔记区

learn to read easily and well at school are whether they have learned the names and the sounds of the letters of the alphabet before they start school. That may seem to imply that letter names and sounds should be deliberately taught to young children, because these skills will not happen 'naturally.'

But in all the research programs where they have done just that—instructed children, *rehearsed* the names and sounds over and over—the results are disappointing. The widely accepted explanation is that knowledge of the alphabet, for it to work in helping one to read, has to be deeply *embedded* in the child's mind. That comes from years of exposure and familiarity with letters, from being read to, from playing with magnetic letters, drawing and *fiddling* with computers.

So parents can do some things to help, although many do these things spontaneously. Instead of reading a story straight through, the reader should pause every so often and ask questions—but not questions which can be answered by a yes or no. Extend their answers, suggest *alternative* possibilities and pose progressively more challenging questions.

And with arithmetic, do not *explicitly* sit down and teach children about numbers, but all through those early years count when walking up steps. Recite nursery rhymes. Talk to children. Say this is a red apple, that is a green one. Please get three eggs out of the fridge for me.

The technical term in *vogue* for this subtle structuring of children's early learning is '*scaffolding*.' Based on recent extensions of the work of the Russian psychologist Lev Vygotsky, the idea is that there are things a child may be almost ready to do. Anna, for example, cannot tie a shoelace by herself, but if an adult or a competent child forms one of the loops for her, she will soon learn to do the rest. Applying this concept to older children, one wonderful teacher has her children keep lists of 'Words I Can Almost Spell'.

While this has all the *hallmarks* of common sense, it represents a significant change of emphasis from the ideas of Piaget, which have dominated the theory of early childhood learning. The child in Piaget's theory looks, more than anything, like a little scientist—exploring the environment, observing, experimenting, thinking and slowly coming to his or her conclusions about how the world works. The image is of a rather *solitary* pursuit with all the real action in the child's head.

The Vygotsky model re-introduces all the people who also inhabit the child's world—parents, care-givers, relatives, *siblings* and all those other children at play or school. They are not simply noise, clattering in the background while the child's developing mind struggles on its own. The cognitive development of the child, that is, the learning of colours or numbers or letters—depends on learning how to interact

笔记区

socially, how to learn from the people (as well as the things) in the environment.

What is important is that the child develops the range of social skills—being able to express a preference, knowing how to take turns, being able to stand up for themselves, being able to get into a group, being able to make decisions, being able to share, and having confidence to go off on their own. These all require careful nurturing. No one is telling parents not to think about their children's development. It is just that it is more important to think about a child's desire to chat and the importance of social behavior and play activity than the actually more trivial markers of intellectual achievement such as being the first kid in the group to cut out a circle that looks like a circle.

(Words: 683)

Glossary:

recognise: 承认、认可 re + cog +nise
acquire: 获得、学会 get by one's own efforts
rehearse: 排练、练习 practice
embed: 嵌入 em (in) + bed
fiddle: 无意识而不停地拨弄
alternative: 可选择的情况 choice
explicitly: 明白地 clearly
vogue: 流行、普及
scaffolding: 脚手架 (scaffold 绞刑架)
hallmark: 特点、标志
solitary: 孤独的 alone
sibling: 兄弟姐妹

Reading Comprehension:

1. During early childhood, children
   A. like to talk to other children.
   B. develop at different rates.
   C. are keen to learn new things.
   D. find it hard to acquire new skills.
2. Children will generally learn to read easily and well at school if
   A. they have often talked with other children and adults.
   B. they have good teachers.
   C. they have learned their skills 'naturally.'
   D. they have learned the alphabet well.

笔记区

3. Research programs studying how children learn have
   A. tried exposing children to reading, drawing and computers.
   B. proved that children learn best at school.
   C. had poor results.
   D. had good results.
4. If parents wish to help their children learn, they should
   A. rely on their children's spontaneous ability to learn.
   B. ask basic questions about stories they have read to their children.
   C. offer alternative possible endings to stories.
   D. ask increasingly difficult questions.
5. 'Scaffolding' is
   A. a theory created by Lev Vygotsky.
   B. helping children with simple tasks, like tying shoelaces.
   C. helping children with tasks that they cannot quite complete on their own.
   D. helping children improve their spelling.
6. The theories of Piaget
   A. have significant emphasis on the theory of childhood learning.
   B. are based on the work of Lev Vygotsky.
   C. call for the study of the environment.
   D. are no longer as popular as they once were.
7. In Piaget's model of child development
   A. the child learns to spell new words.
   B. the child explores on his or her own.
   C. parents play a key role.
   D. the child needs guidance from teachers.
8. In the Vygotsky model
   A. the people who inhabit the child's world are part of the background.
   B. old friends are re-introduced to the child.
   C. parents and relatives are seen as a key part of the child's development.
   D. the child's mind struggles on its own.
9. The ability of a child to learn depends on
   A. learning from his or her surroundings.
   B. learning about colours, numbers and letters.
   C. being sent to school when young.
   D. knowing how to take turns.
10. When considering their children's development, parents should
   A. set them tests of intellectual achievement.
   B. focus on social behaviour and play.
   C. not to be too concerned.
   D. teach them to cut out a circle.

笔记区

参考译文:

怎样培养一个聪明的孩子

1) 幼儿教育的教师和其他专家发现，儿童的发展速度是不一样的。如果给儿童一个多彩多姿的生活——可以听成人和别的儿童说话，与他们说话，和他们一起做事情——儿童就会自然而然地学会以后学习中所需要的所有技能。

2) 就拿阅读来说，最能说明孩子在学校是否能够轻松阅读的两方面就是看他们是否在上学前已经学会字母的名称和发音。这似乎暗示着父母应该有意教给小孩子字母的名字和发音，因为这些技巧不是自然学会的。

3) 但是所有这么做的研究项目——教小孩子字母，一遍又一遍地反复操练字母的名称和发音——结果都令人大失所望。人们普遍接受的解释是因为字母表是一个人阅读的工具，所以孩子必须牢记字母。而那是需要通过多年接触、熟悉这些字母，通过别人读给他听，通过玩有磁性的字母，通过画画和摆弄计算机才能学会的。

4) 所以父母可以给予孩子们一些帮助，虽然很多父母自然地这么做。不是直接把故事讲给孩子们听，而应该经常停顿并问一些问题——不是那种是非问题。扩充孩子们的答案，提示他们其他的可能性，再慢慢提出更具挑战性的问题。

5) 就算术而言，不要就坐在那里教数字，而要通过孩子小时候爬楼梯时数数让他们学会数字。背诵儿歌。与孩子们交谈。说：这是个红色的苹果，那是个绿色的。请为我从冰箱里拿三个鸡蛋。

6) 这种儿童早期学习建构的时髦术语叫“搭脚手架”。根据俄罗斯心理学家利维·维果斯基的著作的进一步研究，儿童可能已经准备好做一些事情。比如说，安娜不会自己系鞋带，但如果大人或者另一个会系鞋带的儿童为她系了一个圈，那么她会很快学会做剩下的事。一位优秀的老师就将这个理念运用到大龄儿童身上，让孩子们列出“我基本上能够拼写的单词”。

7) 虽然这些都是我们的常识，但却反映了与皮亚杰理论的重大差别。皮亚杰是儿童早期学习研究的权威。在皮亚杰的理论里，儿童看来更像个小科学家——探索环境、观察、实验、思考，然后慢慢得出自己对世界运行规律的结论。整个图像就是儿童在头脑中用真实的行动单独寻求答案。

8) 维果斯基的模式再次提出了占据儿童世界的人——父母、护理者、亲属、兄弟姐妹以及所有和他一起玩或一起读书的儿童。他们绝不仅仅是在儿童智力独自发育时喧嚷、嘈杂的背景。儿童的认知发展(即学会颜色、数字或字母)依赖于学习如何与周围的人发生作用，如何从环境中了解人(和事物)。

笔 记 区

9）重要的是孩子能够学会社会交往技能——能够表达自己的喜好、知道如何轮流做事情、能够坚持自我、能够融入团体、能够做出决定、能够与人分享、有信心独自外出。这些都需要悉心的培养。没有人对父母说不要去关心孩子的成长，不过更重要的是关心孩子说话的欲望和了解孩子的社会行为和游戏，而不是光看重那些微不足道的智商的体现，比如是小组中第一个剪出圆形的小孩。

背景知识：

皮亚杰：日内瓦学派创始人，瑞士儿童心理学家，被誉为心理学史上除了弗洛伊德以外的一位"巨人"。皮亚杰指出，在6岁以前，儿童还无法以抽象的概念来完成对外界事物的认识，必须以实际的感觉来认识与学习，所以他们必须不断地以身体及四肢的动作来增加感官及运动的经验，而这种身体及四肢的协调运作则是以大脑的调控和整合为基础的。由此可见，感觉统合是幼儿时期和今后认知学习的基础。

3. The Value of Driver Training

Most fatal accidents involve a *disproportionately* high number of men under the age of 25. A report on young driver research prepared last year by Monash University's accident research centre found that in 1990 and 1991, almost a third of the people killed in road crashes were drivers under 25, yet this age group represents only 14 percent of the population. The report, which also updated a review of international literature about, among other things, driver training, also reached what many would consider a startling conclusion: training and education where they occur—principally in the U.S.—do not appear to reduce younger drivers' risk of crashing.

The Monash University researchers looked at crash information from New South Wales for 1986 to 1990, from Victoria for 1984 to 1990 and from South Australia for 1986 to 1990. The only Australian evidence which possibly indicates that counter-measures targeted specifically at young/novice drivers have been effective comes from evaluations of zero blood alcohol concentration legislation. (In 1989, all Australian governments agreed from 1991 on, to ban *provisional* drivers from drink-driving at any level, and to extend the provisional licence to three years).

The Monash researchers also looked at United States road-crash information for 1989 on 6.6 million police-reported crashes involving fatalities, injuries and motor vehicle damage. The researchers looked at a sample of 44,000 crashes. The conclusion was that the available literature gives a *pessimistic* view of the efficacy of driver training and education, reflected in the inability to produce drivers safer than those who have

笔记区

not been trained. One study on driver training in the U.S. was conducted in DeKalb county, Georgia between 1977 and 1981. 16, 000 school students were split into three groups: one group received 70 hours practical driver education training, another a brief, school-based course and the third no school-based driver education. Those comprehensively trained were 16 percent more likely to get their licences, but 11 percent more likely to crash and 8 percent more likely to get traffic fines.

In 1985, the researchers who conducted that study then reviewed 14 studies of defensive-driver training courses and concluded that though people who attended such courses received fewer traffic fines, they did not have fewer crashes. Despite the *intuitive* conclusion that safe driving should be teachable (like many practical skills), there is insufficient evidence about the ability of practical driver-training to reduce crashes for the general driving population.

The Monash University report into young drivers concluded that younger drivers were more likely to take risks at night, younger men were more likely to take risks than younger women, but younger women appeared to have 'greater skills deficiency.' Overall, the researchers concluded that it appears that vehicle-control skills improve rapidly with increasing experience but that their development is still incomplete after one or two years and possibly after considerably longer periods.

(Words: 479)

Glossary:

disproportionately: 不成比例地 dis + proportion + ate + ly
provisional: 临时的 temporary
pessimistic: 悲观的 opposite to optimistic
intuitive: 直觉的

Reading Comprehension:

1. Men under 25 years old
   A. are responsible for a third of all accidents.
   B. need more driver training.
   C. represent 14% of the whole population.
   D. represent a third of the population.
2. When young drivers receive training and education
   A. the number of accidents drops.
   B. the number of accidents rises.
   C. the risk of accidents rises.
   D. the risk of accidents stays the same.

笔记区

3. The oldest crash information studied by the Australian researchers came from
   A. Monash University.
   B. New South Wales.
   C. Victoria.
   D. South Australia.
4. One measure that seems to have reduced the number of crashes in Australia is
   A. making it illegal for young drivers to have any alcohol in their bloodstream when driving.
   B. giving provisional licences to men under 25 years old.
   C. evaluating blood tests.
   D. improving driver training and education.
5. When the Monash researchers looked at U.S. data, they
   A. examined 6.6 million records.
   B. examined 44,000 records.
   C. examined drivers in DeKalb county.
   D. examined drivers who had received special training.
6. The drivers who received training for 70 hours
   A. were 11% more likely to get their licences.
   B. were 16% more likely to crash.
   C. were 11% more likely to crash.
   D. were 8% less likely to get traffic fines.
7. Researchers who investigated people who had taken defensive-driver training courses found that
   A. the number of traffic fines rose and the number of crashes rose.
   B. the number of traffic fines dropped and the number of crashes rose.
   C. the number of traffic fines dropped and the number of crashes did not drop.
   D. the number of traffic fines dropped and the number of crashes dropped.
8. Although it should be possible to teach good driving
   A. data does not show that training is effective.
   B. such courses must focus on defensive-driving.
   C. such courses must be taught like other practical skills.
   D. such data only exists for 1985.
9. In the conclusion of their report, the Monash researchers found that
   A. younger drivers drive better at night.
   B. younger women take more risks than younger men.
   C. greater skills deficiency is a key problem.
   D. younger men take risks when driving at night.
10. The researchers also concluded that
   A. young women need as much training as men.
   B. young men and young women need equal training.

笔记区

C. driving ability improves with experience.

D. driving ability does not improve with experience.

参考译文：

驾驶员培训的价值

1）许多致命的交通事故都是由25岁以下的年轻人造成的，这个比例高得惊人。去年莫纳什大学的交通事故研究中心对年轻司机所做的研究报告表明：1990~1991年在交通事故中丧生的司机中，有1/3都不到25岁，而这个年龄段的人总共才占总人数的14%。该报告同时还回顾了国际上关于驾驶培训的资料，得出了让人吃惊的结论：培训和教育——尤其是在美国——看上去并没有减少年轻驾驶员的事故率。

2）莫纳什大学研究员查看了1986~1990年新南威尔士、1984~1990年维多利亚以及1986~1990年南澳的交通事故信息。澳大利亚唯一可以表明针对年轻司机或新司机的防范措施有效的证据是他们遵守血液酒精含量为零这一立法的情况很好。（澳大利亚政府在1989年规定从1991年开始严格禁止实习司机饮酒后驾车，并将实习驾驶证延长至3年。）

3）莫纳什大学的研究员还查看了美国1989年警察局报告的660万起死亡、受伤或车辆损毁的车祸信息，并研究了其中44,000起事故，得到的结论是：现有资料表明，驾驶员培训和教育的效果不容乐观。这些教育无法保证受训司机比未受训者更加安全。美国乔治亚洲的底卡普郡在1977~1981年间对驾驶员培训做了一项研究。将16,000名学生分为3组：一组接受70小时的驾驶操作培训，一组接受短暂的理论学习课程，还有一组没有任何理论知识培训。与其他组相比，那些接受全面培训的学生获得驾驶执照的概率高16%，但出车祸的几率也高11%，被罚款的几率高8%。

4）在1985年，做该项研究的人员回顾了14个有关驾驶培训课程的研究，得到的结论是：虽然参加该课程的司机被罚款的可能性下降，但出车祸的概率并没有降低。尽管人们的直觉是就像许多实际操作技能一样安全驾驶是可教的，但事实上并没有足够的证据证明驾驶培训能够普遍降低事故的发生率。

5）莫纳什大学对年轻司机所做的报告得到的结论是：年轻的司机更容易在晚上出事故；年轻司机中男人比女人更容易出事故；不过年轻的女司机看来“驾车技术比较差”。总体而言，研究者发现驾驶技术随着经验的积累会迅速提高，但即使驾驶一两年甚至是相当长的时间后，人们的技术还是不够成熟。

笔记区

4. Traditional Vietnamese Medical Theory

The beliefs of Vietnamese folk medicine associate illness with the absence of any of the three souls which maintain life, intelligence, and the senses, or of the nine spirits which collectively sustain the living body. A number of *rituals* performed at childbirth, which are aimed at protecting the mother and the infant from medical and magical dangers, derive from these beliefs, but they play a relatively limited role in medical behaviour generally. *Conversely*, Chinese medicine plays a major role in the maintenance and *restoration* of health and is observed by *ethnic* Vietnamese and by Vietnamese-Chinese. Principles from Chinese medicine provide the *scripting* for the management of birth for both groups, and more generally, establish guidelines whereby good health may be maintained.

According to Sino-Vietnamese medical theory, the body has two vital and opposite life forces which capture the essence of yin (breath) and yang (blood) in accordance with the 'five *evolutive* phases' (wood, fire, earth, metal and water). The proper circulation and balance of the yin and yang ensure the healthy circulation of blood and thus good health; *disequilibrium* and disharmony cause ill health. Illness, physical and mental, can be identified by the imbalance or excess of yin over yang or yang over yin. Foods and medicine, also classified according to their reputed *intrinsic* nature as yin (cold) and yang (hot), may be taken *therapeutically* to correct the imbalance resulting from ill health, or to correct imbalance due to the *overindulgence* in a food *manifestly* excessively 'hot' or 'cold', or due to age or changed physiological status (for example, pregnancy).

Foodstuffs may also be identified as tonic or antitonic, toxic or poison, or as having wind. A further small group of foods are *ascribed* magical properties. Other foods may be classified as neutral or remain outside any classification system, and hence have no overt therapeutic use.

While the classification of foods as hot, cold, tonic, poison, windy and neutral is based on the intrinsic nature of the foods, in practice they are identified predominantly according to their physical effects on the body. Ultimately, the system is both individual and *arbitrary*, and there appears no firm *correlation* to the raw and cooked states of the food, the method of cooking, the spiciness, or the *calorific* value of the food.

In general, leafy vegetables and most fruit are classified as cold and are said to cool the body; meat, *condiments*, alcohol, and fatty foods are classified as hot and are said to heat the body. Tonic foods, believed to increase the volume of blood and to promote health and energy, include 'protein-rich' foods, high fat, sugar, and

笔记区

carbohydrate foods (fried food, sweet fruit, honey and rice), and medicines (alcohol and vitamins). Sour foods, and sometimes raw and cold foods, tend to be considered antitonic and are believed to *deplete* the volume of blood. Wind foods include raw foods, leafy vegetables, and fruit, and often are classified as cold; they reputedly cause wind illness such as *rheumatism* and arthritis. Beef, mutton, fowl, fish, *glutinous* rice, and bananas are considered potentially toxic and may cause *convulsions*, skin irritation and infection.

(Words: 522)

Glossary:

ritual: 仪式的 (rite)
conversely: 相反地 contrarily
restoration: 恢复 re + store + ation
ethnic: 种族的
scripting: 脚本
evolutive: 发展的、进化的 evolve + ive
disequilibrium: 不平衡 equi- (相等)
intrinsic: 内在的、本质的 inherent
therapeutically: 有疗效地(therapy)
overindulgence: 过分放纵 over + indulgence
manifestly: 明白地、明显地 apparently
ascribe: 归因于 attribute
arbitrary: 任意的、武断的
correlation: 相关性
calorific: 产生热量的 calorie + ic
condiment: 调味品
carbonhydrate: 碳水化合物 carbon + hydrate
deplete: 耗尽 exhaust
rheumatism: 风湿病
glutinous: 黏性的
convulsion: 痉挛

Reading Comprehension:

1. According to Vietnamese folk medicine
   A. childbirth is caused by magical dangers.
   B. illness is caused by the nine spirits of the body.
   C. illness is caused by the lack of soul or spirit.
   D. illness is caused by magic.

笔 记 区

2. Chinese medicine
   A. is used by Vietnamese people.
   B. is not used by Vietnamese people.
   C. is only used by Sino-Vietnamese people.
   D. is never used when a woman gives birth.
3. According to Sino-Vietnamese theory
   A. 'yin' and 'yang' are the same.
   B. the balance of the 'yin' and 'yang' ensure good health.
   C. there are three souls in the body.
   D. there are nine spirits in the body.
4. According to Sino-Vietnamese medicine
   A. food and medicine cannot be used to correct an overindulgence.
   B. food and medicine should not be used during pregnancy.
   C. food and medicine can be used therapeutically.
   D. 'hot' food and medicine should be used during pregnancy.
5. When a person's physiology changes
   A. medicine should be changed appropriately.
   B. 'hot' food should be increased.
   C. 'cold' food should be increased.
   D. medicine should not be changed.
6. Foods that are classified as 'neutral'
   A. are tonic or antitonic.
   B. lack 'wind'.
   C. are classified as magic.
   D. have no medical use.
7. Sino-Vietnamese medicine is ultimately arbitrary because
   A. food has a physical effect on the body.
   B. food has an intrinsic nature.
   C. preparation methods are not taken into account.
   D. the food often has no calorific value.
8. Among foods that 'heat' the body are
   A. leafy vegetables and fruit.
   B. 'wind' foods.
   C. alcohol.
   D. sour food.
9. Foods such as honey and rice
   A. are 'hot' foods.
   B. can cause 'wind-related' problems.
   C. are condiments.
   D. are carbohydrates.

笔 记 区

10. Rheumatism can reputedly be caused by
    A. raw food.
    B. beef and mutton.
    C. long bananas.
    D. sour foods.

参考译文：

越南的传统医学理论

1）越南民间医学认为，疾病与维持生命、智力和感官的三种灵魂或共同支撑人体的九种精神联系在一起。很多在孩子出生时为了保护母亲和婴儿免受病魔和魔法侵害而举办的仪式都是由此而产生的。不过就整体医疗而言，它的作用相对比较有限。与之相反的是，中医在保持和恢复人体健康方面起到了重要的作用，土生土长的越南人和华裔越南人都使用中医。中医原理告诉他们婴儿出生时该如何做；更多的是建立了保持身体健康的准则。

2）根据华裔越南人的医学理论，人体由两大重要但相互对立的生命要素组成，它们根据五行相生原理(金、木、水、火、土)控制阴(气)和阳(血)。阴阳正常的循环和平衡保证血液循环的畅通，从而确保人体的健康；而阴阳如果失衡或不协调，人就会生病。无论是生理还是心理疾病都是阴盛阳衰或阳盛阴衰此类不平衡造成的。食物和药品也根据人们公认的内在特性分为阴(寒)和阳(热)，它们可以治疗由于身体虚弱或过多食用过“热”或过“寒”的食物，或者年老以及生理状况发生改变(如怀孕)造成的失衡。

3）食物还可以分为滋补的、不利于滋补的、有毒的和阴湿的。还有一小部分食物被认为有神奇的特性。其他食物可以分为中性的或不属于任何分类，因此没有显著的疗效。

4）虽然将食物分为热性、寒性、滋补性、有毒性、阴湿性和中性是基于食物本身的性质，但实际上主要是根据它们对人体的实际功效来确认的。根本上说，这种分类是个别的、任意的，而且看来与食物的生、熟、烹饪方式、香料以及所含的热量都没有固定的关系。

5）一般来说，多叶蔬菜和多数水果都是寒性的，会让身体变冷；肉类、调味品、酒类和脂肪食品是热性的，会让身体发热。人们认为滋补品能够增加血量，促进健康，补充精力。它包括富含蛋白质的食物，高脂肪、高糖、碳水化合物的食物(煎炸食物、含糖多的水果、蜂蜜和稻米)以及药物(酒和维生素)。酸的食品，有时还包括生的和冷的食物，都被认为会抵消滋补作用、消耗血液。阴湿的食物包括生的食物、多叶蔬菜和水果，通常被认为是寒性的。据说它们会引起湿性疾病，如风湿病和关节炎。人们认为牛羊肉、家禽和鱼肉以及糯米、香蕉具有潜在的毒性，可能会导致痉挛、皮肤过敏和传染病。

笔记区

背景知识:

五行生克:

五行相生:金生水,水生木,木生火,火生土,土生金;

五行相克:金克木,木克土,土克水,水克火,火克金。

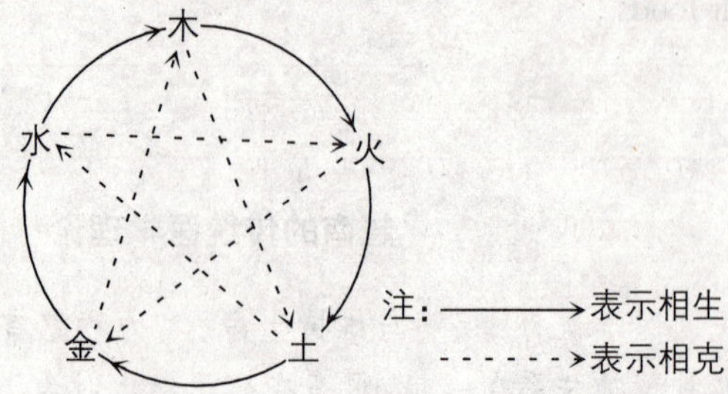

5. The Great Barrier Reef

All along the Queensland coast, *inshore coral reefs*, *smothered* by *silt* and *algae*, are dying. Some lagoons and reefs, once pristine examples of a tropical paradise, now consist of broken skeletons of dead coral, buried in layers of silt. Even the most remote reefs are at risk of pollution from tourist resorts releasing sewage and ships dumping their rubbish. Tourists are so numerous that at one popular reef, urine from swimmers, and droppings from fish they feed have increased the nutrient level in the water so much that algal blooms flourish and threaten the very existence of the colourful corals.

Marine experts say about 70% of coral reefs around the world are dead or severely degraded. Australia's Great Barrier Reef, the globe's largest reef system, stretching 2,300 kilometres and comprising 2,900 separate reefs, is in better shape than most. But experts warn that it requires *concerted* effort and diligence to keep it that way and in some places it is already too late.

The Great Barrier Reef is internationally renowned for its spectacular marine life and the tourist and fishing industries are economically important. Reef-based tourism and fishing have a combined economic worth of more than $1 billion a year. Reef tourism is now more valuable than sugar exports and tourist numbers are forecast to *quadruple* within eight years. The industry depends on protecting a spectacular marine environment that is home to at least 10,000 species of animals (including 400 varieties of coral) and plants. They include such endangered creatures as the *dugong*, the giant *clam* and the *humpback* whale.

It is an environment so little known that thousands more species almost certainly await discovery; during one recent 12 month field study, 200,000 new biological records, information not previously known to science, were made. Many promising

笔记区

compounds for new medical treatments and other products are being discovered on the reef. Compounds derived from *sponges* and other reef organisms are being evaluated in the United States for possible use in drugs to fight cancer and AIDS. Through newly developing technology, corals are giving us an extraordinary insight into past weather patterns.

Scientists have discovered that long-lived corals on the Great Barrier Reef are vast storehouses of weather information. Over the centuries, corals have absorbed *humic* acid from plant material washed into the reef from mainland rivers. By examining bands in coral skeletons (*analogous* to tree rings) under *ultraviolet* light, scientists have been able to trace rainfall levels back to the 1640s; eventually, they will know what the rainfall was at least 1,000 years ago.

Sadly, after several years of research, marine experts agree that inshore reefs are being devastated by a vast *deluge* of *sediment* and nutrients washed into the sea as a result of development on the mainland. Some claim that outer reefs will eventually meet the same fate. As internationally renowned marine scientist Leon Zann sums it up, "It's not the waste on the beaches we have to worry about, it's what we can't see below the surface."

The reef is being assaulted on other fronts:

- Research suggests that a new invasion of crown-of-thorns starfish, a coral *devouring* creature, may be *imminent*. Authorities believe that human activities are implicated in such population explosions.
- Fresh outbreaks of coral bleaching—which occurs when rising temperatures cause polyps to discard the tiny algae that give reefs their colours and which is linked by some scientists to the greenhouse effect, are being recorded.
- Catches of reef fish by commercial and recreational fishermen are falling.
- Ships are illegally discharging oil and dumping garbage; with only one *ranger* per 5,200 square kilometres of the Great Barrier Reef Marine Park, it is difficult to stop them.
- In a controversial move, the oil industry—with the government's blessing—plans to explore waters off the reef for petroleum within the next decade.

Australia is regarded internationally as being in the forefront of reef management and research and is providing $2 million worth of advice on marine issues this year to other countries. Australian scientists have advised Ecuador on how to protect the seas around the famed Galapagos Islands and are helping the Association of South-East Asian Nations to monitor their marine environment, where 80% of reefs are ruined and fish stocks are close to collapse. The hope is that the Great Barrier Reef will avoid a similar fate.

(Words: 728)

笔 记 区

Glossary:

inshore: 沿海的 in + shore

coral: 珊瑚

reef: 暗礁

smother: 窒息

silt: 淤泥

algae: 海藻

concerted: 协定的、一致的

quadruple: 四倍的 quadri（四）

dugong: 儒艮

clam: 蛤

humpback: 驼背 hump + back

sponge: 海绵

humic: 腐殖的

analogous: 类似的 analogue + ous

ultraviolet: 紫外线的 ultra（极端、过度）+ violet

deluge: 洪水、泛滥

sediment: 沉淀物

devour: 狼吞虎咽、破坏 destroy

imminent: 即将来临的 about to occur

ranger: 巡航员

Reading Comprehension:

1. Inshore coral reefs are dying due to
   A. broken skeletons of dead coral.
   B. silt and algae.
   C. pristine tropical paradise.
   D. the remoteness of their location.
2. Marine experts say that
   A. the Great Barrier Reef is 70% damaged.
   B. the Great Barrier Reef is 2,300 km long.
   C. the Great Barrier Reef is the world's largest.
   D. the Great Barrier Reef is relatively undamaged.
3. The Great Barrier Reef
   A. is renowned for its tourism industry.
   B. is renowned for its environment.

笔 记 区

C. is twice as valuable as the sugar industry.

D. will quadruple in eight years.

4. The humpback whale

A. is a danger to coral reefs.

B. is one of 400 species using the reef.

C. is a kind of dugong.

D. is in danger of becoming extinct.

5. One of the key potential benefits of the Great Barrier Reef is

A. its 200,000 new biological records.

B. its information not previously known to science.

C. its possibilities to help medical science.

D. its sponges and other reef organisms.

6. Corals have also helped science

A. fight cancer and aids.

B. investigate past weather patterns.

C. develop technology.

D. evaluate United States research.

7. Humic acid is useful because

A. it is washed into the reef from rivers.

B. it is derived from plant material.

C. it helps scientific study.

D. it helps build up reefs.

8. The destruction of reefs is also being caused by

A. scientific research.

B. plant material washed into the reef.

C. building on the mainland.

D. what is hidden below the surface.

9. Coral bleaching is being directly caused by

A. catches of reef fish.

B. a lack of rangers.

C. the greenhouse effect.

D. a loss of algae.

10. Australia

A. is very concerned about its reefs.

B. is not very concerned about its reefs.

C. spends \$2 million a year on protecting its reefs.

D. has lost 80% of its reefs.

笔 记 区

参考译文:

大堡礁

1）沿着昆士兰海岸，近海的珊瑚礁受到淤泥和海藻的侵害，正在慢慢死去。一些环礁湖和珊瑚礁曾是纯净的热带天堂，现在却满是死去珊瑚的残骸，埋在层层淤泥之下。现在即使是最远处的珊瑚礁也在劫难逃，那些旅游胜地排放出的污水和船只倾倒出的垃圾正威胁着它们。在一片受人喜爱的珊瑚礁附近，不计其数的旅游者在游泳时随处小便，加上鱼的排泄物，增加了水中的营养物质，使海藻迅速生长，威胁了那些五彩缤纷的珊瑚礁的生存。

2）海洋专家说世界上大约70%的珊瑚礁已经死亡或严重受损。澳大利亚的大堡礁是世界上最大的珊瑚礁系统，绵延2,300公里，由2,900个独立的珊瑚礁组成，它比大多数珊瑚礁形状更完好一些。但是专家们警告人们只有齐心协力才能维持它的原状，而且有些地方已经为时已晚。

3）大堡礁由于其壮观的海洋生命而闻名于世，那儿的旅游业和渔业对当地经济有重要的意义。每年依靠珊瑚礁的旅游和捕鱼，综合盈利超过10亿美元。现在，珊瑚礁旅游比糖业出口更加重要，预计8年内旅游人数总量将达到现在的4倍。旅游业有赖于保护这个引人入胜的海洋环境，这里栖居了至少1万种动物(包括400种珊瑚)和植物。其中包括濒临灭绝的生物如儒艮、巨蛤和驼背鲸。

4）人们对这个环境的了解甚少，几乎可以确定的是，还有数千种生物等待着人们去发现。在最近12月内所做的实地研究中，研究者为20万种过去不为人知的生物做了信息记录。人们正在从珊瑚礁中发现许多有望用于新的医疗和其他产品的化合物。从海绵和其他珊瑚生物中提取的化合物正在美国被检测，可能会用于防治癌症和艾滋病的药物。通过新近发展的技术，珊瑚礁正让我们渐渐了解过去的天气模式。

5）科学家发现大堡礁中那些寿命很长的珊瑚礁储存了大量的天气信息。几个世纪以来，植物不断地从陆河被冲进珊瑚礁，而珊瑚礁就从那些植物中吸收腐殖酸。用紫外线检测珊瑚骨骼上的条纹(类似树的年轮)，科学家能够追溯出17世纪40年代的降雨量。最终他们将了解至少1,000年以前地球上的降雨量情况。

6）不幸的是，经过几年的研究，海洋专家们认为由于陆地的发展，大量的沉淀物和营养物质被冲进海洋，因此沿海珊瑚礁正在遭到破坏。一些专家称远海的珊瑚最终也将面临同样的命运。世界知名海洋科学家Leon Zann总结道：“我们所要担心的不是海滩上的垃圾，而是海面下我们看不见的垃圾。”

7）大堡礁还受到其他因素的侵害：

笔记区

- 研究表明棘冠星鱼(一种破坏珊瑚的生物)可能马上要入侵大堡礁。专家们认为人类活动增加与星鱼数量激增不无关系。
- 有记录表明，珊瑚正在爆发大面积白化——温度升高时，珊瑚虫会抛弃那些给珊瑚礁颜色的微藻类，一些科学家认为这和温室效应有关。
- 商业捕鱼和休闲钓鱼捕获的珊瑚礁鱼类数量减少。
- 船只非法排放废油和垃圾；大堡礁海洋公园里每5,200平方千米只有1个巡逻员，很难阻止船只的不法行为。
- 在一份有争议的提案中，在政府支持下，石油业有一项有争议的举动：计划在未来的10年内探测大堡礁附近的水域来开发石油。

8）举世公认，澳大利亚走在珊瑚礁管理和研究的前列。今年它正在向其他国家提供有关海洋问题的建议，这些建议价值200亿美元。澳大利亚的科学家向厄瓜多尔提出了如何保护著名的加拉帕哥斯群岛海域的建议；同时它还在帮助东南亚联盟管理海洋环境，因为东南亚80%的珊瑚礁已被破坏，鱼类资源量急剧下降。人们希望大堡礁不会重蹈覆辙。

背景知识：

大堡礁是澳大利亚东北海岸外一系列珊瑚岛礁的总称。它纵向分布在离岸16~240千米的珊瑚海上，包括约3,000个岛礁，分布面积共达34.5万平方千米，是世界上最大的活珊瑚礁群。1981年，联合国教科文组织将大堡礁作为自然遗产，列入《世界遗产名录》。所谓珊瑚的"白化"是由于气候变暖，给珊瑚虫提供营养的海藻死亡，而造成珊瑚群失去色彩而变白的现象。

6. Earthquake

Earthquakes can *rip* apart entire cities and *outlying* districts, as the 1995 disaster in Kobe, Japan showed. *Seismologists*, scientists who study earthquakes and related phenomena, have records dating back to 1556, from the Chinese province of Shensi, which indicate that earthquakes have been *devastating* our world for centuries. In that instance, a major earthquake is estimated to have killed nearly 830,000 people, while destroying whole towns and villages. More recently, a death toll of more than 66,000 was recorded in northern Peru in 1970, and 23,000 died in the Guatemala quake of 1976.

The destructive forces, which produce earthquakes, usually begin deep below the ground, along a *fault* in weaker areas of the earth's rocky outer shell, where sections of rock repeatedly slide past each other. The speed at which the *fracture* spreads at point of weakness depends upon the type of rock but may average about 3 km a second in granite or other strong rock. At that rate, a fracture may spread more than 560 km in one direction in less than a minute. As the fracture extends along the fault,

笔 记 区

blocks of rock on one side of the fault may drop down below the rock on the other side, move up and over the other side, or slide forward past the other. The violent *shattering* of rock releases energy that travels in waves, and these seismic waves move out from the focus of the earthquake in all directions. As the waves travel away from the focus, they grow gradually weaker, generally resulting in the ground shaking less as distances increase.

Geological movements are not the only occurrences to trigger an earthquake. Human activity, most often the filling of reservoirs with extraordinarily large amounts of water, can also cause earthquakes. Lake Mead, on the Colorado River in the United States, was filled in 1935 and was the first example of an artificial lake being responsible for earthquake activity. Similarly, massive explosions, such as *quarry blasting* and nuclear tests can also *wreak havoc*.

Earthquakes almost never kill people directly, although that fact is not of much *consolation* to relatives and friends who have lost loved ones in an earthquake. Instead, many deaths and injuries result from falling objects and collapsing buildings, while fire resulting from broken gas or fallen power lines is another danger. The Kobe earthquake in January 1995 lasted only 20 seconds, yet resulted in a death toll of over 5,000 and injured approximately 26,000 people. Fires burnt out of control for several days after the earthquake, which was followed by hundreds of after-shocks. Because of fears of damage to gas pipelines and any leaks being potentially disastrous, inhabitants endured freezing winter conditions.

Even though earthquake-*prone* countries spend enormous human and financial resources on seismographic measurement, as a means of predicting earthquakes, there is a danger in paying too much heed to seemingly high risk zones and erecting less stable buildings solely because of their being in a low risk zone. *Prior* to the earthquake, Kobe was not regarded as at serious risk, but after the disaster, investigation of the damage revealed that nearly all deaths occurred in small buildings that shattered rather than twisted when stressed. Coupled with the problem of soft soils, the buildings had little firm support and many *crumbled*. If countries wish to withstand the devastating forces of substantial earthquakes and reduce death, injury and property damage, it is important to design and construct buildings that are earthquake resistant, as well as monitor seismic forces.

（Words：584）

Glossary:

rip: 撕裂 tear apart
outlying: 边远的 distant

笔记区

seismologist: 地震学家
devastate: 毁坏 destroy
fault: 断层
fracture: 破碎 act of breaking
shatter: 粉碎、碎片 cause to break
quarry: 采石场
blasting: 爆破
wreak: 引起 cause
havoc: 大破坏 devastation
consolation: 安慰 comfort
prone: 倾向于 inclined
prior: 优先的、在前的 preceding in the order
crumble: 粉碎、崩溃 break into small pieces

Reading Comprehension:

1. In 1556
   A. an earthquake devastated a city in Japan.
   B. an earthquake killed 66,000 people.
   C. 23,000 people died in Guatemala.
   D. 830,000 people died in an earthquake.
2. Twenty five years before the earthquake in Kobe
   A. an earthquake killed 66,000 people.
   B. an earthquake killed 23,000 people.
   C. an earthquake killed 830,000 people.
   D. an earthquake destroyed many villages in Shenshi.
3. In earthquake terminology, a ‘fault’ is
   A. the earth's rocky outer shell.
   B. a kind of granite or other strong rock.
   C. an area of rock sections that slide over each other.
   D. a destructive force that produces earthquakes.
4. When a fracture spreads along a fault
   A. it moves at 560 km a second.
   B. blocks of rock on either side of the fault may move.
   C. the point of weakness depends on the type of rock.
   D. seismic waves move along the direction of the fault only.
5. With increasing distance from the focus
   A. the fracture speed drops.
   B. the fracture speed increases.
   C. the earthquake becomes stronger.

笔记区

D. the earthquake becomes weaker.

6. Earthquakes are seldom caused by
   A. nuclear tests.
   B. quarrying.
   C. rivers.
   D. dams.
7. Earthquakes cause the highest number of deaths when
   A. the fracture lines move at high speeds.
   B. they are caused by dams and explosions.
   C. people live near the fault line.
   D. they cause buildings to fall.
8. The residents of Kobe had to endure cold weather because
   A. of the hundreds of earthquake aftershocks.
   B. the earthquake only lasted 20 seconds.
   C. they were scared to use heating.
   D. of the high death toll.
9. Countries that often experience earthquakes
   A. can usually predict when an earthquake will occur.
   B. are unable to measure seismographic activity.
   C. avoid building high-risk structures such as dams.
   D. often concentrate too much on certain risk-zones.
10. One of the factors that led to the high death toll in Kobe was
   A. the soft soil of the area.
   B. the lack of heating after the initial earthquake.
   C. the fact that the buildings twisted when the earthquake occurred.
   D. the fact that buildings were earthquake resistant.

参考译文:

地震

1）地震可以毁坏整个城市和其边远地区，就像日本神户1995年那场灾难一样。研究地震和相关现象的地震学家所做的地震记录可以追溯到1556年中国陕西发生的大地震。可见，几百年来地震一直在破坏我们的世界。那次地震摧毁了当地所有的城镇和乡村，大约有830,000人丧生。时期更近一些的1970年秘鲁北部的大地震，死亡人数超过66,000，而在1976年危地马拉的地震中死了23,000人。

2）造成地震的破坏性力量通常从地表深处开始，沿着地壳中较易破碎的断层前进，经过的地方岩石不断错动。岩石的碎裂速度由岩石的类型决定，但花岗岩和其他坚硬岩石的平均碎裂速度高达每秒钟3千米。按照这样的速度，1分钟内，一个方向的碎裂长度能够超过560千米。由于碎裂沿着断层前进，所

笔记区

以断层一边的岩石可能落在另一边岩石下面，向上运动翻过另一边的岩石，或向前擦过另一边。岩石的急剧碎裂会产生地震波，释放大量能量。这些地震波从震源向各个方向发散。随着地震波渐渐离开震源，它们就变得越来越弱；随着距离的增加，产生的震动也越小。

3）地壳运动不是引发地震的惟一原因。人类活动，最常见的是建造巨型水库，也会引起地震。1935年，美国在科罗拉多河上建造米德湖，造成了第一起由人工湖引起的地震。同样，大型的爆炸如开采石头和核试验也会造成严重破坏。

4）基本上地震不会直接造成人的死亡，虽然这个事实对在地震中丧失亲人和朋友的人而言没有多大的安慰。多数的伤亡都是由于坠落的物体和倒塌的房屋造成的，由于煤气的泄露和电线杆的倒塌而造成的火灾也是危险之一。1995年1月神户的大地震为时仅20秒，但死亡人数达5,000，受伤人数达26,000。地震后还遭受了几百次余震，爆发的火灾持续了好几天。由于担心对煤气管道造成了破坏，可能导致煤气泄漏，当地居民只能忍受严寒。

5）虽然多震国家投入了大量人力、物力进行地震测量以便预测地震，但是将过多的注意力集中在地震危险性较高的地区，而在危险较小的地方建造耐震性较差的建筑就很危险了。在地震之前，人们认为神户并不是地震危险区；而地震后的调查表明，几乎所有的死亡都是因为小型建筑受压时彻底粉碎而不是扭曲造成的。由于土质松软，这些建筑没有坚实的基础，许多就崩塌了。如果一个国家希望自己能够承受地震的破坏力，减少伤亡和财产损失，那么最重要的是设计建造防震建筑，并做好地震监测。

7. Why We Can't Afford to Let Asia Starve?

Among the problems *afflicting* a burgeoning world population, overcrowding, poverty and environmental *degradation* are combining to put at risk the very essence of our survival—food.

'If by the beginning of the next century we have failed to satisfy the very basic needs of the two billion very poor and four billion poor, life for the rest of us could be extremely risky and uncomfortable,' predicts Dr. Klaus Lampe of the International Rice Research Institute (IRRI) in the Philippines. This is a highly threatening, even terrifying prediction for Asia, where 70 percent of the world's poor live but where reserves of good quality *arable* land have *practically* run out.

Although the world regards Asia as the focus of an economic and industrial miracle, without adequate supplies of food, Lampe says, *chaos* could easily result in many countries. And the impact will be felt widely throughout the region. In the 1990s alone, he says, the cities of Asia will be swollen by a further 500 million people—

nearly equal to the population of the United States and European Community combined. 'The only growing population in Asia is that of the poor. Prime productive land is being used for city expansion and building roads, while thousands of hectares are being taken out of production each year because of *salinity* or *alkalinity*.'

From the mid-1960s when the Green Revolution began, Asian food production doubled through a combination of high-yielding crops, expanded farming area and greater intensification. From now on, growing enough food will depend almost entirely on increasing yield from the same, or smaller, area of land. However, a mysterious threat is emerging in the noticeably declining yields of rice from areas that have been most intensively farmed. Unless scientists can *unravel* why this is so, food output in Asia may actually *stagnate* at a time when population will double.

Such issues, Lampe argues, while seen as remote by many countries and international corporations, will strike at their economic base as well. Societies that are too poor or driven by internal *strife* and civil war will be bad for investment or as markets for goods. Pressure from a rising tide of environmental and political refugees may also be felt.

One significant factor *undermining* agricultural economies of developing countries has been the farm trade war between the U.S. and the E.C. 'We talk about environmental degradation and dangerous chemicals, yet spend billions of U.S. dollars and ECUs producing things we don't want which ruin local production systems and incomes for poor people,' Lampe says. And instead of developed countries helping struggling nations to develop sustainable food production systems, their policies tend to erode and destroy them.

When world grain prices are bad, farmers in Asia's *uplands* turn from rice to cash crops to supplement falling incomes, or clear larger areas of rainforest with catastrophic environmental consequences within just a few years. Cleared rainforest soils are highly erosive; even where they are not, they rapidly become acid and toxic under intense cultivation and plants die, forcing the clearing of everlarge areas.

Research at the IRRI has indicated that intensive rice production—growing two or three crops a year on the same land—is showing signs of yield declines as great as 30 percent. Evidence for this comes from as far a field as India, the Philippines and Indonesia. At the same time, agricultural research worldwide has been contracting as governments, non-government bodies and private donors reduce funding because of domestic economic pressures. This means, Lampe says, that at risk is the capacity to solve such problems as rice yield decline and research to breed the new generation of super-yielding crops. Yet rice will be needed to feed more than half the human

笔 记 区

population—an estimated 4.5 billion out of 8.3 billion people by 2030.

Compared with the building of weapons of mass destruction or the mounting of space missions to Mars, Lampe says, the devising of sustainable farming systems has little political appeal to most governments: 'To them I say: I hope you can sleep well at night.'

（Words：684）

Glossary:

afflict: 折磨 make suffer
degradation: 退化、降级 de + grade + ation
arable: 可耕种的 fit to be cultivated
practically: 实际上 actually
chaos: 混乱 a disorderly mess
salinity: 盐化 sal-（salt）
alkalinity: 碱化 alkali（碱）
unravel: 拆开 un + ravel（纠缠、混乱）
stagnate: 停滞 stay motionless
strife: 斗争、冲突 conflict
undermine: 破坏 under + mine
upland: 丘陵地、高地 up + land

Reading Comprehension:

1. Extreme poverty
   A. effects 2 billion people.
   B. effects 4 billion people.
   C. effects 70% of the people in the Philippines.
   D. effects overcrowding and environmental degradation.
2. Because there is a lack of good quality arable land in Asia
   A. countries focus on industrial and economic development.
   B. the situation for the rest of the world will become extremely risky.
   C. it is difficult for these countries to produce enough food.
   D. the IRRI has been set up.
3. The populations of the U.S. and Europe
   A. have plenty of arable land.
   B. have lower poverty levels.
   C. grew fast in the 1990s.
   D. are around 500 million.
4. Salinity and alkalinity

笔记区

A. are caused by city expansion.

B. are a prime cause of the shortage of arable land.

C. are caused by road-building.

D. are a prime cause of rapid population growth in Asia.

5. The Green Revolution

A. has led to declining yields of rice.

B. is not fully understood by scientists.

C. is still providing increasingly high rice yields.

D. is no longer providing increasingly high rice yields.

6. Intensive farming

A. led to the beginning of the Green Revolution in 1960.

B. is a mysterious threat to rice yields in Asia.

C. seems to have led to decreasing yields in Asia.

D. led to the creation of high-yielding crops.

7. A significant factor harming developing countries is

A. the fact that the U.S. and the E.C. use too many chemicals.

B. the fact that the E.C. and the U.S. fails to help them.

C. the fact that the U.S. and the E.C. are engaged in a trade war.

D. the fact that the E.C. and the U.S. have their own sustainable food systems.

8. A key problem with clearing rainforests to grow cash crops is that

A. rainforest soils are highly erosive.

B. they are located in Asia's uplands.

C. the fields derived from them are not suitable for certain crops.

D. great environmental damage is caused by the practice.

9. It will be hard to solve the current agricultural problems because

A. scientists do not understand all the problems of rice yield decline.

B. intensive production uses the same land two or three times a year.

C. donors are losing interest in funding scientific research.

D. domestic economic pressures are increasing in many countries.

10. According to Lampe

A. governments spend too much money on space research.

B. spending money on devising sustainable farming systems is uneconomic.

C. government officials need to sleep well at night.

D. governments have the wrong political priorities.

参考译文:

为什么我们不能让亚洲挨饿

1）世界人口不断膨胀，在困扰人类的众多问题中，人口过多、贫穷和环境恶化共同威胁着我们生存的必需品——粮食。

笔记区

2）菲律宾国际粮食研究院的Klaus Lampe博士预言："如果直到下个世纪初(指21世纪初)我们仍然无法满足20亿贫困人口和40亿穷人的最基本需求，那么我们其余的人就会处于极度的危险和不安之中。"对亚洲来说这是一个非常危险的、甚至称得上是恐怖的预言，因为这里生活着世界上70%的贫困人口，而那里多产的耕地几乎已经耗尽了。

3）Lampe说，虽然全世界都认为亚洲是经济和工业奇迹的焦点，但如果没有充足的食物，许多国家都很可能发生混乱，而且一旦发生将影响整个地区。就拿20世纪90年代来说，亚洲的城市将再增加5亿人口——差不多是美国和欧共体所有人口的总和。"亚洲增长的人口都是贫困人口。那些主要的多产耕地正被用于扩展城市和建造公路，而每年还有数千公顷的土地因为盐化或碱化而无法耕种。"

4）自从20世纪60年中期绿色革命开始，亚洲的粮食生产量翻了一番，主要是通过种植高产量作物、扩大耕地面积和更高度的集约化。从现在开始，生产足够的粮食基本上将完全依靠在同样面积甚至更少的耕地上种出更多的粮食。不过，粮食生产正在面临一个难以解释的威胁：在那些原本最集约化种植的土地上，粮食产量明显下降。除非科学家能够找出答案，否则亚洲人口翻番时，粮食产量很可能停滞不前。

5）Lampe认为，虽然很多国家和国际公司觉得这离他们很遥远，但这些问题也会冲击他们的经济基础。贫困至极或饱受内部战乱之苦的社会对投资和其作为商品市场都有害处。人们可能还会感受到日益高涨的环境难民潮和政治难民潮带来的巨大压力。

6）美国和欧共体之间的农产品贸易战是破坏发展中国家农业经济的重要因素之一。Lampe说："我们虽然在讨论环境恶化和有害化学品的问题，但同时却投入数十亿美元和欧币生产我们所不需要的东西，这还破坏了当地的生产体系和贫困人口的收入。"发达国家没有帮助那些苦苦挣扎的国家建立可持续发展的粮食生产体系，而是在对其采取削弱摧毁的政策。

7）当世界粮食价格很低时，亚洲丘陵地带的农民都不种水稻，而转为种植经济作物来贴补减少的收入；或者砍伐更大片的雨林，这在之后的几年造成灾难性的环境问题。雨林被砍伐后，土地被高度侵蚀；即使没有被侵蚀，在密集耕种的情况下它们也会很快酸化有毒，然后农作物就会死亡，这样农民又被迫开垦更多的土地。

8）国际粮食研究院的调查表明：大面积密集的粮食生产——一年在同一块土地上种2～3次庄稼——会导致粮食产量下降多达30%。印度、菲律宾和印尼的大片土地都出现了这种情况。与此同时，由于国内的经济压力，政府机构、非政府团体和个人都减少出资，因此世界范围的农业研究不断减少。Lampe说，这意味着诸如粮食产量下降和培养新一代高产量农作物之类的问题有可能无法解决。到2030年，稻米得维持半数以上人的生活——大约是83

笔记区

亿人口中的45亿。

9）与建造大规模杀伤性武器或登陆火星的航天任务相比，建立可持续发展的耕种系统对多数政府几乎没有政治上的吸引力。Lampe说："我想对他们说：希望你们晚上能睡得着。"

背景知识：

绿色革命：60年代兴起的，以采用农作物高产良种为中心的一场农业新技术革命。主要内容是大规模推广矮秆、半矮秆、抗倒伏、产量高、适应性强的小麦和水稻作物优良品种，并配合灌溉、施肥等技术的改进。这场革命取得了惊人的进展，在发展中国家开展得尤为普遍，因而被称为绿色革命。但是需要指出的是，这场绿色革命在粮食产量大大提高的同时，极大地危害了环境。新种子必须使用大量化肥、杀虫剂和水才能实现全部潜力，这就大大地影响了环境。人们长期生存所需的资源，即土地和水源，受到了损害，在非洲卢旺达有大约一半的耕地出现了流失现象，2/3的可耕地变成酸性和贫瘠土地。因此，一些专家提出了要进行第二次绿色革命——发展生态农业。

8. Intellectual Disability

People with intellectual disability form one of the largest single disability groups in a community. Intellectual disability refers to a general slowness to learn and function within society, and the identification of intellectual disability is usually based on an assessment of a person's performance in a variety of tests. An individual's level of performance, as assessed, can change with time and circumstances. On occasions, an intellectually disabled person may perform better than at other times. Evidence for this inconsistent level of performance comes from modern research and practice which have shown that with skilled training and opportunity for development, people with intellectual disability have much greater potential for acquiring skills and for participation in community life than previously had been thought possible.

In many western societies, five *categories* of intellectual disability have traditionally been used in order to indicate the perceived degree of difficulty an individual has in learning. All five may occur in either children, adolescents or adults, and show as mild, moderate, severe, profound or multiple intellectual disability. However, *undue* reliance on such categories and the consequent 'pigeonholing' of individuals into one of the five categories can result in failure to provide the opportunities for each person to develop.

For the majority of intellectual disabilities, there is no identifiable cause but there are some causes that are well documented. They include: brain damage at birth due to lack of oxygen—prolonged labour during childbirth; brain damage before birth due to

笔记区

factors such as *rubella*, drug or diet-related problems; damage after birth due to illnesses such as *encephalitis* or accidents; *hereditary* defects in the genes, abnormal *chromosome* count resulting in, for example, Down *Syndrome*.

Like everyone else, people with an intellectual disability need a rewarding job, a satisfying place to live and a good social life. But they may need extra support to achieve these things. Good support services are based on the principle of normalisation—which means enabling people to be part of the community like everyone else. In turn, normalisation needs to be well-integrated into the community, in order to be effective. Some of the services needed include assessment centers, training for employment and support to keep jobs once they get them, residential accommodation that is homelike. For children, early education and school education appropriate to the child's needs, are essential. Without a strong community-based system of care, the intellectually disabled run the risk of becoming a huge underclass as in the United States, where thousands of intellectually disabled are homeless because of the American policy of deinstitutionalisation.

With the introduction of the intellectually disabled into communities, there is a need to promote awareness of communication. Although many people may have little experience in talking with an intellectually disabled person, and anticipate great difficulty in communication, there are common guidelines that can simplify the interaction. Firstly, it is useful to remember that people with disabilities have feelings and can usually understand what is said, even though they sometimes may take longer to respond. Speaking in the same friendly manner as you would to anyone else, and using straightforward language and uncomplicated sentences, is also recommended. Being prepared to wait a little longer for replies during a conversation with an intellectually disabled person, would undoubtedly benefit the exchange. Above all, it is suggested not to talk about the person with someone else within their hearing. Ultimately, the idea is to encourage intellectually disabled people to do things for themselves.

(Words: 573)

Glossary:

category: 种类
undue: 不恰当的 excessive, not proper
rubella: 麻疹
encephalitis: 脑炎 encephal-(脑)
hereditary: 遗传的(heredity)
chromosome: 染色体
syndrome: 综合症

笔记区

Reading Comprehension:

1. Intellectual disability is characterized by
   A. being a member of a large group in the community.
   B. changing abilities over time.
   C. difficulty in learning.
   D. performing in a variety of tests.
2. Intellectually disabled people's abilities can change over time because
   A. on occasion, an intellectually disabled person may perform better than at other times.
   B. modern research and practice has led to better tests.
   C. skilled training can help improve their abilities.
   D. participation in community life is possible.
3. 'Pigeonholing'
   A. is the system of dividing intellectual disability into five categories.
   B. is the failure to help intellectually disabled people to develop.
   C. indicates the perceived degree of difficulty an individual has in learning.
   D. is the practice of confining an intellectually disabled person in a single category.
4. In most cases of intellectual disability
   A. no cause can be identified.
   B. rubella is a primary cause.
   C. birth problems are a primary cause.
   D. several causes can be identified.
5. Down Syndrome
   A. is caused by physical factors.
   B. is caused by genetic factors.
   C. is caused by rubella.
   D. has no identifiable cause.
6. People with an intellectual disability
   A. cannot have a good social life.
   B. never have a good social life.
   C. need help to have a good social life.
   D. always have a good social life.
7. A community-based system of care
   A. may cause the creation of a huge underclass.
   B. is part of a policy of deinstitutionalisation.
   C. can help improve the lives of intellectually disabled people.
   D. is provided by intellectually disabled people.

笔记区

8. When talking with an intellectually disabled person
   A. it is helpful to know some common guidelines.
   B. there is often great difficulty in communication.
   C. intellectually disabled people often cannot respond.
   D. intellectually disabled people can be introduced into communities.
9. When talking with an intellectually disabled person
   A. it is best to treat them differently from other people.
   B. you should take a long time to respond.
   C. simple language is recommended.
   D. much experience is required.
10. The overall purpose of introducing intellectually disabled people into society is
   A. to help educate them.
   B. to be able to talk to them.
   C. to teach them to speak more quickly.
   D. to help them become independent.

参考译文:

智力障碍

1）在社会的残疾群体中，有智力障碍的人组成了单一残疾人数最多的残疾人团体中的一个。智力障碍指在社会学习和活动中反应非常迟钝。一般是通过评估一个人在一系列测试中的表现来确定其是否有智力障碍。评估表明，个人的表现可能会随着时间和环境的变化而改变。在某些情况下，一个有智力障碍的人可能会比其他时候表现得好。现代的研究和实践为个人表现的不一致性提供了证据。它表明，如果给智障人士提供技能培训和发展的机会，与人们原来所想像的相比，他们有更大的获得必要的技能并参与社会生活的可能性。

2）在许多西方社会，传统上人们为表示个人学习的困难程度，将智力障碍划分为五个类别。这5种可能发生在儿童期、青春期或成人期；可能是轻度、中度、重度、完全障碍或同时出现多种智力障碍。不过，过分依赖这5种分类而将个人归为其中一类可能导致无法为个人提供良好的改善机会。

3）大多数的智力障碍都没有明确的原因，但有些原因是有证可查的，包括：出生时因为缺氧而使大脑受损——分娩时间过长；出生前由于麻疹、药物或孕妇饮食问题等因素而使大脑受损；出生后由于脑炎等疾病或事故而使大脑受损；遗传基因的天生缺陷，比如染色体数目异常会导致“唐氏综合症”。

4）和每个人一样，智障人士也需要一份有意义的工作，一个满意的住所和正常的社会生活。但是他们可能需要更多的支持才能实现这些。良好的支持服务

笔记区

建立在正常化的原则上——这意味着使他们能够和其他人一样，成为社会中的一分子。反之，正常化需要与社会很好地整合在一起才会奏效。必要的服务包括评估中心、工作培训、维护他们既有的工作和提供温馨的居住条件。对孩子来说，符合孩子需求的早期教育和学校教育是至关重要的。如果没有一个强大的社会维护系统，那么智障人士就会成为社会的底层阶级。例如美国的政策是不设立专门的机构，以至数千位智障人士都无家可归。

5）在把智障人士带入社会的同时必须提高沟通意识。虽然很多人可能没有和智障人交谈过，而且认为与他们交流会有很大的困难，但是有一些通用的准则可以使交流变得简单：首先，要记住，尽管智障人士有时需要更长的时间来做出反应，他们也有感情，一般都能理解别人的话；其次，建议你像和其他人说话一样与他们友好地交谈，使用浅易的语言和简单的句子；最后和智障人交流，你要做好心理准备，需要等待更长的时间他们才会回答，这对交流大有裨益。最重要的是，建议你不要让智障人听到你和别人在谈论他。最终，我们是要鼓励智障人士自食其力。

9. The New Ice Age

Antarctica's long dark winter evokes visions of early explorers barely surviving in huts, their *huskies* and sleds snowbound outside in the harshest conditions imaginable. But times have changed.

Although expeditioners like Mawson, Scott and Amundsen explored and wintered on the continent in the early years of the century, the notion of operating permanent year-round bases in Antarctica was relatively new until the 1950s and 1960s. Even after the Second World War, Antarctica was still being opened up and there were many blank spots on the map. Mawson station, opened in 1954, and Davis in 1957 are Australia's two oldest, continually operated bases on the continent.

In the past, life at these bases was hardly luxurious. It meant camping in *cramped zincalum* sheds, listening to *katabatic* winds scream in the long winter night. Communication with the outside world was restricted to just a few telegraphed lines. Expeditioners heading south were issued with *pamphlets* listing five-letter codes covering almost every conceivable situation so they could communicate with their families and still keep within strict 'word limits' during their year on base. Humour boosted *morale* and was an important element of life there. For instance 'YIKLA' was code for 'This is the life'!

Today, living year-round in Antarctica is considerably easier. The weather hasn't changed of course, but you can pick up a telephone and dial direct anywhere in the world. The cost is very modest and is *subsidised* at 90 cents a minute. All that

笔记区

individuals need to do is to collect the bill at the end of the year.

Because the summer-time work of scientists tends to capture the public's imagination, with revelations about the ozone hole or whale numbers, people tend to overlook the efforts of the 20 or so winterers at each base—mostly tradespeople—who keep the bases going long after 'the *boffins*' (research scientists) have migrated to warmer climates. In doing so, they also keep alive claims to *sovereignty* of sections of the continent and maintain their environmental interest in this sensitive part of the planet. Aside from its wealth of marine resources, Antarctica controls much of the southern hemisphere's climate. As the only other wholly southern hemisphere continent, Australia, more than any other large nation, has the most stake in what happens here.

So what is life like down there? Over the past year, wintering on an Antarctic base has become positively civilised. The conclusion last summer of a 10-year building program has seen the historic zincalum shacks and even older wooden sheds built at an early Antarctic base, on Heard Island in 1947, *supplanted* by vast, bright-coloured buildings with bay-window views and ski-lodge decor. There are video lounges, gymnasiums, bars and libraries. The workshops are *comparable* to anything in modern industrialised countries. The food is plentiful. There are even field huts that double as weekenders for those who feel the need to get away from it all. The money's good and everything from beer to socks is supplied free. Not everyone is pleased with the new luxury. Nowhere were the changes felt more keenly than at Mawson, where the old quarters, with their *rugged outpost* atmosphere, were shut and the last team of huskies removed. To many old Antarctic hands, it marked the end of the great '*Intrepid* Age' in Antarctica.

There are some things about life in Antarctica, however, that even central heating and watching a live-via-satellite sports broadcast cannot change. The Antarctic Territory is still one of the most *exotic* places on Earth. Few people will ever get there. There are no flights which land there—you have to travel as the early explorers did, almost a century ago, by sea. Going to Mawson, for example, means a two-week voyage on an icebreaker such as Aurora Australis, across 5,000 kilometres of the Southern Ocean, one of the roughest stretches of water on Earth. Waves can exceed 15 metres, the ship can *pitch* 40 degrees and, if you're not a good sailor, even the industrial strength Avomine prescribed by Antarctic Division doctors won't keep breakfast down. Most often though, tourist ships sail from South American ports, which offer the easiest access to the spectacular coastal scenery of the Antarctic *Peninsula*.

Once there, after the short shipping season has ended, some time in February when the ice closes in, there is no changing your mind and heading home. You are there for the *duration*, at least until the pack ice breaks up the following November. Like the early explorers, you are *confronted* with the challenge of getting along with a small,

笔 记 区

isolated group of people through the long winter night. Learning to put up with their *foibles* the way they have to put up with yours, which is why everyone applying for a job in Antarctica is interviewed by a psychologist before being accepted. As one veteran *diesel* mechanic at Davis put it, 'If you make an ass of yourself down here, there's no place you can go.'

(Words: 828)

Glossary:

husky: 爱斯基摩狗
cramp: 狭窄的 narrow
zincalum: 锌铝合金
katabatic: 下降的 downward
pamphlet: 小册子
morale: 士气
subsidise: 资助、津贴
boffin: 研究员
sovereignty: 主权
supplant: 代替 take the place of
comparable: 可比较的 compare + able
rugged: 粗糙的 rough
outpost: 前哨 an outlying settlement
intrepid: 无畏的 fearless
exotic: 外来的、奇特的 foreign
pitch: 倾斜
peninsula: 半岛
duration: 持续时间
confront: 面临 con + front
foible: 缺点 weakness
diesel: 柴油机

Reading Comprehension:

1. During Antarctica's winter D
   A. explorers live in huts.
   B. sleds become snowbound.
   C. explorers are often killed by the cold.
   D. the skies are dark.
2. Permanent bases on Antarctica B
   A. were first set up by Mawson and Scott.
   B. were first set up in the middle of last century.

笔记区

C. were set up during the Second World War.

D. were set up for explorers.

3. When the bases were first set up C

A. Katabatic winds were a problem.

B. they were quite comfortable.

C. they were quite uncomfortable.

D. explorers enjoyed living there.

4. Today's bases

A. are difficult to access in poor weather.

B. are much improved.

C. are only operated in summer.

D. are only used by whale scientists.

5. Each base has 'winterers' because

A. 'the boffins' need a holiday.

B. countries need to keep territorial claims.

C. Antarctica controls much of the southern hemisphere's climate.

D. the ozone layer requires year-round study.

6. The recent 10-year building program

A. involved putting sheds on Heard Island.

B. replaced the wooden sheds with zincalum shacks.

C. replaced the wooden sheds and zincalum sheds.

D. involved new construction at mawson base.

7. The recent improvements did not

A. provide free beer.

B. make everyone happy.

C. bring colorful buildings to the area.

D. boost salaries.

8. Getting to Antarctica

A. is difficult due to lack of flights.

B. is difficult due to the cold weather.

C. is difficult due to the expense.

D. is difficult due to the exotic surroundings.

9. When traveling to Antarctica, Avomine is used to

A. make the food taste better.

B. help prepare against the cold.

C. tackle seasickness.

D. help control the ship's pitch.

10. One of the similarities of life in Antarctica today to life there in the past is that

A. psychological tests are used.

B. the shipping season runs between February and November.

笔记区

C. applying for a job there is difficult.

D. living with small groups of people is difficult.

参考译文:

新冰河时代

1）南极洲的漫漫冬夜让人们眼前浮现出这样的画面：那些早期的探险家在小屋里勉强度日，他们的爱斯基摩狗和雪橇被困在所能想像的最恶劣环境中。不过，时代已经变了。

2）虽然探险家如Mawson, Scott和Amundsen在本世纪初（指二十世纪初）就去探索南极洲，并在那里过了冬，但在南极洲建立永久的基地直到二十世纪五六十年代还是个新鲜的想法。甚至在二战结束后，南极洲还在开发之中，在地图上还有很多人们未曾到达的地方。1954年建立在南极洲的Mawson观察站和1957年建立的Davis观察站是澳大利亚两个最古老的南极站，至今仍在工作中。

3）过去，南极站生活艰苦。那意味着在狭窄的锌铝合金棚里扎营，在漫长的冬夜听狂风呼啸。与外界的联系仅限于几行电文。凡是去南极的探险家都发到一些小册子，上面的五字代码几乎覆盖了所有可能的情况，这样，在南极站工作的一年里他们就能在严格的"字数限制"内与家人交流。幽默鼓舞着他们的士气，也是在那里生活的重要的一部分。比如"YIKLA"代表"这就是生活"！

4）如今，在南极洲住上一整年可容易多了。当然天气还是老样子，不过你可以直接拿起电话，直接拨到世界上任何一个地方。费用很合理，每分钟还能得到90美分的补贴。个人要做的就是年末去取账单。

5）由于人们往往注意了科学家夏天的工作，比如那些关于臭氧空洞和鲸鱼数量等发现，因此很容易忽略每个南极站里大约20个在那儿过冬的人员的工作，其中大部分是技术工人，他们在科学家们移居温暖的地区后维持着南极站的正常运行。这样做的同时，他们也保持着自己在南极洲对该地区的主权，在这个星球的敏感地区保证他们的环境利益。除了丰富的海洋资源，南极洲还控制着南半球的主要气候。与其他任何一个大国相比，澳大利亚作为南半球惟一的一片大陆，与南极洲最为息息相关。

6）那么，那儿的生活究竟是怎样的呢？去年以来，南极站的过冬已经变得相当文明。去年夏天长达10年的建造工程终于结束，带有观景凸窗和滑雪小屋的宽敞明亮的建筑取代了1947年在Heard岛上建造的早期南极站的锌铝合金的小屋和更古老的木头小屋。里面有录像室、健身房、酒吧和图书馆。工作室可以与现代工业国家的任何一间媲美。食物非常充足。甚至为满足那些周末想逃离基地的人，还建造了野外小屋。在这儿，薪水丰厚，而且从啤酒到袜子，

笔记区

一切都是免费供应。并不是每个人都喜欢这种奢侈。在Mawson观察站更能感觉到变化的无处不在。那些带着粗野的边区村落气息的老旧的房间都被关闭了，最后一队爱斯基摩狗也撤离了。对许多早期在南极洲工作的人而言，这标志着南极洲"无畏时代"的终结。

7）即使有中央空调和卫星现场直播的体育节目，南极洲生活中的有些东西也是无法改变的。南极洲仍然是地球上最奇特的一角。将来也很少会有人到那里去。没有飞往南极洲的航班——你还得像差不多一个世纪以前的探险家一样乘船去那里。比如说到Mawson观察站，就得在Aurora Australis这样的破冰船上航行两个星期，穿越5,000公里的南大洋，这是地球上最汹涌的海域之一。波浪可能超过15米，轮船可能倾斜40度，如果你不是个好水手，即使是南极洲研究所的医生开给你的特效晕船药Avomine也无法让你吃下早餐。不过，游客通常是乘坐从南美港口驶出的旅游船旅行，那是前往南极半岛观赏壮观的海岸风景最方便的路线了。

8）一旦南极洲短暂的航运期结束，就是在2月水面封冻的时候，你就无法改变主意回家了。你得在那儿等待，至少得等到浮冰11月碎裂了才行。就像早年的探险家一样，你会面临同样的挑战，那就是和一小撮远离城市的人度过漫漫冬夜。就像他们要忍受你的缺点一样，你也得学会忍受他们的缺点。这就是为什么每个申请去南极洲工作的人在被批准之前都得进行心理测试。正如一个在Davis南极站工作的经验丰富的柴油机械师所说："你要在那儿干了蠢事，连个逃的地方都没有。"

10. Tools for Tomorrow's Telecommunications

For some time yet, much of our telecommunicating will continue to depend on the existing web of thin copper wires that telephonically link most of our homes and workplaces. Making it possible for that network to match the communications demands of the near future will require new technologies that widen the lanes on the information highway.

The standard telephone service is something we take for granted in today's modern world. The public telecommunications network provides a reliable and highly accessible service—we have high expectations and react strongly when the service is unavailable. To meet the demand for high reliability, and to provide services economically, the public network is being progressively upgraded.

Yet consumers are still waiting for the widespread use of new services such as the videophone, which was first demonstrated 30 years ago. What then is required to make new services such as video telecommunications possible and widely available? Apart from the availability of inexpensive video terminal equipment, the key requirement is increased bandwidth (that is, more available frequencies for

笔 记 区

transmission) which must be provided by the network at an affordable cost. Understanding how this objective might be achieved requires review of the existing telecommunications network and the new technologies that are expected to improve and extend its capacity.

The traditional telephone network consists of a pair of copper wires connecting the customer *premises* to a local exchange. This is known as the customer access network. The local exchange is connected to other local exchanges through a series of intermediate exchanges, using *coaxial* cable, microwave or satellite transmission links. This part of the network is referred to as the core network. Within the core network, a technique known as *multiplexing* is used so only a small number of physical connections are needed between each telephone exchange. As a result, each transmission link may carry thousands of telephone conversations simultaneously.

Traditionally the telephone network used *analogue* switching and transmission techniques. Since the 1970s, the core network has been progressively changed from an analogue to a digital network. Digital technology offers better quality, with the capability to actively regenerate the original transmitted signal even when buried in unwanted noise. Pulse Code Modulation (PCM) is the process in which analogue telephone signal is converted to a digital one. Each analogue voice signal is sampled at a rate of 8,000 times a second, with one sample represented by eight bits of digital information. Each voice signal therefore requires a 64 kilobits/second transmission channel.

The physical connections in the core network have in recent years been changed to fibre optic cable. A large fibre optic network can connect many major metropolitan centres. Fibre optic cable is fundamentally the most important transmission technology because of high bandwidth that it offers.

The shift from the analogue to digital world within the core network exchanges means that majority of local exchanges are now digital exchanges. What then of the customer access network? A long term goal is to upgrade the customer access network using fibre optic cable, which will allow the delivery of new high bandwidth services such as video-on-demand. However, this final step from the local exchange to the customer is an expensive one, due to the large number of connections involved. Only when the demand for these new services is well established can the cost of large scale *deployment* of fibre optic cable in the customer network be justified.

(Words: 569)

Glossary:

笔记区

premise: 房屋

coaxial: 同轴的 co + axial

multiplexing: 多路技术 multi-（many）

analogue: 模拟的、类似的

deployment: 配置 deploy + ment

Reading Comprehension:

1. Currently, telecommunications
   A. use new technologies.
   B. use wide lanes on the information highway.
   C. use traditional wires.
   D. use video phone technology.
2. Because the current telecommunication network is highly reliable,
   A. new technologies are not immediately required.
   B. people will not put up with breakdowns.
   C. the public network is being progressively updated.
   D. new services can be provided economically.
3. Video phones are not yet common because
   A. the technology is 30 years old.
   B. demand is not widespread.
   C. video terminals are inexpensive.
   D. bandwidth is not sufficient.
4. A customer access network is
   A. the network of wires connecting up customers.
   B. a local exchange connected to other exchanges.
   C. a series of intermediate exchanges.
   D. a series of microwave or satellite links.
5. The process of multiplexing
   A. uses coaxial cable.
   B. links the core network to the customer network.
   C. carries thousands of telephone conversations.
   D. enables exchanges to use few physical connections.
6. Analogue switching
   A. was invented in the 1970s.
   B. regenerates the original signal.
   C. is giving way to digital switching.
   D. use pulse code modulation.
7. Analogue voice signals
   A. are repeated 8,000 times a second.
   B. use eight bits of digital information.

笔 记 区

C. are generated by PCM.

D. use transmission at 64 kilobits a second.

8. The key benefit of fibre-optic cables is that

A. they offer excellent bandwidth.

B. they connect major metropolitan centers.

C. they are fundamentally important.

D. they create physical connections in the core network.

9. Most telephone exchanges are now digital because of

A. the shift towards analogue.

B. the shift away from analogue.

C. the use of fibre optic cable.

D. the use of core network exchanges.

10. The final problem facing video-on-demand services is

A. bandwidth in the core network.

B. customer unwillingness to use them.

C. the expense of converting analogue to digital.

D. the large number of connections in the customer access network.

参考译文：

未来的通讯工具

1）在未来一段时间内，我们大多数的通信还将依赖现在连接着我们的家和工作场所的电话铜线网。要使这个网络满足在不久的将来的通讯要求，就得使用拓宽信息高速公路的新技术。

2）在当今社会，我们认为标准的电话服务是理所当然的。公共电信网为人们提供了可靠便捷的服务——我们对它充满希望，一旦无法使用便会强烈抗议。为了满足人们对高度的可靠性的需求，提供经济的服务，公共信息网正在不断升级。

3）不过消费者仍然期待着新服务的广泛应用，如30年前首次面世的可视电话。那么普及像可视通信这样的服务需要什么条件呢？除了便宜的可视终端设备外，关键是必须增加网络带宽（即更高的传输频率），而且成本必须合理。要理解如何实现这一目标，首先要回顾一下现有的通信网和可能改善、提高其通信能力的新技术。

4）传统的电话网由连接用户的房屋和当地交换机的两根铜线组成。这就是我们所知的用户接入网。当地的交换机又通过一系列中间交换系统，如同轴电缆、微波或卫星传播器，与其他地区的交换机相连。这部分网络被称为核心网络。核心网络使用多路技术，所以电话转接之间需要很少的物理连接。因此，每个传播器能同时处理几千个电话。

笔记区

5）传统的电话网使用模拟转换传播技术。从20世纪70年代开始，核心网络已经从模拟技术渐渐转变为数字网络。数字技术能够提供更好的质量。即使原始的发送信号被淹没在噪音中，数字技术也能使信号再生。脉冲编码调制（PCM）是模拟语音信号转化为数字信号的过程。每个模拟声音信号都以每秒钟8,000次的速率取样，单个取样用8字节的数字信号表示，所以每个语音信号需要64千字节/秒的传送通道。

6）近些年，核心网络中的物理接线已经换成了光纤电缆。一个光纤网络就能连接许多主要城市。由于光纤电缆能提供高带宽，所以它是最重要的信息传送技术。

7）核心网络交换机从模拟信号转变为数字信号意味着大多数的当地交换机也使用数字信号。那么用户接入网会怎么样呢？长远的目标是用光纤电缆升级用户接入网，这样就能提供高宽带的服务，如视频点播等。不过，从当地交换机到用户升级换代的最后一步因为牵涉到许许多多的连线，所以非常昂贵。只有确定人们需要这些新服务后，才能铺设用户网络所需的光纤电缆，这样付出的成本才是合理的。

11. Associations Provide Therapy for Society

A century and a half ago, Alexis de Tocqueville traveled across the United States to learn more about democracy. One of its underpinnings, he came to believe, was a phenomenon he had not observed in Europe, namely membership by citizens in voluntary social groups.

By the 1950s '*voluntarism*,' as it came to be known in the U.S., was being studied diligently by sociologists. Uniquely, Americans continued to increase their participation in organisations such as the parent-teacher associations, league baseball, girl and boy *scouts*, *choral* societies, bowling leagues, junior leagues of women voters—the list seemed endless.

Then, in the 1960s, voluntary participation began a steep slide. Robert Putnam, a political scientist, in an *ingenious* study entitled: *Bowling Alone: Democracy at the End of the Twentieth Century*, began to interpret the implications of the falling figures. Not surprisingly, he forecasts a threat to democracy in the decline of a once vital part of American life.

The reasons for these continuing changes are as numerous as the organisations experiencing them. The rapid movement of women into the workforce is often cited incorrectly, I believe, as the primary reason for the drop in participation, because they are no longer free to volunteer for community activities or school meetings.

Obviously, it is only one variable. Beginning in the 1970s, real income dropped,

笔记区

which led to the increase in the numbers of people working at more than one job—it now requires two incomes to maintain a similar standard of living that one income provided in 1970. The apparent social isolation has also been *abetted* by the explosion of new technologies.

Television, tapes, CDs, VCRs and audio-visual cameras have turned the home into an entertainment centre. Another giant leap is occurring through the use of the Internet, the electronic network, that is ultimately likely to be the most revolutionary of all behaviour-modifying technologies.

Putnam's *provocative* study provides the context within which to consider the implications. No eye-to-eye contact, not even the voice recognition of the phone. Just a *depersonalized* screen with its written messages on thousands of electronic bulletin boards. Worldwide, the 'community' of Internet users is growing. More than 26 million are already wired in. According to one electronic pioneer, by 2005, if the growth rate continues, every country in the world except Africa will be connected to this global network. It seems unlikely that there will be much time for group activity. Why might this social isolation make a difference? Putnam's figures reveal that being socially connected yields benefits for individuals and society. It is good for your health.

Joining one group cuts your mortality risk in half, two groups are twice as good. If you are part of a social network, someone will notice whether you look well or have been absent from the group. Voluntarism cuts crime. If you know your neighbours' first names it is more of a *deterrent* to crime than more police. Increasing parent-teacher-association involvement in schools is more effective than increasing teachers' salaries 10 percent. Living on a block where people go to church, even if you do not go, means that you will hear about jobs and consequently, will be less likely to be on drugs. Areas with high social connectedness produce better government services, less corruption and more efficiency. The drop in membership in voluntary associations is marked with a *concomitant* rise in *cynicism* and alienation. The *convergence* of these two growing trends—dropping out and logging on—exacerbates the serious consequences of a drop in political involvement and a rise in social isolation. Life on the Internet is unlikely to lead to the downfall of democracy by itself. Nor is the act of joining groups a guarantee that democracy will thrive. Growth of membership in right-wing religious groups, *unbuffered* by membership in other voluntary or religious groups, could undermine the very democracy that has thrived on diverse interests.

It is going to require a lot of consciousness-raising to drive home the critical role that social interactions contribute to society, or just as importantly, what their absence could lead to. Even one of the already mythical founders of the electronic revolution,

笔记区

John Perry Barlow, wonders: 'How can you guess what lies in hearts, when you can't see their eyes?'

(Words: 712)

Glossary:

voluntarism：自愿主义 voluntary + ism
scout：侦察员
choral：合唱团的（chorale赞美诗）
ingenious：有创造性的 clever
abet：帮助、煽动 help, urge
provocative：煽动的 provocate + ive
depersonalized：失去个性的 de + person + al + ize + ed
deterrent：威慑
concomitant：伴随物 attendent
cynicism：愤世嫉俗 cynic + ism
convergence：集中 converge + ence
unbuffered：无缓冲的 un + buffer + ed

Reading Comprehension:

1. When Alexis de Tocqueville travelled to the U.S.
   A. he decided to learn more about democracy.
   B. he had not yet been to Europe.
   C. he was struck by similarities to Europe.
   D. he was struck by the existence of volunteer groups.
2. 'Voluntarism'
   A. was invented in the 1950s.
   B. is the name for parent-teacher associations.
   C. was a subject keenly studied by social scientists.
   D. spread to Europe after the 1950s.
3. According to Robert Putnam
   A. voluntary participation began to slide in the 1960s.
   B. democracy was threatened by changes in social behaviour.
   C. political science required ingenious study.
   D. volunteerism was vital to American life in the 1960s.
4. The author of the article
   A. denies the entry of women into the workforce is a key problem.
   B. cites the entry of women into the workforce as a key problem.
   C. denies the numerous number of organisations is a key problem.
   D. cites the numerous number of organisations as a key problem.

笔 记 区

5. Because real income has dropped since the 1970s
   A. social isolation has risen.
   B. standards of living have dropped.
   C. people have to work much harder.
   D. current incomes are not enough to live on.
6. In the future, it is likely that the biggest changes in social behaviour will be created by
   A. a continued decline in real income.
   B. continued use of CDs, VCRs, tapes and television.
   C. giant entertainment centers.
   D. the Internet.
7. When the article focuses on the 26 million Internet users, the implication is that
   A. this number will continue to grow.
   B. the new community it creates replaces the old.
   C. bulletin boards are driving the increase.
   D. direct contact between people suffers as a result.
8. Reduced social activity
   A. cuts social isolation.
   B. is good for health.
   C. increases crime.
   D. benefits individuals.
9. Areas that have good government services also tend to have
   A. rising cynicism and alienation.
   B. high social activity.
   C. good salaries for teachers.
   D. plenty of jobs.
10. Democracy
   A. is directly threatened by modern technology.
   B. is directly protected by modern technology.
   C. is directly neither threatened nor protected by modern technology.
   D. is directly threatened by social interaction.

参考译文：

社会疾病的社团疗法

1）一个半世纪以前，Alexis de Tocqueville走遍美国以更多地了解民主。他后来相信，民主的基础之一是他在欧洲所没见过的一个现象，那就是公民自愿参与社会组织。

2）到20世纪50年代，随着美国人渐渐知道“自愿主义”这个名词，社会学家开始

笔记区

对其进行坚持不懈的研究。特别地是，越来越多的美国人参与各种组织机构，如家长老师协会、棒球协会、男生女生童子军、合唱团、保龄球协会和年轻女性投票联盟等等，多得不计其数。

3）然后到20世纪60年代时，自愿参加社团的人数陡然下降。政治科学家Robert Putnam在其极富创造性的研究报告——《仅看保龄球：20世纪末的民主》中开始解释这一数字减少的意义。他预言美国人生活中曾经重要的一部分的衰落，将对美国的民主产生威胁。这个说法一点也不奇怪。

4）导致不断发生变化的原因与那些经历这些变化的组织一样多得数不清。通常人们会提到大量妇女外出工作是参加社会团体的人数下降的主要原因，因为她们没时间去参加社团活动和学校的会议了，在我看来这并不正确。

5）显然，这只是其中的一个因素。从20世纪70年代开始，人们的实际收入下降了，这迫使更多的人不只做一份工作——因为在1970年以一份工作收入达到的生活水平，现在得靠两份工作的收入才能维持。而随着新技术的不断诞生，社会也变得更加孤立。

6）电视、磁带、光盘、录像机和摄像机已经把家变成了娱乐中心。而互联网（电子网络）的使用又让人们实现了巨大的跳跃，这可能是一切改变人类行为的技术中最具革命性的技术了。

7）Putnam煽动性的研究报告激发我们考虑这些技术的意义。没有眼神交流，甚至没有语音识别，只有一个非个性化的屏幕，上面充斥着成千上万的公告牌上的信息。从全世界来看，互联网用户的队伍正在日益壮大，目前已经有2,600多万人使用互联网。据一电子业先辈预言，如果互联网用户的数量继续以相同的速度增加，那么到2005年，除非洲外，其他地区的国家都将与全球网络相连。看来人们将没有多少时间参加团队活动了。为什么这样的社会孤立的影响会如此重大？Putnam的数据表明，参与社会活动对个人和社会都有好处，对健康有益。

8）参加一个团队可以将你的死亡风险降为原来的1/2，参加两个团队对你就有双倍的好处了。如果你是社会网络的一分子，那么别人就会注意你看上去是否健康，有没有缺席。自愿主义还能降低犯罪率。如果你知道邻居的名字，对犯罪分子而言，这比多一些警察还有威慑力。在学校让教师参加“家长老师协会”比给老师加10%的薪水更有效。生活在人们定期去做礼拜的街区里，即使你不去教堂，也能听到人们举行的各种活动，那你吸毒的可能性就小了。社会活动集中的地区，政府服务比较好，腐败情况少，工作效率高。自愿参加社会组织的人数减少后，社会中就出现了日益增长的疏远感和愤世嫉俗的情绪。这两种渐长的趋势——脱离现实和登陆网络——共同影响，将使更多的人退出政治活动，加剧社会孤立感。但是互联网上的生活本身不可能导致民主的衰败。参加社会团体也不是民主昌盛的保证。如果参加保守宗教

笔记区

组织的人数增加，而又没有参加其他的自愿的或宗教的团体的成员加以平衡，就会破坏原本基于不同利益而蓬勃发展的民主。

9）人们需要提高自己的觉悟，才能充分理解社会活动对社会的重要意义，或者缺少社会活动所造成的损失。连电子革命传奇的奠基人之一，John Perry Barlow都会怀疑："当你看不到对方眼睛的时候，你怎么能够知道他们心里想什么？"

12. Sustainable Production

Sitting on my desk are two ball-point pens. One seems *unremarkable*, just another white, *disposable*, plastic pen. The second is more curious. It's a small rolled tube of brown cardboard which pulls apart into a body and a lid; only the *protruding* plastic and brass of the writing tip gives its nature away. It looks like something you might expect to find in a kit of *stylish* recycled paper envelopes and stationery. But it is planned for more *ubiquitous* usage to meet the purchasing requirements of many government bodies and companies in Europe; requirements which are increasingly based on environmental criteria.

This cardboard pen is (supposedly) recyclable; the black plastic parts of the pen are from already recycled material (from a shampoo bottle, or a disposable razor, or possibly even another pen). It is a small example of a new trend to design products that can be disassembled and recycled. Pull it apart the body and lid can be dropped into the recycling bin.

The white pen is a manufacturer's demonstration, a prototype. Produced for a European plastics convention, it illustrates another approach to the production of an environmentally acceptable product. The silky feel and the flexibility of the plastic suggests that this is no ordinary stationer's item; so does the *embossed* 'green' and 'biodegradable' stamp on the barrel. It is made from a plastic derived entirely from corn, manufactured in Italy under the trade name Mater-Bi. If you are prone to chewing the end of your pen, you would find this one quite edible, perhaps even nutritious. Mater-Bi *dissolves* in water and the manufacturers claim that it leaves only harmless biodegradable organic compounds. After removing the *cartridge* this pen can go back to fertilize the crops whence it came. These are just two examples of the transformation taking place in almost all areas of product design; a *tantalizing* glimpse of a sustainable future composed of objects which will be familiar, yet radically different, having evolved, like species, to adapt to new environmental conditions.

笔记区

Consumer products, small disposable items, cleaning agents, domestic appliances, white goods, TVs, computers and cars, clothes and packaging, are all being redesigned to reduce their environmental impact. There is some superficial greening, just the latest *ploy* from the advertising and marketing division. Many of the more reputable green products, however, represent very large investment in research and design, and in new materials and technology.

These developments are so potentially significant in the light of global environmental problems that government research and development programs in many countries now have new categories of 'eco-design', 'design for the environment' and 'life-cycle analysis'. Recently, *Scientific American* included 'environmental design' in its list of the 12 critical new challenges for research in the coming years.

'Design for the environment seeks to stir engineers to think about the environmental implications of a product and of its manufacture during the earliest phases of design. These considerations may embrace a sweeping collection of issues: the environmental distress caused by obtaining the raw materials, the toxicity of using and discarding chemicals during production, the likelihood that the production itself can be *refurbished*, reused or recycled once the consumer has decided to abandon it.'

(Words: 531)

Glossary:

unremarkable:寻常的 un + remark + able
disposable:一次性的 dispose + able
protruding:突出的 pro- 向前
stylish:时髦的、漂亮的 style + ish
ubiquitous:普遍存在的 being everywhere
emboss:装饰 to decorate
dissolve:溶解 melt
cartridge:笔芯
tantalizing:非常着急的 tantalize (逗弄) + ing
ploy:策略 action
refurbish:磨光、刷新 re + furbish (磨光、擦亮)

Reading Comprehension:

1. In comparing the 'white' pen and 'brown' pen, the author says that
   A. the white pen is made of plastic and brass.
   B. it is not obvious that one of them is a pen.
   C. the brown pen can be found in stationary kits.
   D. the white pen can be found in stationary kits.
2. European governments and companies

笔记区

A. are likely to ensure the popularity of the brown pen.

B. have different requirements for the brown pen.

C. have individual purchasing requirements.

D. lack environmental criteria in their purchases.

3. The brown pen can be easily disassembled because

A. it is made from shampoo bottles.

B. it is made of used materials.

C. it allows ease of recycling.

D. it is made of cardboard.

4. The white pen

A. is not recyclable.

B. is not made of cardboard.

C. is not derived from corn.

D. is not biodegradable.

5. Before the white pen goes back 'whence it came'

A. it must be dissolved in water.

B. it must be chewed.

C. it must be embossed 'green'.

D. it must be disassembled.

6. The author likens future new products to species because

A. they are specifically adapted to their environments.

B. they biodegrade at the end of their lives.

C. the different products have different shapes and functions.

D. they are made of organic compounds.

7. When the author talks about 'superficial greening,' he is referring to

A. consumer products, cleaning agents and white goods.

B. the white pen and the brown pen.

C. products that are not truly environmentally friendly.

D. products that are truly environmentally friendly.

8. Many environmentally friendly products

A. require extensive advertising and marketing.

B. require large sums of money to buy.

C. require large sums of money to create.

D. require large sums of money to recycle.

9. The new environmentally friendly products are important due to

A. current environmental concerns.

B. the search for 'eco-design'.

C. *Scientific American's* list of challenges.

D. government research programs.

笔记区

10. According to *Scientific American*,
   A. environmentally friendly design requires discarding chemicals.
   B. environmentally friendly design is driven by environmental distress.
   C. environmentally friendly design is important at the beginning of the creation process.
   D. environmentally friendly design requires skilled product engineers.

参考译文：

可持续生产

1）我的桌上放着两支圆珠笔。一支看上去普普通通，只不过是支白色的一次性塑料笔。另一支有点奇特。它是一个棕色硬纸板卷起来的小圆筒，分成主体和盖子两部分，只有突出的塑料和金属笔尖暴露了它的真实身份。看上去，你可能会在一套漂亮的可循环利用的信封和文具里找到它。但是它是为满足欧洲许多政府机构和公司正逐渐基于环境标准而增长的更为广泛的购买要求而设计的。

2）这支硬纸板笔(应该)能够循环利用；黑色的塑料部分本身就出自再生的材料(洗发水瓶、一次性刀片，甚至可能是另一支笔)。它是设计可拆卸、可循环利用产品新趋势的小典范。把它拆开，就可以把它的主体和盖子扔进纸张回收利用桶了。

3）那支白色的笔是生产商提供的模型。它是为欧洲塑料会议生产的。它展示出另一种生产环保型产品的方法。它塑料外壳的丝般触感和柔韧性表明它不是一件普通的文具；外壳上印的“绿色”和“可分解”标志也不寻常。它的制作材料是完全用谷物制成的塑料，产于意大利，名叫Mater-Bi。如果你喜欢咬笔头，那么你会发现这支笔居然可以吃，说不定还很有营养。Mater-Bi可溶解于水。生产商说这支笔溶解后留下的是可分解的无害有机化合物。去掉笔芯，这支笔就能做庄稼的肥料，而它本身就来自于庄稼。这两支笔代表了几乎在所有的产品设计领域中发生的改变；看一眼我们未来实现可持续发展的诱人的前景，未来要生产的产品将是看起来熟悉其实截然不同，将能够像物种一样不断进化以适应新的环境。

4）为了减少产品对环境的破坏，人们正在重新设计消费品、一次性小物品、清洁剂、家用设施、大型家用电器、电视机、计算机、汽车、衣服和包装材料。有些表面看起来环保的绿色产品只不过是广告和营销的最新手段罢了。但许多著名的绿色产品意味着在研究、设计方面以及新材料和新技术方面的巨大投资。

5）这些发展对全球环境问题有潜在的重要意义，因此许多国家的政府研究发展项目都特地设立了“生态型设计”“环保型设计”和“生命循环分析”等项目。最近，《科学美国人》杂志将“环境设计”列为未来12项新挑战之一。

笔记区

6）“环保型设计”是为了鼓励工程师在开始设计时就考虑产品及其生产对环境造成的影响。对于这些因素的考虑可能包括一连串的其他问题：原材料的获得对环境的破坏；生产过程中使用和丢弃的化学物质的毒性；以及一旦消费者决定不用该产品，生产本身的可循环性和再利用性。

13. A Different Taste of Things to Come

The French are turning their noses up at wine and rejecting their *croissant* in favour of breakfast *cereal*, the English are turning from tea to mineral water and the Spanish are turning to pizza at an alarming rate. In short, we are beginning to see the evolution of the Euro-consumer. That seems to be the message from research conducted by Europanel, an association of research companies across 23 countries which monitors buying patterns using consumer panels.

Social and demographic factors and the marketing strategies of multinational food and drink companies are combining to make the lifestyles of different European nations more alike. The main demographic factors leading to this increasing uniformity across the continent are falling birth rates and easier divorce, according to one member of Europanel. He said: ‘The result is smaller households, which rely more on things such as microwaves and convenience foods, whatever the nationality.’

Even the French, who are proud of their *cuisine*, are turning to the microwave. Latest Europanel figures show that 38% of French kitchens house a microwave, just under the figure of 40% in western Germany. In Britain, the figure is 57%.

The French are also becoming ‘less French’ as they continue to shy away from wine. Wine consumption in France fell by an average of 6% a year between 1986 and 1992. By contrast, the British are drinking more.

A key demographic factor is average household size, measured by the number of adult residents. Already the spread between nations is quite narrow. Western Germany has the lowest figure in western Europe at 2.2 adults, and Spain the highest at 3.2, followed by Italy at 2.8. The gap will narrow still further because, surprisingly enough, the birth rates in Catholic countries such as Spain and Italy are falling.

Another factor is the rise of the one-person household, frequently misinterpreted to mean harbouring an unmarried or divorced man or woman living alone. Statistically, one-person households include single-parent households, the numbers of which are shooting up. The phenomenon is growing. 40% of Swedish homes are now one-person households, compared with 29 % ten years earlier. In western Germany

笔记区

the figure is 35% (30% ten years ago), in the Netherlands 29% (16%), and in Ireland 21% (17%).

In Spain, the one-adult household was so rare a decade ago it did not register statistically; now the figure is 10%. Hence the growth in demand for convenience foods. In Spain, the annual growth rate for pizza sales between 1986 and 1992 was 34% while growth last year slowed a little to 16%. Other factors affect consumer habits. For instance, Piper says that the wider *prevalence* of central heating in chilly Britain is the chief cause of the decline in the popularity not just of tea, but of all hot drinks. Another major factor is aggressive multinational marketing. After all, the French cannot indulge a craving for sliced bread if all that is on offer is a baguette. The products have to be on the supermarket shelves. In fact, there have to be supermarket shelves. There must be enough space to put new choices on offer.

Once a major manufacturer has won a dominant share in a mature market, it will look abroad for *pastures* new. Breakfast cereals are one such product. With growth opportunities in the mature British market slowing, manufacturers crossed the Channel. As a result, cereal sales in France grew by 18% a year between 1986 and 1992, and continued to grow by 10% last year. Similarly, tomato ketchup sales have boomed in such unlikely places as Spain and France, with growth rates of 28% and 18% respectively.

How far the process will go is anybody's guess. Increased choice is all very well, but the prospect of every kitchen in Europe serving up milk-*sodden* cereal in the morning and microwaved pizza in the evening is surely a depressing one.

(Words:657)

Glossary:

croissant: 羊角面包

cereal: 谷物

cuisine: 烹饪

prevalence: 流行 prevail + ence

pasture: 草原、牧场

sodden: 浸透的 thoroughly soaked

Reading Comprehension:

1. In Europe

   A. breakfast is becoming less popular in France.

   B. people are beginning to eat less healthily.

笔记区

C. tea is becoming less popular in England.

D. people are beginning to eat more healthily.

2. One of the key factors driving changing tastes in Europe is

A. the activities of the Europanel association.

B. the buying patterns of consumer panels.

C. the activities of large food companies.

D. the lifestyles of different European nations.

3. Statistics about microwave use reveal that

A. France and England have similar usage patterns.

B. microwaves are less popular in Germany than England.

C. microwaves are much less popular in France than Germany.

D. microwaves are less popular in England than in Germany.

4. Statistics about wine consumption reveal that

A. the French are shy about buying wine.

B. wine consumption in England began to grow in 1986.

C. wine consumption in France has risen since 1992.

D. wine consumption is rising in England.

5. Statistics about household size reveal that

A. it is less in western Germany than Spain.

B. it is second highest in Italy.

C. there is a significant gap between western Germany and Spain.

D. it is 2.2 in western Europe.

6. The fact that Spain and Italy are Catholic countries

A. would lead one to expect different household size figures.

B. explains the different household size figures.

C. explains the different figures between those countries and Germany.

D. is a matter of surprise to the author of the article.

7. One-person households

A. are frequently the result of divorce.

B. have increased most in Sweden.

C. have increased least in western Germany.

D. have increased most in the Netherlands.

8. Pizza consumption in Spain

A. grew fastest in 1986.

B. is still growing.

C. is growing less fast.

D. is influenced by the weather.

9. Tomato ketchup sales have risen in Spain because

A. pizza is popular there.

笔记区

B. British manufacturers are looking for new markets.

C. Spanish manufacturers are beginning to promote it.

D. Spain used to be an unlikely market for the product.

10. The author concludes that

A. in the future, most households will eat cereal and pizza.

B. increased choice is a good thing.

C. the change in eating habits has a negative side.

D. microwave use has a negative side.

参考译文：

未来人们不同的口味

1）法国人现在对葡萄酒不屑一顾，对羊角面包置之不理，他们感兴趣的是燕麦早餐；英国人也正从饮茶转向矿泉水；而西班牙人正以惊人的速度投向比萨的怀抱。总之，我们开始看到欧洲消费者的饮食变化。这看来是Europanel的研究结果，Europanel是23个国家的研究公司的联盟，它通过消费者讨论小组监测消费模式。

2）社会、人口因素和国际饮食公司的市场策略使不同的欧洲国家的生活方式趋于同化。据Europanel的成员说，导致欧洲大陆这种一致性的迅速增长的主要人口因素是出生率的降低和离婚率的升高。他说："结果是家庭规模变小，这样无论在哪个国家，家庭都更加依赖诸如微波炉和方便食品之类的东西。"

3）即使是以烹饪为傲的法国人也开始使用微波炉。最近的Europanel数据表明38%的法国家庭使用微波炉，仅次于德国40%的比例。在英国，使用微波炉的家庭占到57%。

4）随着法国人越来越远离葡萄酒，他们也变得越来越不"法国"了。1986到1992年间法国葡萄酒的年消费量平均下降了6%。不过相反，英国人喝得倒多起来了。

5）一个关键的人口因素是以成人人数为依据的家庭平均规模。各国间的差异已经很小了。在欧洲，家庭规模最小的是德国，平均每家2.2人；最大的是西班牙，每家3.2人；其次是意大利，每家2.8人。这个差距还会继续缩小，因为如西班牙和意大利等天主教国家，出生率正在下降，这着实让人吃惊。

6）还有一个重要因素是单人家庭增多了，人们往往把它误解为未婚或离婚的男女一个人生活。其实数据统计的单人家庭还包括单亲家庭。单亲家庭的数目呈飞速上升状态。这种现象还在不断增加。现在40%的瑞士家庭是单人家庭，而10年前才29%。在德国，单人家庭占35%(10年前为30%)，荷兰为29%(10年前16%)，爱尔兰为21%(10年前17%)。

笔记区

7）在西班牙，10年前几乎没有单人家庭，所以都没有数据记录；但现在的比例达到10%，因此对方便食品的需求也增加了。在西班牙，1986年到1992年比萨的年消费增长了34%，不过去年的增长稍有下降，为16%。还有其他因素也在影响消费者的消费习惯。例如，Piper说，在寒冷的英国，中央空调的更广泛使用是人们对茶和一切热饮降温的主要原因。还有一个主要因素是激烈的国际市场竞争。毕竟，如果只有棍子面包，法国人也无法培养出对切片面包的感情。所有的产品都得在超市的架子上等待出售。事实上，必须使用超市的摆架，因为必须容下足够多的新选择。

8）大厂商一旦在成熟市场获得了主要的份额，它就转向国外寻求新的发展空间。早餐麦片就是其中之一。随着英国国内市场成熟，发展机会逐渐减少，厂商们就跨越海峡开辟新天地。结果，法国1986~1992年麦片的销量年增长达到18%，去年继续以10%的速度增长。同样，番茄酱也在那些看似不可能的地方（如西班牙和法国）销售得红红火火，销量增长分别为28%和18%。

9）人人都在猜这种改变会持续多久。消费选择增加当然是好事，不过将来欧洲的每个厨房早餐都是牛奶麦片，晚餐都是微波炉加热的比萨，那绝对是倒胃口的事。

14. Fire Tests

Most fires start in a building's contents, not its structure. Understanding how fire grows indoors—in enclosed spaces—is the first step in limiting its potential for death and destruction. Fire tests have been around for years, and most building codes make reference to them. Some, however, are *obsolete*, in the sense that they can't accommodate a growing number of new materials in new *configurations*. Nor can they rank items in order of *flammability*. What is needed are graded tests that attach numbers to the degree of flammability. These numbers could then be plugged into suitable computer models. The computer could work out the total flammability of an item, depending on what it's made of, how it's put together, and where it's placed.

Computer models are becoming important in research. Scientists are hoping that one day, with enough data and sufficiently powerful computers, they will be able to calculate, without actually setting fire to anything, the way a fire will spread in any given building.

A fire indoors is a very different animal from the one outdoors. When you put a match to *incinerator*, the flames build up steadily. Most of the heat is lost to the atmosphere, so you have no trouble staying close by.

Inside a room, it obeys different and more complex physics, and the danger quietly multiplies. First, instead of a match, imagine a cigarette dropped into the back of a

笔记区

lounge chair. Cigarettes, you should know, are among the major causes of fires in houses. A carelessly discarded cigarette can stay alight in a concealed *crevice* for as long as 45 minutes. Then, after *smouldering* away, the chair's *upholstery* suddenly *ignites*. Within perhaps 30 seconds, smoke, combustion gases, and heat begin curling upwards, and before 1 minute has passed, they have started building up in a trapped layer under the ceiling.

As the chair continues to burn the layer gets hotter and thicker, and after 2 minutes it starts radiating heat back down to the chair and other furniture in the room. After 3 minutes or so the trapped heat can become so intense that we see 'flash-over'—everything in the room, including combustible gases, has reached ignition point and bursts into flame.

Experiments have shown that some *polyurethane* armchairs can, 5 minutes after ignition, give out 1-2 megawatts of heat. That's no more than a lively incinerator produces; but when it's confined in a room it can easily induce flash-over. After flash-over anybody still in the room would be dead. People rarely appreciate how quickly a small fire indoors can turn into a deadly *inferno*. They waste time going to the laundry to get a bucket of water instead of making sure everybody else is out of the house. By the time they get back, the fire will almost certainly be out of control. *Billowing* clouds of smoke and toxic gases quickly spill through doorways and along halls, enveloping and *incapacitating* sleeping occupants in the rest of the house.

You can appreciate that modelling the entire course of an indoor fire on a computer is a *daunting* task. The program needs to consider the flaming combustion zone, the rising thermal plume above there beneath the ceiling, and ventilation. Turbulence of air is very difficult to model because large *eddies* can grow from features as small as 0.1mm across.

Nevertheless, fire researchers overseas have simplified models to study aspects of fire behaviour in homes, hospitals, aircraft, tunnels, stadiums, shopping malls and airports. For example, the Fire Research Station in Britain has spent 7 years developing 'Jasmine,' which can show how air circulates into a burning building and how the smoke layer deepens with time.

In the United States, the National Bureau of Standards has developed ASET, which calculates 'available safe *egress* time.' This fire-growth model requires figures for rates of mass loss, smoke release, production of toxic gases, and heat build-up. Most existing tests, as we have noted, fail to provide the necessary data. They will need to be modified, or a whole new generation of tests devised.

(Words: 675)

笔记区

Glossary:

obsolete：过时的，荒废的 no longer in use
configuration：配置 configure + ation
flammability：可燃性 flame + able + ty
incinerator：焚化炉
crevice：裂缝 narrow crack
smouldering：冒烟燃烧
upholstery：装潢
ignite：点燃 cause to burn
polyurethane：聚氨酯 (poly- 多个的)
inferno：地狱
billow：翻腾 surge in huge waves
incapacitate：使无能力 in + capacitate
daunt：沮丧 discourage
eddy：漩涡 water or air current
egress: 出口 an exit (e- out)

Reading Comprehension:

1. The majority of fires in buildings are caused by
   A. materials left in the buildings.
   B. poor building structure.
   C. outdated fire regulations.
   D. enclosed spaces.
2. The increased number of new materials used to construct buildings
   A. leads to increasing number of fires.
   B. means fire rules need to be updated.
   C. requires many new construction configurations.
   D. uses graded tests to determine risk.
3. The risk of flammability in a given material
   A. is due to computer modeling.
   B. is due to what the item is made of.
   C. is due to a variety of factors.
   D. is due to graded tests.
4. Due to insufficient computing power
   A. scientists do not understand the risks of fire.
   B. scientists cannot update fire regulations.
   C. scientists cannot recommend using new materials.
   D. scientists have to test materials by setting fire to them.
5. Fires in houses

笔记区

A. are always caused by cigarettes.
B. take between 45 minutes and 2 hours to spread.
C. are very different to fires outdoors.
D. often start suddenly.

C

6. When a chair has been burning for about 3 minutes
A. smoke becomes trapped under the ceiling.
B. the temperature rises.
C. the rest of the room ignites.
D. people in the room will die.
7. The article suggests that if a person encounters a burning chair D
A. it won't put out as much heat as an incinerator.
B. the person should try to put it out.
C. the person will become incapacitated.
D. the person should remove all people in the area.
8. Because indoor fires have many aspects, A
A. they are difficult to understand.
B. air turbulence is increased.
C. eddies cannot be understood.
D. they are difficult to put out.
9. Overseas fire researchers B
A. are particularly interested in fires in homes and hospitals.
B. study certain features of fires rather than the whole process.
C. understand how air circulates in a burning building.
D. have enough computer power to do complete research.
10. The National Bureau of Standards in the U.S. C
A. fails to provide necessary data.
B. needs to be modified.
C. requires a wide range of data.
D. helps control fires.

参考译文：

火灾测试

1）很多火灾是因为建筑内的物品，而不是大楼结构引起的。要减少火灾带来的死亡和破坏，首先要明白它是如何从室内这个封闭的空间开始燃起的。人们已经进行了多年的火灾测试，大多数建筑条例对此也有明文规定。不过有些已经过时了，因为它们不适应新建筑中使用的新材料；也不能根据物品的可燃性分级。现在需要的是分级测试，将可燃性量化。然后这些数字就能输入适当的计算机模型，让计算机根据物品的材料、结构和摆放的位置计算物品的总体可燃性。

笔记区

2）计算机模型在消防研究中越来越重要。科学家们希望有朝一日，能够利用足够的数据和功能强大的计算机，在无需点燃任何东西的情况下，得出火在建筑中的蔓延方式。

3）火灾发生在户内户外，情况是完全不同的。当你把点燃的火柴扔进炉子，它会安静地燃烧。大部分的热量都散发到空气中，所以你站在炉子旁边不会有任何问题。

4）但在屋子里，火的运动遵循不同的、更为复杂的运动方式，而且危险是悄悄地增加。首先，不要想火柴，想像一截掉进安乐椅背部的香烟。你知道，香烟是家庭火灾的罪魁祸首之一。一支不小心丢掉的香烟会在隐蔽的裂缝中持续燃烧长达45分钟。然后冒烟燃烧一段时间后，椅子的外饰突然开始燃烧。30秒之内，烟、可燃性气体和热量一股脑儿地向上蹿；不到1分钟的时间内，它们可能已经充满了天花板下的夹层。

5）椅子继续燃烧，夹层变得越来越热、越来越厚，2分钟后它开始将热量辐射到椅子和房间里的其他家具上。大约3分钟之后，积聚的热量越来越多，我们会看见“火焰飞蹿”——房间内所有的东西，包括可燃性气体，都达到燃点开始燃烧。

6）实验表明一些聚氨酯扶手椅在着火后5分钟内能释放出1~2兆瓦的热量。这和真的火炉产生的热量相差无几；但如果它在封闭的房间里燃烧，就很容易烧着所有东西。那样的话，留在房间里的人就可能无法生还。很少有人明白户内的小火怎么会变成致命的火焰地狱。他们只会浪费时间，跑到水房去提水，而不是先确定所有的人都离开着火的房子了。等到他们把水提回来的时候，火势已经基本上失去控制。波浪般翻滚的浓烟和毒气迅速溢出门口，沿着走廊，笼罩屋内其余还在睡觉的人，使他们葬身火海。

7）你会明白用计算机模拟户内火灾的整个燃烧过程是多么的困难。整个程序必须考虑燃烧带、不断上升的热空气、天花板下的热空气层和通风情况。空气的紊乱运动很难模拟，因为巨大的气流漩涡可能是从直径小到0.1毫米的漩涡发展来的。

8）不过，国外的火灾研究者将测试模型简化，研究家庭、医院、飞机、隧道、体育场、购物街和机场发生火灾的情况。比如说，英国火灾研究站花了7年时间研制出名为“Jasmine”的火灾模型，它可以显示空气如何在燃烧的建筑里流动以及烟层如何随着时间不断变厚。

9）在美国，国家标准局开发了ASET，它可以计算“安全逃离时间”。不过这个火势增长模型需要知道质量亏损、烟尘释放、有毒气体产生和热量积聚的速度。正如我们所注意到的，许多现有的测试模型都无法提供必要的数据。它们需要改进，或者人们应该开发新一代的测试模型。

笔记区

背景知识：

计算机火灾模化和模拟技术的开发与利用，为人们了解火灾发生和发展的过程提供了新的方法和手段，它使人们可以通过在计算机上建立火灾模型，运用工程计算和计算机模拟的方法，对不同空间和环境条件下火灾的发展和蔓延进行模拟和预测；并根据设定的火灾场景，测算和确定各种建筑构件、材料与组件、消防设备以及空间内的火灾特性参数。国外在火灾模化理论成果的基础上，已开发出一批具有实用价值的计算机火灾模型和消防安全评估软件，例如美国的HAZARD、CFAST，加拿大的FIRECAM，英国的JASMINE、SMARTFIRE，澳大利亚的CESARE-RISK，日本的BRI，德国的KOBRA-3D等等。

Directions: *Read the following passage and figure out the hierarchy of the dinosaur family.*

15. What Is a Dinosaur?

Although the name dinosaur is derived from the Greek for 'terrible *lizard*,' dinosaurs were not, in fact, lizards at all. Like lizards, dinosaurs are included in the class Reptilia, or reptiles, one of the five main classes of *Vertebrata*, animals with backbones. However, at the next level of classification, within reptiles, significant differences in the skeletal *anatomy* of lizards and dinosaurs have led scientists to place these groups of animals into two different superorders: *Lepidosauria*, or lepidosaurs, and *Archosauria*, or archosaurs.

Classified as lepidosaurs are lizards and snakes and their prehistoric ancestors. Included among the archosaurs, or 'ruling reptiles,' are prehistoric and modern crocodiles, and the now extinct *thecodonts*, *pterosaurs* and dinosaurs. Palaeontologists believe that both dinosaurs and crocodiles evolved, in the later years of the *Triassic* Period (248 –208 million years ago), from creatures called pseudosuchian thecodonts. Lizards, snakes and different types of thecodont are believed to have evolved earlier in the Triassic Period from reptiles known as eosuchians.

The most important skeletal differences between dinosaurs and other archosaurs are in the bones of the skull, *pelvis* and limbs. Dinosaur skulls are found in a great range of shapes and sizes, reflecting the different eating habits and lifestyles of a large and varied group of animals that dominated life on Earth for an extraordinary 165 million years. However, unlike the skulls of any other known animals, the skulls of dinosaurs had two long bones known as vomers. These bones extended on either side of the head, from the front of the snout to the level of the holes in the skull known as the *antorbital fenestra*, situated in front of the dinosaur's orbits or *eyesockets*.

笔 记 区

All dinosaurs, whether large or small, *quadrupedal* or *bipedal*, fleet-footed or slow-moving, shared a common body plan. Identification of this plan makes it possible to differentiate dinosaurs from any other types of animal, even other archosaurs. Most significantly, in dinosaurs, the pelvis and *femur* had evolved so that the hind limbs were held vertically beneath the body, rather than *sprawling* out to the sides like the limbs of a lizard. The femur of a dinosaur had a sharply in-turned neck and a ball-shaped head, which *slotted* into a fully open acetabulum or hip socket. A supra-*acetabular* crest helped prevent *dislocation* of the femur. The position of the knee joint, *aligned* below the acetabulum, made it possible for the whole hind limb to swing backwards and forwards. This unique combination of features gave dinosaurs what is known as a 'fully improved *gait*.' Evolution of this highly efficient method of walking also developed in mammals, but among reptiles it occurred only in dinosaurs.

For the purpose of further classification, dinosaurs are divided into two orders. *Saurischia*, or saurischian dinosaurs, and *Ornithischia*, or ornithischian dinosaurs. This division is made on the basis of their pelvic anatomy. All dinosaurs had a pelvic *girdle* with each side comprised of three-bones: the *pubis*, *ilium* and *ischium*. However, the *orientation* of these bones follows one of two patterns. In saurischian dinosaurs, also known as lizard-hipped dinosaurs, the pubis points forwards, as is usual in most types of reptile. By contrast, in ornithischian, or bird-hipped dinosaurs, the pubis points backwards towards the rear of the animal, which is also true of birds.

Of the two orders of dinosaurs, the Saurischia was the larger and the first to evolve. It is divided into two suborders: *Therapoda*, or therapods, and *Sauropodomorpha*, or sauropodomorphs. The therapods, or 'beast feet,' were bipedal, *predatory carnivores*. They ranged in size from the mighty *Tyrannosaurus rex*, 12m long, 5.6m tall and weighing an estimated 6.4 tonnes, to the smallest known dinosaur, *Compsognathus*, a mere 1.4m long and estimated 3kg in weight when fully grown. The sauropodomorphs, or 'lizard feet forms,' included both bipedal and quadrupedal dinosaurs. Some sauropodomorphs were carnivorous or *omnivorous* but later species were typically *herbivorous*. They included some of the largest and best-known of all dinosaurs, such as Diplodocus, a huge quadruped with an elephant-like body, a long, thin tail and neck that gave it a total length of 27m, and a tiny head.

Ornithischian dinosaurs were bipedal or quadrupedal herbivores. They are now usually divided into three suborders: *Ornithipoda*, *Thyreophora* and *Marginocephalia*. The ornithopods, or "bird feet", both large and small, could walk or run on their long hind legs, balancing their body by holding their tails stiffly off the ground behind them. An example is *Iguanodon*, up to 9m long, 5m tall and weighing 4.5 tonnes. The thyreophorans, or 'shield bearers,' also known as armoured

笔记区

dinosaurs, were quadrupeds with rows of protective bony *spikes*, studs, or plates along their backs and tails. They included *Stegosaurus*, 9m long and weighing 2 tonnes. The marginocephalians, or 'margined heads', were bipedal or quadrupedal ornithischians with a deep bony frill or narrow shelf at the back of the skull. An example is *Triceratops*, a *rhinoceros*-like dinosaur, 9m long, weighing 5.4 tonnes and bearing a prominent neck frill and three large horns.

(Words:827)

Glossary:

lizard: 蜥蜴
Vertebrata: 脊椎动物 vertebra(脊椎骨)
anatomy: 解剖
Lepidosauria: 有鳞目 lepido-(鳞片)
Archosauria: 祖龙目 archaeo- (古老的、原始的)
thecodont: 槽齿类的
pterosaur: 翼龙 pter=ptero-(羽翼)
triassic: 三叠纪 tri- (3)
pelvis: 骨盆
antorbital fenestra: 眶前小孔 ante- (在…之前), fenêtre (法语:窗)
eyesocket: 眼眶
quadrupedal: 四足 quadr- (4) + pedal (foot)
bipedal: 两足 bi (2) + pedal
femur: 大腿骨
sprawl: 四肢伸开
slot: 放置
acetabular: 吸盘的
dislocation: 脱臼 dis + locate + ion
align: 排成一行
gait: 步态、步伐
Saurischia: 蜥臀类 saurian (蜥蜴类)
Ornithischia: 鸟臀类 ornith- (鸟)
girdle: 腰带
pubis: 耻骨
ilium: 髂骨
ischium: 坐骨
orientation: 定位、方向 orientate + ion
Therapoda: 兽孔类 pod (足)
Sauropodomorpha: 蜥脚类
predatory: 食肉的
carnivore: 食肉动物

笔 记 区

Tyrannosaurus rex: 暴龙
Compsognathus: 细颚龙
omnivorous: 杂食的 omni (all)+ vorous
herbivorous: 食草的 herb (草药) + vorous
Ornithipoda: 鸟脚龙 ornith- + pod
Thyreophora: 甲龙
Marginocephalia: 肿头龙 margin + cephal- (头)
Iguanodon: 禽龙
spike: 长钉
Stegosaurus: 剑龙
Triceratops: 三角龙
rhinoceros: 犀牛

参考译文:

恐龙是什么?

1) 虽然恐龙这个名字起源于希腊，意思是“恐怖的蜥蜴”，但事实上，恐龙根本就不是蜥蜴。不过，像蜥蜴一样，恐龙也被归为爬行动物，是5大类脊椎动物之一。不过在爬行纲下一层次的分类上，科学家们根据蜥蜴和恐龙骨骼的明显区别将它们列入两个不同的总目：有鳞目和祖龙目。

2) 有鳞目包括蜥蜴、蛇和它们的史前祖先。而祖龙目或“爬行动物统治者”包括史前和现代的鳄鱼以及现已绝迹的槽齿类动物、翼龙和恐龙。古生物学家认为恐龙和鳄鱼都是在三叠纪晚期（据今2亿4,800万年到2亿800万年）从 槽齿类动物(pseudosuchian thecodonts)进化而来。而蜥蜴、蛇和各种槽齿类动物都被认为是在三叠纪早期从爬行动物eosuchian进化而来。

3) 恐龙的骨骼与其他祖龙最重要的区别在于头骨、骨盆和肢骨。人们发现恐龙头骨的形状和大小不尽相同，这反映出1亿6,500万年前主宰地球的巨型动物不同种群的饮食习惯和生活方式。不过，与其他所知动物的头骨不同，恐龙的头骨有两根长长的犁骨。它们位于恐龙头部两侧，从嘴的前部延伸到头骨的空洞，就是恐龙眼眶前面的眶洞。

4) 所有的恐龙，无论大小，无论是四足还是两足，无论动作敏捷还是迟缓，都有同样的身体构造。只有确认了恐龙的骨骼构造，人们才有可能将恐龙与其他动物，甚至是其他祖龙区别开来。很重要的是，恐龙的盆骨和腿骨已经进化到后肢骨是垂直在身体下这一程度，而不像蜥蜴的四肢是摊开在身体四周的。恐龙的腿骨有一个内转的颈部和球状的圆头，与它的完全开放的髋臼相吻合。尾端的骨锤构造可以防止骨盆脱臼。髋臼下的膝关节排成一行，这样恐龙的后肢才能前后摆动。这些特征独一无二的组合给了恐龙“完全进化的走路姿态”。哺乳动物同样也采用这种高效率的走路方式，但在爬行动物

笔记区

中，只有恐龙是这样。

5）为了进一步分类，恐龙被分为两个目：蜥臀目和鸟臀目。这是根据恐龙的盆骨构造来分的。所有恐龙的骨盆带每边都由耻骨、髂骨和坐骨3根骨头组成。不过，这些骨头的生长方向都遵循下列两种模式之一。蜥臀类恐龙的耻骨向前伸，就像大多数的蜥蜴一样；不同的是鸟臀类恐龙的耻骨向后伸，这和鸟是一样的。

6）在这两种恐龙中，蜥臀类恐龙体形比较大，进化也比较早。它又分成两个亚目：兽孔类和蜥脚类。兽孔类又叫“兽脚类”，是两足的食肉动物。它们的体形大到长12米、高5.6米、重约6.4吨的暴龙，小至最小的长1.4米、重仅3公斤的成年细颚龙。蜥脚类恐龙包括两足和四足恐龙。其中有些是食肉或杂食恐龙，但后期进化的种类基本上是食草恐龙。它们包括最大最出名的恐龙，如全长27米的四足梁龙，它长着大象般的身体，拖着又细又长的尾巴，细长的头颈撑起它小小的脑袋。

7）鸟臀类恐龙是两足或四足的食草恐龙。现在人们一般把它们分为三个亚目：鸟脚龙亚目、甲龙亚目和肿头龙亚目。鸟脚类恐龙有大有小，都是靠长长的后肢行走或奔跑，靠尾巴撑在地上保持平衡。比如说禽龙，最长可达9米，高5米，重4.5吨。甲龙亚目或“有盔甲的恐龙”又叫装甲恐龙，四足行走，背上和尾巴上都长有尖刺或铠甲。其中包括长9米、重2吨的剑龙。肿头龙的头顶向外隆起，是两足或四足的鸟臀类恐龙。它们的头骨后部有一个穹隆。比如说三角龙，是长得像犀牛的恐龙，长9米，重5.4吨，它的颈部高高隆起，还长着3个巨大的角。

背景知识：

分类等级：界—门—纲—目—科—属—种。早期的古生物学家认为恐龙是自成一类的爬行动物，因此将其统一分类在“恐龙目”当中。后来才发现它们实际上包括了两个不同的爬行动物目，即蜥臀类和鸟臀类。二者区别在于腰臀部的骨骼结构不同。两个目的恐龙分别在三叠纪晚期起源于槽齿类。蜥臀目分为3个亚目：古脚亚目、蜥脚亚目和兽脚亚目。我国云南发现的禄丰龙就属于古脚亚目。蜥脚亚目的著名代表有产于我国四川、甘肃晚侏罗纪的马门溪龙，由19节颈椎组成的脖子长度约等于体长的一半。翼龙是恐龙同时代的近亲，与恐龙差不多同时在距今6,500万年前从地球上绝迹。翼龙骨骼比较脆弱，一般来说很难作为化石流传后世。
http://www.booksofa.com/infobase/dinosaur.htm（恐龙名中英文对照）

Directions: *Read the following passage and design 15 questions to test the understanding of your fellow students.*

笔记区

16. Freshwater Runoff into Arctic Is on the Rise

The six largest Eurasian rivers are dumping a lot more freshwater into the Arctic Ocean now than they were several decades ago, according to an international team of scientists. Their finding gives teeth to the long-held prediction that freshwater runoff into the ocean would increase in the Arctic as a result of global warming.

"The mechanism is most likely due to increased precipitation as forecast by global climate models,"said Bruce Peterson, a researcher at the Marine Biological Laboratory in Woods Hole, Massachusetts. Other factors for the observed 7 percent increase in runoff from 1936 to 1999 could be changes in ice and permafrost melt or changes in the seasonality of precipitation and runoff, he said.

If this current rate of freshwater influx into the oceans continues to rise, it could have a large-scale impact on ocean circulation patterns in the North Atlantic. The influx could slow down or shut off the North Atlantic Deep Water (NADW) formation, the driving factor behind the conveyor belt current known as thermohaline circulation, which brings large amounts of warm water to the North Atlantic region.

Co-author Stefan Rahmstorf of the Potsdam Institute for Climate Impact Research in Germany said stoppage of the NADW could cause temperatures in continental Europe to drop by 3.6 to 9 degrees Fahrenheit (2 to 5 degrees Celsius). "However, you have to take into account that the Earth will have warmed a lot by the time this happens, so depending on how much that is, most of Europe may not get colder than it is now," he said.

Long-term records

Climate models have long predicted that as global temperatures rise, evaporation of surface water will increase and more moisture will be held in the atmosphere. This moisture will lead to more precipitation at high latitudes, such as the Arctic, and subsequently more river runoff. If these models are correct, the researchers suggest, the 1 degree Fahrenheit (0.6 degree Celsius) rise in temperature over the last century should have caused a corresponding increase in Arctic river discharge. Until now, however, researchers have not been able to obtain good observational data on regional trends.

Previous observational studies have focused on specific areas and time periods. Peterson and his colleagues obtained their data by looking at discharge trends of the six largest Arctic rivers over a 64-year period. "Use of the combined discharge rather than the single river discharge makes the test for continental scale more robust and

笔记区

comprehensive," said Peterson. According to the researchers' analysis, the average annual discharge from these six rivers is currently about 31 cubic miles (128 cubic kilometers) greater than it was when routine measurements of discharge began in the 1930s.

Less density

Scientists are particularly interested in the potential impacts of this increase in freshwater on thermohaline circulation. The circulation is driven by differences in density of sea water, which is controlled by temperature and salinity.

Historically, thermohaline circulation brings warm, salty water to the North Atlantic, where it is cooled and sinks. "Cool and salty water is dense, it can sink to great depths," Peterson explained. This newly formed deep water is subsequently exported southward. This ocean circulation, which brings warm waters northward and ships cooler water south, is thought to be responsible for the warming of northern Europe by several degrees. "One thing that can slow this circulation down," said Peterson, "is, if you add freshwater to that area of the North Atlantic, it lowers the density. It counteracts the process that is increasing density."

According to several ocean circulation models, if enough freshwater is added to the Arctic Ocean, over time it will shut down the NADW. "If you stop the process, you stop the conveyor that brings warm water north," said Peterson. The paradoxical result, he added, would be a cooling of northern Europe. However, most of the rest of the world gets warmer when NADW is shut down, said Rahmstorf, who is an expert in ocean current modeling. Ocean currents don't generate heat, they just move it around, he said. In fact, a shut down of the NADW "would probably enhance global warming, since shutting down NADW will also reduce the ocean's uptake of carbon dioxide, so that more of our emissions remain in the air," said Rahmstorf.

Temperature rise

According to the Intergovernmental Panel on Climate Change, which was established in 1988 to assess the risk of human-induced climate change, global surface air temperature is expected to rise between 2.5 to 10.4 degrees Fahrenheit (1.4 and 5.8 degrees Celsius) by 2100. "This would represent an 18 to 70 percent increase in Eurasian Arctic river discharge over present conditions," the researchers write in *Science*. That would make for what Peterson calls an "interesting amount of water relative to what modelers predict."

While the researchers say their extrapolation of Arctic river discharge data should not be taken as a prediction, they suggest that such increases "are potentially important with respect to NADW formation." Going forward, the researchers will work to better understand the links between the atmospheric, continental, and oceanic components of the Arctic hydrologic cycle. Peterson and his colleagues plan to measure chemical

笔 记 区

tracers in major Arctic rivers, so that, in collaboration with oceanographers, they can find out where the river water is going in the ocean. "If we can do that, we can make a more rigorous test of ocean circulation simulation models," said Peterson. Such tests will make predictions more robust.

(Words: 911)

参考译文:

越来越多的淡水正在涌入北冰洋

1）国际研究小组的科学家说，欧亚大陆最大的6条河流现在注入北冰洋的淡水量比过去几十年来注入的总量还要多得多。长期以来，人们预言全球气候变暖将导致注入北冰洋的淡水量增加，而他们（国际研究小组）的发现更有力地支持了这一预言。

2）马萨诸塞州Woods Hole的海洋生物实验室研究员Bruce Peterson说："全球气候模型预测降水量会增加，这很可能是海洋中淡水量增加的原因。"他还说："根据我们的观测，1936年至1999年淡水溢流量增加了7%，这也可能是因为冰层和永冻层的融化或季节性降水量和淡水流量发生了变化。"

3）如果注入海洋的淡水量不断增加，那么北大西洋的海洋环流模式将受到极大的影响。依靠北大西洋深层水（NADW）推动的北大西洋输送带环流，即人们现在所知的热盐环流，将大量温暖的水流带到北大西洋地区，而大量淡水流入海洋将使北大西洋深层水的形成速度放慢甚至停止。

4）德国波斯坦气候影响研究所的Stefan Rahmstorf认为北大西洋深层水如果无法形成，那么欧洲大陆的气温可能会下降华氏3.6至9度（2到5摄氏度）。他补充说："不过我们必须考虑到那时（不再形成北大西洋深层水时），地球气候已经变暖了许多。所以（欧洲大陆气温比现在下降多少）取决于到时候地球升温多少。因此，可能欧洲大部分地区不会比现在冷。"

长期记录

5）长期以来，气候模型预测，随着全球气候变暖，地表水的蒸发量将会增加，大气中所含的水分也会增加。这些水分将增加高纬地区的降水量，如北冰洋地区，从而增加淡水河的流量。研究者提出，如果这些气候模型是正确的，那么上个世纪气温升高了1华氏度（0.6摄氏度），北极圈周边河流的流量也该相应增加。不过，至今为止他们并没有取得充足的地区气候变化趋势的观察数据。

6）以前的观察研究都针对特定的区域和时期；而Peterson和他的同事得到的数据是建立在北极圈周边6大河流64年来的流量趋势记录之上。Peterson说："在大陆规模的测试中使用综合流量比单用一条河流的流量更加有效、更加全面。"根据研究者的分析，这6条河流现在的平均年流量比20世纪30年代以来常规测量测得的数据增加了31立方英里（128立方千米）。

笔记区

密度降低

7）科学家们尤为关注淡水量增加对热盐环流的潜在影响，因为热盐环流由海水的密度梯度驱动，而海水密度由温度和盐度决定。

8）过去，热盐环流将温暖含盐的水流带到北大西洋，水流在那儿冷却下沉。Peterson解释说："盐水变冷后密度增大，会沉到海洋深处。"然后，这样的深层水团向南溢流。人们认为北欧气候之所以升高了几度，就是因为这种海洋环流将暖水流向北输送的同时将冷水流向南输送。Peterson还说："如果你将淡水注入北大西洋，就可以减缓这种环流的循环速度。因为淡水会减小海水的密度。它会抵消环流增加海水密度的作用。"

9）根据多种海洋环流模型显示，如果北冰洋中加入足够多的淡水，慢慢地，就不会形成北大西洋深层水。Peterson说："如果终止这个过程，那就等于割断了将暖水流北送的（北大西洋）输送带。"他又补充说，这将导致一个看似矛盾的结果，即北欧气温可能下降。不过，洋流模式专家Rahmstorf认为当北大西洋深层水不再形成的时候，全球其他地区可能变得更加暖和。他说，海洋流不会产生热量，它只是传递热量。事实上，Rahmstorf认为北大西洋深层水的不复存在"很可能加速全球变暖趋势。因为如果北大西洋不能形成深层水的话，它所吸收的二氧化碳的量也会下降。那么我们排放出来的二氧化碳将更多地残留在空气中。"

气温升高

10）根据气候变化政府间合作小组（该小组于1988年成立，负责评估人为引起的气候变化的危险）预计，到2100年全球地面气温将上升华氏2.5~10.4度（1.4~5.8摄氏度）。这些研究者们在《科学》杂志上写道："这可能意味着北冰洋附近欧亚大陆的河流流量与现在相比将增加18%~70%。这与Peterson所说的'气候模型家预测的令人关注的水量'相吻合。"

11）虽然研究者说他们根据北冰洋淡水注入量所做的推断不能作为一种预测，但他们认为淡水量的增加"对北大西洋深层水的形成可能非常重要"。今后，研究者们将继续努力，以便更深入地了解北冰洋水文循环系统中大气、陆地和海洋之间的关系。Peterson和他的同事将测量北冰洋附近主要河流中的化学示踪物，然后与海洋研究者合作，找出淡水河在何处注入海洋。他说："如果我们可以做到这一步，那么我们就能对海洋循环模型进行更精确的测试。"这将使由此得出的预测更加可靠。

背景知识：

全球变暖对欧洲大陆的影响遵循着这样一条因果链：全球气候变暖，气温升高——高纬冰川融化，海洋地区的降水量和降雪量增加——排入格陵兰海和拉布拉多海的淡水增多——表层海水变淡，密度减少——表层海水下沉减弱，"水泵"功率变弱甚至停止运转——墨西哥暖流改变方向，达不到高纬海域——北极冷空气肆虐欧洲——欧洲出现区域性冰期。

笔记区

第六章　雅思阅读参考答案

Answer Key

第一章 雅思阅读介绍篇

Ⅱ.

Example 4/A: False　　**4/B:** False

Example 6:

1. photographic negatives; printing plates
2. eating habits; lifestyles
3. temperature; salinity
4. algae

Example 7: environmental factors

Example 9/A: C　　**9/B:** A, C, F

第二章 雅思阅读基础篇

Ⅰ.

Exercise A–C: 略

Exercise D: 1. fragile　2. earned　3. recover　4. betray　5. rescue

Exercise E: A, B

Exercise F :

1. unfavorable	2. unfavorable	3. unfavorable
4. unfavorable	5. favorable	6. neutral, favorable
7. unfavorable	8. favorable, unfavorable	9. unfavorable
10. unfavorable	11. unfavorable	12. unfavorable

ExerciseG–H: 略

Exercise I : authenticated & verified

Exercise J : 略

Exercise K : All are refusals.

Exercise L: 略

Exercise M: B, D, E, F

Exercise N: C, G, D, H, A

Exercise O: FALSE

笔记区

Exercise P:

1. NOT GIVEN 2. FALSE

Exercise Q:

1. B 2. A 3. C 4. A

Ⅱ.

Exercise A:

1. 7 2. 5

Exercise B–F: 略

Exercise G :

1. the urban concentration
2. car transport
3. to create a mental image
4. societal attitudes
5. difficult characters
6. giving oneself comfort food, or doing nice things; to wrap themselves in positive thoughts or mother themselves
7. wood; lignin
8. the destructive force; in weaker areas of the earth's rocky outer shell

Exercise H:

1. NOT GIVEN
2. Reasons and organization.
3. No illustrated stimuli, those who pointed at the words, those who pointed at the pictures.
4. Modelers' assumption
5. No.
6. FALSE
7. NOT GIVEN
8. Snakes.

Exercise I:

1. 4 2. 8% 3. 1:3 4. 80%
5. Britain 6. Netherlands 7. 44,000

8.

Date	Location	Casualty
1556	Shensi/China	830,000
1970	Northern Peru	66,00
1976	Guatemala	23,000
1995	Kobe/Japan	/

9. 略

Ⅲ.

Exercise A:

1. However, allowing their time dominated by computers has progressively eroded children's independent thinking ability.

笔记区

2. What types of volcanic hazards might they face? These questions are difficult to answer because there are many types of volcanic eruptions which produce different types of volcanic hazards.
3. We have identified three distinct value discipline, so called because each discipline produces a different kind of customer value.
4. But other desires kept them active: four in particular, which we can label acquisitiveness, rivalry, vanity and love of power.

Exercise B:

1. Read a poem more than once.
2. Reaching that goal requires that they challenge themselves in three ways.
3. The value of snobbery in general, its humanistic 'point', consists in its power to stimulate activity.

Exercise C:

1. B
2. To support the topic that many deaths and injuries result from fire.
3. B

Exercise D:

1. C 2. C 3. B
4. C 5. A 6. D

Exercise E :

1. Chronological 2. Chronological 3. Chronological
4. Location 5. Problem + Causes + Solutions
6. General to specific 7. Comparison and contrast
8. Hierarchy 9. Parallel

Exercise F :

1. ① Antiquity ③ Population
2. ② The first Australians were still thought of as...
   ③ The authoritative view was that...
   ④ Though Aborigines might see themselves as indigenous, there is no doubt that they were in fact...

Exercise G: 略

Exercise H: 略

Exercise I:

1. (1)Borrowing (2)Narrowing
   (3)Widening (4)conditions
   (5)Three (6)Nature
   (7)Latin (8)Greek
   (9)contact (10)Resistance
   (11)Assimilation

笔 记 区

2.

Origin	Class	Words
French	cosmetics	***perfume/rouge***
German	***food***	***hamburger/delicatessen***
Italian	***musical words***	piano
Indian	***exotic dress items***	sari
Arabic	***al-***	alcohol
Latin and Greek	***formal learned items***	***magistrate/secure***
Danish	***'everyday' words***	them

Exercise J:

1. B　2. D　3. C　4. A
5. D　6. B　7. C　8. D

第三章　雅思阅读实战篇

Exercise A–C: 略

Exercise D: B

Exercise E: A

Exercise F: B

Exercise G: 略

Exercise H: 略

Exercise I:

1. Higher frequency　2. Slow rolling
3. Deep sleep / Normal sleep　4. Huge slow
5. Still　6. Dart / Rapid
7. Paralyzed

Exercises J–R: 略

第四章　雅思阅读补充习题

Ⅰ.

Exercise A:

1. C　2. G　3. I
4. D　5. A

Exercise B:

1. E　2. B　3. C　4. F
5. G　6. I　7. D　8. H
9. J　10. A

Exercise C:

1. B 2. F 3. H 4. A
5. K 6. M 7. O 8. G

Exercise D:

1. a 2. f 3. b 4. h
5. k 6. l 7. c 8. e
9. m 10. g 11. j 12. i
13. d 14. n

Exercise E:

1. acceptable 2. domestic
3. property 4. wages
5. husband 6. divorce
7. claims 8. legal
9. suit 10. permitted
11. make 12. excluded
13. lacked 14. belonged
15. determined

Exercise F:

1. step 2. acknowledge
3. prevent 4. essential
5. physician 6. due
7. physical 8. emotional
9. symptoms 10. confidence
11. disease 12. thorough
13. psychosomatic 14. upsetting

Exercise G:

1. solve 2. communities
3. creative 4. prevention
5. disposal 6. resources
7. recycling 8. waste
9. increase 10. place
11. measures 12. amount

Exercise H:

1. devastating 2. deterministic factors
3. stochastic factors 4. a natural cycle

Ⅱ.

Exercise A: 略

Exercise B:

1. B, E, F 2. B 3. B 4. A

笔记区

5. C　　6. D

Exercise C:

1. D　　2. A　　3. C　　4. A
5. A　　6. C　　7. B　　8. B
9. C　　10. A

Ⅲ.

Exercise A:

1. three　　2. productive activities
3. classroom　　4. classwork
5. maintenance　　6. napping
7. leisure　　8. three
9. home　　10. school
11. public places　　12. automobile
13. alone　　14. family members
15. friends

Exercise B:

1. Attitudes　　2. Introversion
3. Rational　　4. Feeling
5. Sensing　　6. Understand
7. Evaluate　　8. Apprehend/discover

Exercise C:

1. E　　2. F　　3. A　　4. D
5. C　　6. I　　7. H

Exercise D:

1. timber and stone　　2. modernism
3. international style　　4. badly-designed buildings
5. preservation　　6. high-tech
7. co-existence of styles

Exercise E:

B–E–H–F–I–G–D–A–C

Exercise F:

1. Offices　　2. sorted
3. (Re)pulped　　4. De-ink / make white
5. Refined

Exercise G:

1. C　　2. D　　3. C　　4. A
5. B　　6. B

笔 记 区

IV.

Exercise A:

1. NF 2. NF 3. F 4. F
5. F 6. F 7. NF 8. F
9. NF 10. F 11. NF 12. NF

Exercise B:

1. TRUE 2. TRUE
3. FALSE 4. FALSE
5. TRUE 6. FALSE

Exercise C:

1. TRUE 2. NOT GIVEN
3. NOT GIVEN 4. FALSE
5. NOT GIVEN 6. FALSE
7. TRUE 8. TRUE
9. NOT GIVEN 10. FALSE

Exercise D:

1. FALSE 2. FALSE
3. TRUE 4. NOT GIVEN
5. TRUE 6. NOT GIVEN
7. TRUE 8. TRUE

Exercise E:

1. NOT GIVEN 2. TRUE
3. NOT GIVEN 4. FALSE
5. TRUE 6. TRUE
7. NOT GIVEN 8. NOT GIVEN

V.

Exercise A: 略

Exercise B:

1. travertine, limestone, basalt, turquoise
2. pink flamingos, parrots, toucans
3. the Pampas, the veldt, the steppes, and the great prairies
4. the Himalayan Mountains, the Alps, Fijiyama
5. navy, azure, turquoise
6. kangaroo, platypus, koala, kookaburra
7. victoria Falls, Horseshoe Falls

Exercise C:

2–10–3–5–1–7–4–9–11–8–6

Exercise D: Reggie

Exercise E: 略

笔记区

Ⅵ.

Exercise:

1. Ⅴ　2. Ⅰ　3. Ⅷ　4. Ⅲ
5. Ⅸ　6. Flood basalts
7. Gases, water　8. Long period earthquakes
9. ground　10. magma
11. cracks　12. transport
13. volcanic tremor

第五章　雅思考试扩充阅读

Reading 1:

1. B　2. D　3. B　4. A
5. C　6. B　7. B　8. C
9. D　10. A

Reading 2:

1. B　2. D　3. C　4. D
5. C　6. A　7. B　8. C
9. A　10. B

Reading 3:

1. C　2. D　3. C　4. A
5. B　6. C　7. C　8. A
9. D　10. C

Reading 4:

1. C　2. A　3. B　4. C
5. A　6. D　7. C　8. C
9. D　10. A

Reading 5:

1. B　2. D　3. B　4. D
5. C　6. B　7. C　8. C
9. D　10. A

Reading 6:

1. D　2. A　3. C　4. B
5. D　6. C　7. D　8. C
9. D　10. A

Reading 7:

1. A　2. C　3. D　4. B
5. D　6. C　7. C　8. D
9. D　10. D

笔记区

Reading 8:

1. C	2. C	3. D	4. A
5. B	6. C	7. C	8. A
9. C	10. D		

Reading 9:

1. D	2. B	3. C	4. B
5. B	6. C	7. B	8. A
9. C	10. D		

Reading 10:

1. C	2. B	3. D	4. A
5. D	6. C	7. D	8. A
9. B	10. D		

Reading 11:

1. D	2. C	3. B	4. A
5. C	6. D	7. D	8. C
9. B	10. C		

Reading 12:

1. B	2. A	3. C	4. B
5. D	6. A	7. C	8. C
9. A	10. C		

Reading 13:

1. C	2. C	3. B	4. D
5. A/B	6. A	7. D	8. C
9. B	10. C		

Reading 14:

1. A	2. B	3. C	4. D
5. C	6. C	7. D	8. A
9. B	10. C		

附录 1

雅思(IELTS)与新托福(iBT TOEFL)考试的异同

考试形式

新托福: 新托福通过互联网与ETS总部组成局域网,为每个人发出不同的考题,而且考题一次有效,不再会有题库。此外,网考通过电子方式记录答案后,将答案传输到人工评分网络,并予以客观、可靠的评分,从而确保考试的公平合理性。

雅　思: 目前官方并未公布采用"机考"的消息,中国考生所参加的雅思考试仍然是以笔试的方式进行,考试会有一定的题库,部分题目会在考试中重复出现。2006年雅思作文的评分标准将会更加细化。

考试结构——听力

新托福: 原来的短对话被取消。听力部分内容更加学术化,演讲篇幅大大加长。此外,听力部分出现了5种新题型:选择两个正确答案的题目、听部分文章摘要后完成的细节题、根据文章内容点击图片相应位置的题目、通过拖动来选择答案的多选题以及点击表格的题目。

雅　思: 听力部分出现多个经典场景,对细节的考核更贴近国外生活要求。此外,听力部分将出现一些新场景,比如商业场景、超市、纪念品销售点等。考核题型也趋向多样化,不再是单纯考查填空或选择题。

考试结构——口语

新托福: 口语部分采用人机对话,模拟正式的上课讲演来考查学生。考试共有6道题目,一、三、五针对的是校园生活,而二、四、六都是相对学术性的题材。

雅　思: 口语采用"人人对话"形式,客观性相对减弱。2006年的考试不仅会在原有话题的基础上增加部分新问题,而且会将第二部分的话题具体化。

考试结构——阅读

新托福: 阅读部分内容变得更加学术化,其涵盖的题材也更加广泛,包括了历史、科学、教育、商业、社科、艺术文学、工程技术、体育文娱八个方面。此外,阅读部分还出现两种新题型:插入句子题和拖动选择的多选题。

笔记区

雅　思: 文章内容基本来自传统的题库,比如有关古代文明、移民史的社会科学话题，英国农业和动物特征介绍的自然科学话题等。新题的出现都比较有规律，阅读部分新题约占20%~30%。

考试结构——作文

新托福： 作文部分新增一篇考查综合能力的文章。要求考生用3分钟的时间读一篇学术性文章，然后听2到3分钟的相关演讲的录音，最后要求考生在20分钟内写下一篇字数在150到225的短文。大作文部分基本不变，字数比旧托福要求稍长。

雅　思： 一大一小两篇作文，小作文中的各种常规图表、柱状图、线图、饼图等交替出现。大作文的话题比较全面，包括了政府、环境、科技、媒体、犯罪、文化、动物等各种争议性话题。

托福雅思认可度异同

美　　国： 两者都承认，3,000多所大学中有接近700所承认雅思成绩（根据雅思官方网站，有380多所学校正式认可）。

澳大利亚： 两者都承认。大学承认托福成绩，但政府签证要求雅思成绩。

日　　本： 两者都承认，但偏向承认托福。

韩　　国： 两者都承认，但偏向承认雅思。

加 拿 大： 两者都承认。

英　　国： 两者都承认。

新 西 兰： 两者都承认。

新 加 坡： 两者都承认。

欧　　洲： 两者都承认。

新托福最低分数线为80分

近日，美国教育考试服务中心（ETS）官方网站公布了北美各大学对新托福网考成绩要求及新旧托福分数换算表，部分大学对申请就读美国大学本科和研究生院的学生的托福成绩划出最低分数线。从公布的新托福网考成绩分项要求可以看出，各高校均十分重视考生的口语与写作能力，具有良好的自我表达能力的留学申请者将在考试和申请过程中有较大优势。

笔记区

附录 2

中国内地雅思考试中心

北京语言大学

考点代码：1
地　　址：100083 北京市海淀区学院路15号
笔试考场：教1楼
口试考场：逸夫楼
电　　话：(010)82303550
交　　通：乘坐 331，375，398路

天津外国语大学

考点代码：2
地　　址：300204 天津市河西区马场道117号 天津外国语大学
笔试考场：逸夫教学主楼
口试考场：逸夫教学主楼
电　　话：(022)23286085
交　　通：乘坐4，13，26，871，904，906路

黑龙江大学

考点代码：3
地　　址：150008 哈尔滨南岗区学府路74号
笔试考场：试验楼
口试考场：外事处3号楼
电　　话：(0451)86608579
交　　通：乘坐11，106路

辽宁师范大学

考点代码：4
地　　址：116029 大连市黄河路850号
笔试考场：南院田家炳书院
口试考场：南院外语楼
电　　话：(0411)84258728
交　　通：乘坐101，708，705，715路或522，534路小公共汽车

沈阳师范大学

考点代码：5
地　　址：110032 沈阳市皇姑区黄河北大街253号

笔试考场：信息技术中心四楼
口试考场：信息技术中心四楼
电　　话：(024)86909660，86892233-161
交　　通：乘坐255，236，326，338，4301，4302路

山东大学

考点代码：6
地　　址：250061　济南经十路73号
笔试考场：南校区(原山工大)东配楼
口试考场：南校区(原山工大)东配楼
电　　话：(0531)8903388
交　　通：乘坐K51，K93，K56，2，8，16，18路

中国海洋大学

考点代码：7
地　　址：266071　青岛市香港东路23号
笔试考场：外语学院A区
口试考场：外语学院A区
电　　话：(0532)5901710
交　　通：乘坐501，11，801，321，304路

西安外国语学院

考点代码：8
地　　址：710061　西安市长安南路437号
笔试考场：2号教学楼
口试考场：6号教学楼
电　　话：(029)85309384
交　　通：乘坐603，504，527，215，19路

新疆财经学院

考点代码：9
地　　址：830012　乌鲁木齐市新市区北京北路15号
笔试考场：5号教学楼
口试考场：信息化中心
电　　话：(0991)7843882
交　　通：乘坐2，54，152路或民航班车

郑州轻工业大学

考点代码：10
地　　址：450002　郑州市东风路5号
笔试考场：国际教育学院

笔记区

口试考场：国际教育学院
电　　话：(0371)3836837
交　　通：乘坐2，28，64，86，87路

湖南大众传媒学院
考点代码：11
地　　址：410007　长沙市雨花亭新建西路77号
笔试考场：教学楼
口试考场：教学楼
电　　话：(0731)5602228，5602476
交　　通：乘坐7路到雨花亭

湖北大学
考点代码：12
地　　址：430071　武汉市武昌区学院路11号
笔试考场：3号楼南楼
口试考场：外国语学院
电　　话：(027)87122395
交　　通：乘坐573，215，543，554路

吉林大学
考点代码：13
地　　址：130021　长春市前卫路10号
笔试考场：前卫校区南区第三教学楼
口试考场：前卫校区南区第三教学楼
电　　话：(0431)5651004
交　　通：乘坐13，222，154，239路

华东师范大学
考点代码：14
地　　址：200062　上海中山北路3663号
笔试考场：文史楼
口试考场：文科楼四楼或心理学二楼
电　　话：(021)62233151
交　　通：乘坐69，224，524，567，754，765，829，909路

东南大学
考点代码：15
地　　址：210096　四牌楼2号
笔试考场：礼东楼
口试考场：外语系3楼

笔记区

电　　话：(025)83793242，83791474

交　　通：乘坐31，2，特1，52，11，15，304路

浙江省高等教育自学考试办公室

考点代码：16

地　　址：310007　文晖路321号浙江教育大厦

笔试考场：省教育厅内一层

口试考场：省教育厅内一层

电　　话：(0571)88008098，13600511882

交　　通：乘坐6，42，45，74，203，316，534路公交车到市交警支队站下车

安徽中澳科技职业学院

考点代码：17

地　　址：230031　合肥市濉溪路312号

笔试考场：学院办公楼

口试考场：学院办公楼

电　　话：(0551)5148001

交　　通：乘坐112，124，131，143，22，300路

仲恺农业技术学院

考点代码：18

地　　址：510225　广州市纺织路东沙街24号

笔试考场：新教学楼

口试考场：新教学楼

电　　话：(020)89003878，89003877

交　　通：乘坐8路公共汽车可到达考点

深圳赛格人才培训中心

考点代码：19

地　　址：518031　深圳市华强北路赛格经济大厦7楼

笔试考场：深圳市华强北路赛格经济大厦7楼

口试考场：深圳市华强北路赛格经济大厦7楼

电　　话：(0755)83780139，83217093

交　　通：乘216，225，212，9，410，446，466，469，470，407，411，413路公共汽车可达

福建师范大学

考点代码：20

地　　址：350001　福州市仓山区上三路

笔试考场：外国语学院

笔记区

口试考场：外国语学院
电　　话：(0591)87676583，87616544
交　　通：乘1，4，20，702，726，813，815，945，963，978路公共汽车可达

厦门大学

考点代码：21
地　　址：361005　厦门市思明南路
笔试考场：基金楼
口试考场：基金楼
电　　话：(0592)2185305
交　　通：乘1，15，17，21，29，43，87路公共汽车可达

海南大学

考点代码：22
地　　址：570228　海口市人民大道
笔试考场：旅游学院2号教学楼
口试考场：旅游学院2号教学楼
电　　话：(0898)66521995，66521985
交　　通：乘5，11，17，18，20，26，30，207，209路公共汽车可达

广西大学

考点代码：23
地　　址：530004　南宁市大学路100号
笔试考场：中加国际学院
口试考场：中加国际学院
电　　话：(0771)3233884
交　　通：乘4，222，218，28路公共汽车可达

四川外国语学院

考点代码：24
地　　址：400031　重庆市沙坪坝区烈士墓
笔试考场：出国留学人员培训部教学B区
口试考场：出国留学人员培训部教学B区
电　　话：(023)65385446
交　　通：乘坐210、801路

四川大学

考点代码：25
地　　址：610065　成都市一环路南一段24号(四川大学北门磨子桥方向)
笔试考场：出国留学人员培训部(四川大学西区)
口试考场：出国留学人员培训部(四川大学西区)

笔记区

电　　话：(028)85407413
交　　通：乘坐27、34路

云南大学
考点代码：26
地　　址：650091 昆明市翠湖北路2号
笔试考场：外国语学院（英华园）
口试考场：外国语学院（英华园）
电　　话：(0871)5032252
交　　通：乘坐22，64，84，96路

贵州大学
考点代码：27
地　　址：贵州省贵阳市花溪区
笔试考场：外国语学院
口试考场：外国语学院
电　　话：(0851)8292035
交　　通：乘公交210，202，203，204路，中巴89，90，97，109路可达

附录 3

INTERNATIONAL ENGLISH LANGUAGE TESTING SYSTEM

Test Report Form ACADEMIC

NOTE *Admission to undergraduate and postgraduate courses should be based on the ACADEMIC Reading and Writing Modules. GENERAL TRAINING Reading and Writing Modules are **not** designed to test the full range of language skills required for academic purposes. It is recommended that the candidate's language ability as indicated in this Test Report Form be re-assessed **after two years** from the date of the test.*

Centre Number	CN001	Date	23/OCT/2004	Candidate Number	002853

Candidate Details

Family Name	HE
First Name	GANG
Candidate ID	332621720820005

Date of Birth	20/08/1972	Sex (M/F)	M	Scheme Code	Private Candidate
Country of Origin	China (People's Republic of)	First Language	Chinese		

Repeating IELTS (Y/N)	Y	Previous Test Date	13/SEP/2003	Previous Test Centre	BRITISH EMBASSY, BEIJING

Test Results

Listening	Reading	Writing	Speaking	Overall Band Score
9.0	9.0	8	8	8.5

Administrator Comments

idp Education Australia

Centre stamp: BRITISH EMBASSY CULTURAL & EDUCATION SECTION BEIJING

Validation stamp: IELTS VALIDATION STAMP CAMBRIDGE ESOL/BRITISH COUNCIL/IDP

Writing Examiner Number	003246	Administrator's Signature	
Speaking Examiner Number	997892	Date	03/11/2004

Test Report Form Number: 04CN002853HEG001A

BRITISH COUNCIL · idp IELTS AUSTRALIA · UNIVERSITY of CAMBRIDGE ESOL Examinations